CREATING CHRIST

How Roman Emperors Invented Christianity

by

JAMES S. VALLIANT

&

WARREN FAHY

Table of Contents

"For now we see only a reflection as in a mirror;
then we shall see face to face.
Now I know in part; then I shall know fully,
even as I am fully known."

—Corinthians 13:4-13

Introduction

Religious fanatics from the Middle East are waging an assault on Western civilization and have just struck a demoralizing blow to the very capital of foreign "decadence." Leery of war with an entire people, the West acknowledges only advocates of peace to be "true" followers of the terrorists' religion. Indeed, Western leaders proclaim that their attackers' own dogma *commands* peace.

The year is 66 CE. The civilization under attack is the Roman Empire. And the terrorists: an ancient fanatical sect of Judaism.

Today, religious intolerance is readily associated with Islam. Before the last two or three centuries, however, Christianity is known to have justified the same practices: heretics burned alive, holy inquisitions torturing and executing those suspected of deviant beliefs, priceless books burned and lost to posterity, pagan temples and art destroyed, and sacrilegious sex acts punished by death. For many centuries Europe was plagued with brutal and bloody wars waged decade after decade merely between different *sects* of Christianity. On a scale of sheer insanity, those atrocities equal those committed in the name of Islam today.

Predating both Christianity and Islam, however, monotheistic Hebrews in the 1st Century divided into querulous factions and rebelled against their ruthless Roman conquerors, ultimately igniting the first Jewish War and altering the course of Western Civilization forever.

By the middle of the 1st Century CE, the Romans had carved out an empire through their military conquest stretching from Spain to Turkey and from Egypt to the Scottish border. Cosmopolitan, multinational and multiethnic, Rome was, at first, a religiously diverse leviathan that endured through its military skills, no doubt, but also through its political genius.

One way the Roman Empire tried to integrate its many diverse peoples was by actively supporting local religions and cultural traditions. Romans not only allowed but built temples to regional gods and shrines that embraced their various theologies within the

hierarchy of official Roman state religion. Both local and Roman deities were venerated together—inscriptions throughout the Empire
record their side-by-side worship, including dedications made by
wealthy or political Romans to a number of regional gods.

At the Empire's zenith, a wide variety of international deities
were worshipped by Romans of all classes and sexes—even in the
capital city of Rome itself. The most remote provinces saw alien
cults emerge that had first developed thousands of miles away in
some distant part of the Empire, deities such as the Egyptian Isis
and Serapis, and Cybele from present-day Turkey.

At this time, religion and politics were one, and the Romans'
policy of comparative religious tolerance proved to be a political
advantage that helped their empire endure for centuries. The strict
monotheism of Judaism, however, would present Roman policy with
its greatest challenge.

At first, cultural and religious compromises with the Jewish people were attempted, such as the granting of special exemptions
from the public worship of Roman state deities. However, so strict
had the traditions of Jewish monotheism become that *any* cultural
integration was emotionally repulsive "pollution" to many pious
Hebrews. Meanwhile, many Romans developed an ugly anti-Semitism as they accused Jews of being anti-social "haters of all humanity." Violent conflict—religious, cultural, political and military—was
inevitable.

The first Roman census and tax in Judea immediately resulted in
the emergence of rebel groups, who the ancient historian Josephus
went so far as to label philosophical "innovators" although they are
more properly understood as extreme cultural conservatives within
Judaism. They were resisting what was, in their eyes, the corrupting
influence of foreign paganism.

Violent conflicts between Hebrews and Greeks exploded in
Alexandria during the reign of the notorious Emperor Caligula during the 1st Century. In the reign of his successor, Claudius, still
more violent disturbances between Romans and messianic Jews
erupted in the capital of Rome itself, as we will see. In the end,
two prolonged, bloody wars were fought in Judea in the 1st and
2nd Centuries, wars that cost hundreds of thousands of lives, the
enslavement of thousands more, the complete and final destruction

of the Jewish Temple at Jerusalem and a legal expulsion of the Jewish people from Judea that extended the Diaspora for two thousand years. Though obscured by the passage of time, the conflict between Romans and Jews was a cultural and military cataclysm that would reverberate through the centuries to this day.

According to an eyewitness historian of the 1st Century Jewish Revolt against Rome, Flavius Josephus—himself a Jewish priest and aristocrat who fought first for the Jewish rebels and then went over to the Roman side—the underlying causes of the conflict were religious in nature. The sacred literature of the Hebrews, he explained to the pagan audience of his histories, contained prophecies that a Deliverer would come, a Savior, a world ruler who would emerge from Judea and lead them to victory. At several desperate moments in their long history, Josephus writes in his later works, they had known great leaders, sometimes miracle-workers, who defeated the foreign enemies of the Hebrews and achieved for them the political and cultural independence that their strict form of monotheism required of them.

So, despite the heavy odds against taking on Rome's powerful war machine in the 1st Century, they rebelled and kept fighting even after defeat was certain. Though Josephus described it as a misinterpretation of their messianic prophecies, their xenophobia had been compelled by strict adherence to Mosaic Law—and their rallying cry was "Messiah!"

It was at this moment in history that a new religion emerged, one that was at once radically different from messianic Judaism and yet seemed to be an offshoot from it. It would come to be known as Christianity, the world's second major monotheistic religion.

The letters ascribed to the Apostle Paul, or at least some of them, may have been written within a decade or so before open warfare in Judea broke out. The Gospels and most of the rest of the New Testament were probably composed in the decades following the First Jewish-Roman War (66-71 CE) during the imperial rule of the Flavian dynasty of Roman emperors and immediately after. The oldest of the Gospels, Mark, may have been written during or shortly after the First Jewish-Roman War. The latest material in the Bible may not have been written until a few decades later, although a process of fine editing would continue for some time. That is to say, the New Testament was written in the years *just before* and *in between* the two great Jewish Revolts, from the middle decades of the 1st Century through the early decades of the 2nd.

An apparent outgrowth of messianic Judaism, the emergence of Christianity during this period of intense religious conflict between messianic Jews and the Roman Empire cannot be a coincidence. The only mystery is the nature of the causation: exactly how and why did this conflict between the Jewish people and the Romans frame the emergence of Christianity? Just how closely are these two historical movements related? That is the topic this book explores.

For most of their ancient history, Romans had never legally required the worship of any single deity or cult, and this is why religious tolerance was never a major problem in their empire—until the monotheism of Judaism. This new conflict between cultures and religions in 1st Century Rome makes it easy to understand why the Roman state began to encourage solar cults like those of Mithras or Sol Invictus. Ironically, such gods tended to be worshipped exclusively and began to prefigure a new imperial monotheism.

As gods like these flourished across the Empire at this time, as far north as Roman Britain and as far east as Syria, the Romans came to seek a single unifying political force in religion for themselves. And, over time, the consolidation of the many faiths of their diverse peoples was regarded as increasingly desirable for political order and stability.

The opening centuries of the Common Era were rife with religious innovations, including outright religious fraud practiced nakedly as political statecraft. The audacious deification of Roman emperors is only one example. Arguably, this was the most religiously dynamic period in all of Western history.

Modern readers readily acknowledge religious fraud in long-dead faiths from this period, like the gaudy emperor cults. When even educated 2nd Century Roman historians report with credulous sincerity that the 1st Century Roman Emperor Vespasian miraculously cured the blind and lame, a 21st Century audience readily sees this as outright religious fraud and simultaneously crass political propaganda. During this time, however, Christians were also engaging in religious improvisation.

Through literary forensics we now know, for example, that some letters attributed to St. Paul are not likely to have been written by him. The letters' author(s) may have been influenced by Paul's theology—but his language, his concerns and context, and some of the ideas that he developed, all suggest that someone other than Paul wrote them at a later date. Scholars of Christian literature actually have a term for this type of material. They call it "Pseudepigrapha." As the name suggests, this material is considered to be *falsely attributed.* The letters ascribed to St. Peter and the names that tradition credited as the authors of the Gospels have also been persuasively challenged.

After these Christian fictions were revealed, even more creative liberties by editors' activities in the New Testament were discovered. During the first two or three centuries we can see that there was a veritable explosion of Christian creativity that displays a remarkable range of bold innovations and bald contradictions.

In this book, we will see how, by the 4th Century, Christians began modifying the actual text of previous writers (such as the historian Josephus) in order to make those older texts more consistent with their current views. We will also reinvestigate the apocryphal letters between St. Paul, author of what may be the oldest material in the New Testament, and the Roman Stoic philosopher, Seneca the Younger, tutor and advisor to the Emperor Nero himself. So similar were the ideas of these two contemporaries that such a correspondence seemed to help explain why there are such uncanny echoes between them. Today, however, this correspondence is known to be a fraud, again simply by language and content. And it must have been a relatively early fraud since it was already known to St. Jerome, who wrote about it around the year 400.

Explanations for this kind of "creativity" among early Christian writers, to put the matter generously, range from so-called "pious fraud" (e.g., sincere Christians who had themselves had ecstatic visions or other religious experiences that personally confirmed for them, for example, that it was Paul's words that they were writing down and not their own), to innocent misattribution or simple error, and, finally, to outright fraud (e.g., it is hard to imagine the phony correspondence between Seneca and Paul, or the enhancement of existing texts like that of Josephus, to be anything less than conscious and deliberate).

For both the Roman state and the early Christians, this was a period of liberal religious invention in which practicing outright religious fraud was a matter of routine. Against this historical backdrop, the first Gospels of the New Testament were being set down on paper for the first time.

In this book, we will reveal how and why the calamitous clash of civilizations between the Romans and the Jews brought into existence a new religion. For the first time, we will present astonishing new evidence proving beyond any reasonable doubt that the Roman government, in direct response to this bitter clash of cultures, created the religion known today as "Christianity."

Although we will in the course of this book agree with nearly all of the accepted factual conclusions of historians who have covered the subject of Christianity's origins, we will require no conspiracy-theory-like leaps of faith or logic to establish what we are suggesting—quite the opposite. The theory presented reconciles all of the seemingly contradictory evidence of Christianity's origins for the first time with none of the convolutions employed by scholars and historians for centuries.

Over the 30 years of research that produced this book, it was only at the very end, when we discovered the last piece of the puzzle we had suspected would be there at the beginning, that this hypothesis, which resolves mysteries concerning the history of Christianity that are age-old, was at last confirmed by *physical evidence*. Not only did our theory and all of the other evidence predict it must exist, but by the current understanding of Christianity's origins it was impossible that it could exist. And, though we anticipated it, what we discovered was far more conclusive than we ever imagined.

During the 30 years since we began our research what can only be described as a new school of thought regarding Christianity's origins has been emerging—one that is starting to reveal a long-buried secret. In various ways, an increasing number of scholars are recognizing that most of the New Testament has a *Roman* provenance.

First and foremost, in 1996 came the work of Prof. Robert Eisenman, a pioneer of this school. His works, such as *James the Brother of Jesus* and *The Dead Sea Scrolls and the First Christians*, note the strange way that the New Testament appears to invert the and even the New Testament itself are often boldly reinterpreted rather than simply taking them literally. As we shall see, even scholars' interpretations of the first symbols that archeology and Church historians recognize as "Christian" have been inverted in a way that has disguised what the evidence tells us.

Ironically, any questioning of the Gospels' scenario of Jesus as an itinerant preacher and healer in pastoral Galilee is itself automatically branded a *Da Vinci Code*-like "conspiracy theory." Considering how Hellenized and *non*-Jewish Christ's own teachings actually are, and how pro-*Roman* the positions of Paul and all of the Gospels happen to be, what is surprising is that scholars could accept as unquestionable the central tradition of a purely Jewish origin for the Gospels.

It has always been tempting to search for obscure, hidden and ulterior meanings in the New Testament. Even Jesus's own words are themselves blatantly conspiratorial:

> When he was alone, the Twelve and the others around him asked him about the parables. He told them, "The *secret of the kingdom of God* has been given to you. *But to those on the outside everything is said in parables* so that, "'they may be ever seeing but never perceiving, and ever hearing but never understanding; otherwise they might turn and be forgiven!'" (Emphasis added.) (3)

Jesus sometimes instructs his disciples, and those he heals, not to reveal his miracles to anyone. (4) He even orders his disciples not to tell anyone that he is the Messiah. (5)

Mystery surrounds why code-names were adopted by so many of the first Christians in the New Testament. Simon was renamed Peter by Jesus, since he was to be the "rock" (*petra* or πέτρα means "rock" in Latin or Greek) upon which the early Church would be founded. Barnabas, Paul's associate, was really named Joseph. Paul was originally Saul. (6) While it may have been true that many 1st Century Jews had second "Greek" names, sometimes the name of the disciple is completely suppressed in the literature, as in the case of the famously unnamed "disciple whom Jesus loved." (7)

Notably, members of the rebellious Jewish sect that preserved the famous Dead Sea Scrolls used titles such as "Teacher of Righteousness" rather than reveal the names of any individuals. Secrecy more emblematic of war than religion marks both the Dead Sea Scrolls and the New Testament.

In the following pages we will embark on the opposite of a "conspiracy theory." By considering the simplest answer from all of the evidence, we will ask the reader to take all of it at face value. In the process we will advance a theory that uniquely integrates all of the seemingly contradictory evidence without tortured reasoning or the unprovable speculations employed in much of Christian scholarship.

What follows is not, therefore, a conspiracy theory. It is, however, the story of a conspiracy hatched almost two millennia ago that had consequences far outlasting any intended purpose. For we will demonstrate that most of the "new" Testament—a text full of magic, mystical visions, astrological portents, demonic possessions, resurrections of the dead, the fulfillment of ancient prophecies, and allegorical mystery—was known by its authors to be a work of fiction.

This book does not address the questions of the existence of God. Nor does it explore the origin or content of the Hebrew Bible. Such matters stand well outside our purview. (8)

Many may wonder why the subject of this book, if it is so readily observable, has never been explored in such comprehensive detail before in the 20 centuries since Christianity's inception. One simple answer is that, since Christianity became the official religion of the Roman Empire, it has only been legally possible in the last three centuries for anyone to publicly question Christianity's origins without incurring a charge of heresy—for which a sentence of death was not uncommon.

Even today, many biblical academics and other specialists have concluded that approved scholarly qualifications are required to grasp the history of Christianity. However, after 30 years of research, 60 years cumulatively between the authors of this book—an effort well beyond what most could ever devote to such an investigation— we must deny this cloistered view. In this respect, some modern scholars are nearly as guilty of dogmatism as the mystics they often critique from a modern vantage.

Part I

Dolphin and Anchor

I. *Crux Dissimulata*

At the center of Christianity, according to the first three Gospels, Jesus Christ seems to have made an impossible mistake.

While only God knew the precise date, Jesus proclaims that the Messiah, the "Son of Man," in "great power and glory" would return *within the lives* of some of the people listening to him.

This strange misstatement has caused consternation almost since the expiration date of this prophecy passed.

But *was* it a mistake? What if we take Jesus Christ at his word?

In his prophecy, Jesus links the blessed event of his Second Coming with the destruction of Jerusalem and its famous Temple, which we know did in fact occur within his prophecy's timespan. Both events are predicted by Jesus to transpire, definitively, within the living memory of those to whom he made these predictions. Jesus even accurately describes the future Jewish War that would begin in 66 CE and correlates it to the destruction of the Temple that was to signal his return in power and glory.

The verbal description of the war that Jesus renders in the Gospels eerily mirrors that given by the historian Flavius Josephus of the actual events 40 years later as the Roman general and future Emperor Titus fulfilled Jesus's prophecy, right down to the "armies in the clouds" that Jesus foretold would appear in the sky before that brutal war's climactic siege and the Temple's destruction.

The Gospels were written after the Temple was demolished and the Flavian generals Vespasian and his son Titus rose from the East to become emperors of Rome and rule "the world" as a new era of peace did, in fact, return—a "Pax Romana." In short, the Jewish prophecy of the messiah had been fulfilled—and so had the prophecy of Jesus.

Moreover, the Roman emperors Vespasian and Titus openly proclaimed that they were the messiahs of Jewish prophecy, as part of their official propaganda and imperial cult. Few today realize that even important Jewish leaders at the time (officially if not always sincerely) recognized these pagan Romans as messiahs.

Was their arrival in power and glory as princes of peace the advent of Jesus's prophecy? Or is it possible that Jesus's prophecy was written while these Flavian emperors ruled *in order to prove* their messianic pretentions *after* they had conquered Judea? In either case, Jesus's prediction in the New Testament may not be the mistake many assume it to be, after all.

For decades, based on the striking possibility suggested by this historical coincidence, we searched for further links between the Flavian dynasty and the formation of Christianity. In the process we found so many connections that they exceeded our most outlandish expectations.

At first, we were struck by the sheer quantity of what, in this light, appears to be Roman propaganda in the Gospels themselves. Not only does Jesus advocate peace with Rome in an age of Jewish rebellion—even calling for the payment of taxes—but he acknowledges the faith of a Roman centurion with his most lavish praise. Indeed, the New Testament thoroughly removes the special status of Hebrews as God's Chosen People altogether and opens to the whole world the worship of the Jewish God.

Writing in the years just before the outbreak of the first Jewish War, St. Paul himself identifies political rebellion as a sin in the New Testament and proclaims that submission to the Roman government *is* obedience to God and his own appointed agents on earth.

According to the Gospels, Jesus not only calls for an end to the contemporary purity regulations that so alienated the Jewish people from the pagan world (as does St. Paul), but Pontius Pilate, the Roman governor at the trial of Jesus, vividly washes the Romans' hands of any culpability for his crucifixion. And, as readers will see, at every turn Christ's own story seems to have been shaped by the Roman political agenda of the time.

Just how much of the New Testament comprises such pro-Roman propaganda? It soon became obvious while searching for an exception to the startlingly pro-Roman attitude in the New Testament that there is no exception anywhere to be found. (1)

Most people today do not know that the writing of the Gospels has been dated to the era of the Flavian dynasty of Roman rulers, who rose to power after crushing the massive religion-inspired rebellion of messianic Jews some 40 years after the alleged death of Jesus. Most Christians are also unaware that close friends of these same Flavian rulers appear in the New Testament itself, or that the oldest Christian catacombs were the original burial site of the Flavian Emperor Vespasian's granddaughter (the niece of the Emperor Titus, his son), or that her husband would be counted among the first "popes" of the first Christian church in Rome.

All of this evidence, when unflinchingly placed together in its historical context, suggests what is today considered completely impossible: that Christianity is somehow intertwined with imperial Rome.

However, actual *physical* evidence directly linking the Flavian dynasty to Christianity had never been shown to exist and continued to elude us during three decades of research. With all of the propaganda typically generated by Roman emperors, it seemed certain that, if such a radical hypothesis were correct, at least some physical link between Flavian emperors and Christianity must have survived, even after the many centuries during which evidence could have been lost or purposely destroyed. An imperial Roman form of Christianity may have been aimed at a specific audience, and it may have been only a single aspect of imperial propaganda, but, if the inference is correct, we realized that some visual trace should remain even to this day.

Of course, all of the Flavian temples have been demolished, and the vast majority of documents from that era have disintegrated. Surely, however, some *coins*, a leading device used by Romans to promote their political objectives, must have endured to reveal this connection if it in fact existed.

Unfortunately, scattered across museums and catalogs previously isolated in libraries and universities and in segregated collections around the world, a complete inventory of Roman coins was not readily available to us—until the advent of the Internet. It was then, after three decades of looking, without knowing in advance what the coin we were searching for would look like, that we found it.

And this is *it*. It is a coin issued in the millions by the Flavian Emperor Titus, who conquered Jerusalem and sacked the Temple just as Jesus had prophesied. The symbol it bears, a dolphin wrapped around an anchor, is the very symbol Christians used to symbolize Christ for the first three centuries before the Emperor Constantine replaced it with the symbol of the Cross. In the middle is the flipside of the Roman coin of the Emperor Titus, and on the right is the first symbol of Jesus Christ:

Coin of the 1st Century Flavian Emperor Titus (left and middle); and the symbol of Jesus Christ used by Christians for the first three centuries (right)

We had to study the entire literary, historical, archeological and numismatic context of Christianity for three decades before we could even recognize this coin as the evidence we were looking for. This is the first time such evidence has been presented side-by-side.

As mentioned, this coin was the last piece of the puzzle to fall into place after years of researching. And it filled the final gap in a mosaic. That it would be so conclusive a link between the Flavians and Christianity as to be a *literal match* was astonishing, even to us.

This book will fill in the rest of the mosaic of evidence that led us to this coin as we explore the startling truth that it reveals about the origins of Christianity.

* * * * * * * *

How could Christians represent themselves with any symbol stamped on the coins of a Roman emperor while those coins were still circulating in Rome?

How is it possible that the first symbol Christians chose to represent Jesus Christ was used by a Roman emperor—the very emperor who fulfilled Jesus's prophecy by destroying the Jewish Temple and who proclaimed himself to be the Jewish Messiah so recently?

Let us assume, at the start, that Jesus was correct in his otherwise baffling prophecy. Let us assume that he did *not* make a mistake and that he meant exactly what is recorded in the Gospels.

If Jesus did indeed "return" to punish the Jews who unjustly rejected and killed him to sack their Temple within the lifetime of those who heard Jesus foretell it, as he predicted, then he must have returned as Vespasian and Titus. If he did come back to rule the world within his audience's lifetime, just as he foretold, he clearly did so as the Roman emperors who came from the East to fulfill both Jewish and Christian prophecy by bringing a new era of peace to the war-weary world. If a final End of Days is still pending, the glorious Second Coming, at least as predicted by Jesus, must have already come and gone—nearly 2,000 years ago.

The simultaneous existence of more than one "messiah," or indeed more than one manifestation of God, may strike some readers as strange. How can Vespasian *and* his son Titus both be the Jewish Messiah—and embodiments of the Jewish God—at the same time? How could the lives of Jesus Christ and Vespasian have overlapped, if they were incarnations of the same divine Being? (2)

This question imports contemporary Christian ideas on the subject of Jesus's divinity into this context where they did not yet exist, however. According to Hebrew scripture, the Jewish people had already experienced multiple messiahs and, within Hebrew tradition, there is nothing whatever to prevent the existence of more than one (mortal) messiah at the same time. God's messenger, Moses, named the "messiah" Joshua his successor, just as Elijah named Elisha, and just as the Maccabees, all of whom were messianic figures, could all be of the same family.

The sectarian documents of the Dead Sea Scrolls even suggest that at least some Jews of the period were expecting not just one, but two "messiahs," perhaps a priestly (although hardly a pacifist) leader, along with a military/political figure. However miraculous their deeds and whatever communications they might receive from God, both were to be mortal, of course. (3)

In the pagan context there is no problem with this, at all. On their coins, Romans identified multiple emperors as manifestations of the divine Apollo or Sol Invictus, for example. The problem we might have with two emperors simultaneously being the "Messiah" would emerge only later as Christians wrestled with the conflict between Christ's divinity and monotheism. Early Christian documents implying Christ's divinity also posit the simultaneous existence of more than one divine figure. Thus, the author of Colossians 1:15-16 (whether he was Paul or an early follower of his), wrote that Jesus, "the Son," was the first of God's creations and, at the same time, the image of the invisible God Himself. Although divine, Jesus is also the Son of God, and again, still within an allegedly monotheistic tradition.

This is not a problem in either a Jewish or pagan context for the theory we are testing, though it would be a major and logically insurmountable problem for early Christians. The concept of a "Trinity" in the three-fold identity of the single God—Father, Son and Holy Spirit—was their somewhat ungainly solution to the fundamental paradox of what would seem to be the worship of more than one deity by a group still claiming to be monotheistic. (4)

In order to test the theory that the Flavians were the validation of Jesus's prophecy, or that Jesus's prophecy was a validation of the Flavians' rule, we must first take a closer look at the physical evidence we have just presented that directly links the Flavian Emperor Titus to those who worshipped Jesus Christ.

Where did this symbol, a dolphin and an anchor, come from? How common was it to both pagans and Christians? Was it specific to Titus, the man who sacked the Temple in accordance with Jesus's prediction, or was it popular enough at the time that it could have been used by both Titus and Christians as a simple historical coincidence?

Where our journey ended is where we will now begin.

* * * * * * * *

What were the first symbols used by Christians? Although the symbol of the Cross has been, by far, the dominant symbol of Christian belief for the last one-and-a-half-thousand years and remains Christianity's most recognized emblem, it is widely understood that the most common symbol used by the earliest Christians was not a cross but a fish:

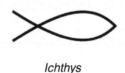

Ichthys

Some of the underlying reasons for using this symbol are also well-known. Spelled out in Koine Greek (the common language of the ancient eastern Roman Empire, the original language of the New Testament and an ancestor of modern Greek), the word for *fish* ("ichthys" or ΙΧΘΥΣ) forms an "acrostic"—that is, a word puzzle in which each letter is the first letter of the words "Jesus Christ, Son of God, Savior."

Another Christian adaptation of "ichthys" is a circle comprising the letters ΙΧΘΥΣ, which, when overlapped, make a wheel with eight spokes fusing both fish and Cross, as in this early example from Ephesus in Asia Minor:

The ichthys wheel

The symbol of a *fish*, therefore, comprised a name-game that referenced Jesus Christ with an abbreviation of his name and some of his titles.

There were other reasons for Christians to adopt a fish as their symbol. Fish allegories abound in the Gospels. Jesus recruits some of his first disciples from among the fishermen who work on the Sea of Galilee, including St. Peter. "Follow me," Christ says to them, "and I will make you fishers of men." (5)

Jesus's miracles and activities on the Sea of Galilee are also significant. The New Testament tells us that Jesus ministered near that "lake." Jesus, we are told, taught his disciples while standing in a boat on those waters. According to the Gospel of Luke, Jesus facilitated a miraculously large catch of fish on the waters of Galilee early in his ministry. And he would do so again following his Resurrection, according to the Book of John. (6) Jesus is not only said to have walked on water on the Sea of Galilee (7) but also to have calmed a raging storm there that endangered his disciples. (8)

In addition to healing miracles performed around this body of water (9), the Gospels tell us that, having driven a multitude of demons from one man, Jesus allowed those malignant spirits to possess a herd of pigs that stampeded down a steep bank into the Sea of Galilee, where they all drowned. (10)

When some question whether Jesus paid the famous "Temple Tax," which all Jews were commanded to pay in accordance with the Torah (11), another fish symbol appears in the Gospel of Matthew 17:24-27:

> After Jesus and his disciples arrived in Capernaum, the collectors of the two-drachma Temple tax came to Peter and asked, "Doesn't your teacher pay the Temple tax?"
> "Yes, he does," he replied.
> When Peter came into the house, Jesus was the first to speak. "What do you think, Simon?" he asked. "From whom do the kings of the earth collect duty and taxes—from their own children or from others?"
> "From others," Peter answered.
> "*Then the children are exempt*," Jesus said to him. "But so that we may not cause offense, go to the lake and throw out your line. Take *the first fish you catch;* open its mouth and you will find a four-drachma coin. Take it and give it to them for my tax and yours." (Emphasis added.) (12)

So a fish is seen providing the Jewish Temple tax for the followers of Jesus.

The Romans had repeatedly attempted to suppress the payment of the Temple tax, but it was not until the Flavians actually destroyed the Second Temple in 70 CE, about 40 years after the death of Jesus, that they abolished the payment of this tax altogether by faithful Jews across the Empire. Therefore, it seems that Jesus himself is predicting the demise of this tax within a generation—by exempting "the children" from it—just as he elsewhere famously predicts the destruction of the Temple itself will happen within that same period. (Referring to his second coming, Jesus states in the Gospel of Mark (13): "Truly I tell you, this generation will certainly not pass away until all these things have happened.")

There are many more fish references in the New Testament. Jesus transforms a mere five loaves of bread and "two fishes" into enough food to feed a multitude of 5,000 men plus women and children, with twelve baskets of leftovers, according to all of the Gospels (14). According to Mark (15), Jesus fed a multitude with seven loaves and "a few fish," leaving seven baskets of leftovers. The Gospel of Matthew (16) specifies that 4,000 people were fed fish on that miraculous occasion.

The fish symbolism is significant in a number of ways. Just as early Christians considered Christ to be "the Bread of Life," as Jesus describes himself no less than three times in the Gospel of John (17), Jesus is also said to be the "Water of Life" according to John (18). Just as Jesus is the *fish* that he feeds to the multitudes, so is he the bread and the water, the satisfaction for those who "hunger and thirst for righteousness."

Jesus's feeding miracles also foreshadow the Last Supper, where he feeds his disciples (at least symbolically) with his flesh and blood. Jesus claims of the bread on this occasion, "[t]his is my flesh (or body)," and of the wine, it is "my blood" (19).

Although not a direct part of the Eucharist, as the bread and wine are, a fish became symbolic of Jesus himself. We can see the fish directly symbolizing the Eucharist in the Sacraments Chapel of the Catacombs of St. Callixtus (one of the very first artistic depictions of the Last Supper):

Eucharist depicting fish on the table, 3rd Century

One of the earliest Christian writers, Tertullian (c. 160-225 CE) argued for baptism by saying (and here we can see all of the fish allegories brought together in one conceit): "But we, being little fishes, as Jesus Christ is our great Fish, begin our life [in Christ] in the water, and only while we abide in the water are we safe and sound." (20)

The first historical naming of the fish as an official visual symbol of Christianity is by St. Clement of Alexandria (whose full name was Titus Flavius Clemens, c. 150-215 CE). In his work, *Christ, the Instructor*, St. Clement advises Christians to use a dove or a fish or an anchor among other symbols as their identifying "seal":

> And let our seals be either a dove, or a fish, or a ship scudding before the wind, or a musical lyre, which Polycrates used, or a ship's anchor, which Seleucus got engraved as a device; and if there be one fishing, he will remember the apostle, and the children drawn out of the water. (21)

It is interesting that the "Polycrates" mentioned by St. Clement here was a *pagan* tyrant of the Greek island of Samos who flourished around 530 BCE and who especially revered the god Apollo, to whom the lyre was sacred. This tyrant's execution by the Persians (probably by being impaled or crucified) was foreseen in a prophetic dream by his daughter, who saw him "washed by Zeus [rained on] and anointed by Helios [sweated out under the sun]." (22)

Seleucus I Nicator (ca. 358-281 BCE)

The "Seleucus" curiously mentioned by St. Clement of Alexandria was a Macedonian general of Alexander the Great. As a founder of the Hellenistic "Seleucid Empire" following the division of Alexander the Great's conquests, he chose to use the symbol of an *anchor and fish*, as on this 2nd Century BCE silver bowl (produced by one of his descendant-successors):

Silver-gilded Seleucid bowl with dolphin-and-anchor

We must ask ourselves: why would St. Clement recommend using symbols with *pagan* origins as Christian seals?

Fully aware of the Crucifixion, St. Clement of Alexandria instead nominates images closely associated with the Greek god Apollo and certain pagan rulers. He does not even mention the Cross at all in his list of appropriate Christian symbols, though he is writing in the late 2nd/early 3rd Centuries.

Of course, as a literary metaphor, at least, the Cross can still be counted in the earliest Christian symbolism. According to the Gospels, Jesus himself used it allegorically even before he was crucified: "Then he called the crowd to him along with his disciples and said: 'Whoever wants to be my disciple must deny themselves and take up his cross and follow me.'" (23) Therefore we know that the earliest Christians were clearly aware of the symbolic importance of the Cross. And St. Clement himself refers to the Cross in a literary context. Yet he does not suggest using it as a graphic Christian symbol. (24) Why not?

Many symbols in the New Testament recur again and again: bread, water, wine, rocks/pillars, etc. Fish are among the most common. Why, then, would Clement refer to pagan sources like Seleucus for a fish symbol instead of sourcing his suggestions to the New Testament itself? While he is clearly aware of the Bible stories, St. Clement seems to cite the "fishing" of the "apostle" in order to justify using the earlier pagan precedent.

To explain why the first Christians used symbols like a fish

instead of the Cross, Christians often suggest that a secret symbol—a so-called *"crux dissimulata"*—had been necessary in the
first centuries because Christians were being persecuted by the
Roman Empire.

According to this explanation, Christians used the fish as a
means of recognizing a fellow Christian by quickly scratching it into
the sand without any fear of discovery by Roman authorities. And,
certainly, Christians who refused to worship Roman state deities
could be subject to criminal prosecution and even execution.

Yet, while it may have been convenient at certain times to have a
secret code, it is not clear at all that pagans would have recognized
the Cross as a Christian symbol during the first two centuries of
Christian history. According to *The Catholic Encyclopedia*, not more
than 20 examples have ever been found of the Cross being used as
a Christian symbol during the entire first *four* centuries.

It would seem that an outsider would need the same knowledge
of an insider to recognize a cross as a Christian symbol at all considering how rarely it was ever used. An outsider had a much better
chance of recognizing a fish as a Christian symbol at this time since
it was far more commonly used. How could the Cross be so recognizable during this period that disguising it would be necessary?
And were these early Christians really in danger of discovery and
persecution by the Roman government?

We now know much more about the treatment of Christians by
the Roman Empire. Recent scholarship, such as that of Candida
Moss, has revealed that traditional claims about Christian persecution have been greatly overstated. (25) The first Christian catacombs
in Rome, dated to the early 2nd Century, were burial sites—not hiding places—just as the Jewish catacombs in Rome were before
them. The symbols used by early Christians at their gravesites do
not appear to have been any secret, but quite the opposite. They
were used to identify the occupants as Christians. And the symbols
they used most predominantly were *fish* and *anchors*, the same
symbols stamped on the Emperor Titus's coins.

We will take a close look at these earliest Christian symbols
later. First, we need to consider why our modern understanding of
Christianity's origins makes it so difficult to believe that Romans,
let alone Roman emperors, could be involved in the creation of

Christianity. Our modern impression of persecuting Romans and oppressed Christians has built in a natural aversion to any such possibility.

Christians fed to lions, "The Triumph of Faith,"
by 19th Century painter Eugene Thirion

The new discovery of this coin's link to Christianity proves that within a decade or so of Flavian rule, starting in the early 2nd Century, Christians were publicly memorializing their faith on tombs, with no fear of imperial persecution, even as they used symbols associated with the emperor himself. And prominently buried in one of these tombs, indeed the *oldest* Christian catacombs, was the granddaughter/niece of three Flavian emperors. Today they are named after her (the Catacombs of St. Domitilla, although her remains were later moved to the basilica of *Santi Nereo e Achilleo* in Rome).

Facts like these already cast extreme doubt on the idea that Romans were persecuting Christians in the 1st Century. However, we know that some instances of Christian persecution by Roman authorities did in fact occur. According to our ancient sources, the late 3rd-4th Century Roman Emperor Diocletian and, later, Julian (the notorious "Apostate" from his family's Christian faith) were explicitly and harshly anti-Christian emperors. Yet, before them, only Decius in 250 CE had enacted any law against Christians. And even under Diocletian, the evidence tells us that by the end of his second year of rule "the ferocity of the persecution [of Christians] had eased off again, and the *earlier tradition of tolerance* had begun to reassert itself." (Emphasis added) (26)

More and more, the evidence suggests that the persecution of Christians was not at all common before the Christian faith started to become the official state religion of the Roman Empire under the Emperor Constantine in the 4th Century. By the reign of Emperor

Gratian (359-383) paganism would be vigorously suppressed by the Roman Empire. There is simply no evidence that Christians were driven underground, as commonly depicted in movies and novels—at least not for any extended periods of time.

The first and only existing documentation of official Roman policy on Christians, dating prior to the brief reign of the hostile Emperor Decius, is this correspondence between Pliny the Younger, governor of the Roman province of Pontus-Bithynia (in modern-day Turkey), and the Emperor Trajan in 111 CE.

Pliny the Younger, façade of the Cathedral of St. Maria Maggiore

Pliny the Younger to Emperor Trajan:

> It is my custom to refer all my difficulties to you, Sir, for no one is better able to resolve my doubts and to inform my ignorance.
> I have never been present at an examination of Christians. Consequently, I do not know the nature or the extent of the punishments usually meted out to them, nor the grounds for starting an investigation and how far it should be pressed. Nor am I at all sure whether any distinction should be made between them on the grounds of age, or if young people and adults should be treated alike; whether a pardon ought

to be granted to anyone retracting his beliefs, or if he has once professed Christianity, he shall gain nothing by renouncing it; and whether it is the mere name of Christian which is punishable, even if innocent of crime, or rather the crimes associated with the name. For the moment this is the line that I have taken with all persons brought before me on the charge of being Christians. I have asked them in person if they are Christians, and if they admit it, I repeat the question a second and third time, with a warning of the punishment awaiting them. If they persist, I order them to be led away for punishment; for, whatever the nature of their admission, I am convinced that their stubbornness and unshakeable obstinacy ought not to go unpunished.

There have been others similarly fanatical who are Roman citizens. I have entered them on the list of persons to be sent to Rome for trial.

Now that I have begun to deal with this problem, as so often happens, the charges are becoming more widespread and increasing in variety. An anonymous pamphlet has been circulated which contains the names of a number of accused persons. Amongst these I consider that I should dismiss any who denied that they were or ever had been Christians *when they had repeated after me a formula of invocation to the gods and had made offerings of wine and incense to your statue (which I had ordered to be brought into the court for this purpose along with the images of the gods),* and furthermore had reviled the name of Christ: none of which things, I understand, any genuine Christian can be induced to do.

Others, whose names were given to me by an informer, first admitted the charge and then denied it; *they said that they had ceased to be Christians two or more years previously, and some of them even twenty years ago.* They all did reverence to your statue and the images of the gods in the same way as the others, and reviled the name of Christ. They also declared that the sum total of their guilt or error amounted to no more than this: they had met regularly before dawn on a fixed day to chant verses alternately amongst themselves in honor of Christ as if to a god, and also to bind themselves by oath, not for any criminal purpose, but to abstain from theft, robbery, and adultery, to commit no breach of trust and not to deny a deposit when called upon to restore it. After this ceremony it had been their custom to disperse and reassemble later to take food of an ordinary, harmless kind; but they had in fact given up this practice since my edict, issued on *your instructions, which banned all political societies*. This made me decide it was all the more necessary to extract the truth by torture from two slave-women, whom they call deaconesses. I found nothing but a degenerate sort of cult carried to extravagant lengths.

I have therefore postponed any further examination and hastened to consult you. The question seems to me to be worthy of your consideration, especially in view of the number of persons endangered; for a great many individuals of every age and class, both men and women, are being brought to trial, and this is likely to continue. It is not only the towns, but villages and rural districts too which are infected through contact with this wretched cult. I think though that it is still possible for it to be checked and directed to better ends, *for there is no doubt that people have begun to throng the temples which had been entirely deserted for a long time; the sacred rites which had been allowed to lapse are being performed again, and flesh of the sacrificial victims is on sale everywhere, though up till recently scarcely anyone could be found to buy it*. It is easy to infer from this that a great many people could be reformed if they were given an opportunity to repent. (Emphasis added.)

Emperor Trajan

What we appear to be witnessing in this correspondence between the emperor and his governor is the first formulation of a Roman response to New Testament Christians. Here is Emperor Trajan's reply to Pliny the Younger:

> You have followed the right course of procedure, my dear Pliny, in your examination of the cases of persons charged with being Christians, for it is impossible to lay down a general rule to a fixed formula. *These people must not be hunted out;* if they are brought before you and the charge against them is proved, they must be punished, but in the case of anyone who denies that he is a Christian, and makes it clear that he is not by offering prayers to our gods, he is to be pardoned as a result of his repentance however suspect his past conduct may be. But pamphlets circulated anonymously must play no part in any accusation. They create the worst sort of precedent and are quite out of keeping with the spirit of our age. (Emphasis added.) (27)

Pliny's ignorance of an existing policy concerning Christians is clear, along with his personal hostility toward them. Interestingly, Pliny thinks the Christians' meetings are properly forbidden under

Trajan's ban on *political* groups. But Pliny clearly does not know what the emperor will think about this new problem.

Any sacrifice or prayer in the presence of pagan images would have been a form of idol worship forbidden in the Hebrew scripture, including the Ten Commandments' famous prohibition against "making" or "bowing down" to the graven images of polytheistic deities. In this way, Gentile Christians could be detected immediately, Pliny presumes. Jews had been exempted from the requirement to worship Roman state deities. However, as such worship was required of Roman citizens and officials, the failure to do so restricted their social mobility within the Roman world.

It's unclear, however, whether these early New Testament Christians would have had the same problem since we now know they were already using both symbolic representations of the divine and pagan religious images themselves, even images related to pagan gods like Apollo, as the examples of St. Clement of Alexandria demonstrate.

Trajan's reply reassures the governor that he acted wisely by consulting him about the treatment of Christians and that he has ruled appropriately. He directs Pliny that Christians need only offer prayer with incense and wine to Caesar in order to acquit themselves. Emperor Trajan does not require Christians to recognize Caesar's divinity but merely to make an offering to the divine for Caesar's well-being. And, while the offensive images of pagan gods would be present, their official offering would not require an animal sacrifice of any kind. Above all, Christians are not to be hunted down, but ignored as much as possible. The official imperial attitude toward Christians, even as this earliest record shows, is actually rather benign and consistent with the policy of religious tolerance usually favored by the Romans.

Pliny's letter also tells us that the Christian movement was at least 20 years old in 111 or 112 CE. This is most interesting because it dates the existence of Christianity in Bithynia to the time of the Flavian Roman emperors who preceded Trajan.

What else does this oldest surviving discussion of Christianity by Roman officials reveal? Pliny states that Christianity's popularity seems to have waned since the Flavian era. He also mentions that the Christians he is dealing with, even at this early stage of Christian history, appear to come from *all classes* of Roman society. All of these facts challenge the conventional view of Christian history.

Pliny also reveals that the traditional or established forms of Roman worship became "entirely deserted" at one time in the recent past but that they were now staging a comeback. Even if this report is exaggerated, a great many people, it seems, had gotten over a "Christian phase" that had peaked and started fading during the reign of the Flavian Emperor Domitian, who succeeded his father Vespasian and brother Titus.

The archeological evidence tells us that the coin issued by Titus that mirrors the first symbol of Christ was discontinued by his brother Domitian only a few months into his reign. Titus ruled for only 2 years, 2 months and 20 days, yet he had managed to issue millions of coins bearing that symbol during this brief reign. His younger brother Domitian ruled for 15 years and was known to have conducted a harsh purge of the upper class, even executing and banishing some of his own family members who, as we shall see, may have been Christians—including his nephew-in-law Titus Flavius Clemens and his niece, the afore-mentioned Domitilla, even though he had previously adopted their children as his own heirs.

What is most vivid in this early correspondence between the Emperor Trajan and Pliny the Younger is the contrast between imperial Rome's careful policy toward the new Christian religion on the one hand and its violent suppression of militant messianic Judaism on the other.

Outside the New Testament itself (and, possibly, the writings ascribed to St. Clement of Rome, St. Ignatius of Antioch and Papias of Hierapolis), this correspondence is the earliest primary evidence of Christianity that exists anywhere in the historical record with one controversial exception that we will examine in detail in Part II.

Among the earliest surviving mentions of Christianity we have an official statement of how the Roman Empire will *not* persecute Christians—written by the Roman emperor himself. The evidence from almost the whole of the two centuries that follow conforms to Emperor Trajan's quasi-toleration of Christians. His approach seems to have become the standard operating policy of the Roman government toward Christianity, despite later fictional depictions of Roman mistreatment of Christians.

So what is the basis for the assertion that Christians were being systematically hunted down and slaughtered by Romans as early as the 1st Century, as we have been led to believe by tradition, books, movies and popular culture? The answer turns out to be a key to understanding what has been puzzling Christian scholars for centuries.

* * * * * * * *

According to the famous account of the 2nd Century historian Tacitus, Nero, the notorious 1st Century emperor, tried to pin the blame for the Great Fire of Rome in 64 CE on "Christians." In *The Annals*, Tacitus writes:

> But all human efforts, all the lavish gifts of the emperor, and the propitiations of the gods, did not banish the sinister belief that the conflagration was the result of an order. Consequently, to get rid of the report, Nero fastened the guilt and inflicted the most exquisite tortures on a class hated for their abominations, called *Christians* by the populace. Christus, from whom the name had its origin, suffered the extreme penalty during the reign of Tiberius at the hands of one of our procurators, Pontius Pilatus, and a most mischievous superstition, thus checked for the moment, again broke out not only in Judaea, the first source of the evil, but even in Rome, where all things hideous and shameful from every part of the world find their center and become popular. Accordingly, an arrest was first made of all *who pleaded guilty*; then, upon their information, an immense multitude was convicted, not so much of the crime of firing the city, as of *hatred against mankind*. Mockery of every sort was added to their deaths. Covered with the skins of beasts, they were torn by dogs and perished, or were nailed to crosses, or were doomed to the flames and burnt, to serve as a nightly illumination, when daylight had expired. Nero offered his gardens for the spectacle, and was

exhibiting a show in the circus, while he mingled with the people in the dress of a charioteer or stood aloft on a car. Hence, *even for criminals who deserved extreme and exemplary punishment*, there arose a feeling of compassion; for it was not, as it seemed, for the public good, but to glut one man's cruelty, that they were being destroyed. (Emphasis added.) (28)

Such a characterization of Christians—*criminals who deserved extreme and exemplary punishment*—by a Roman senator and historian like Tacitus makes no sense if we understand the term "Christian" in the sense of Gospel-believing, tax-paying advocates of peace with Rome who render unto Caesar what is Caesar's and turn the other cheek while walking the extra mile for Romans. Who, then, are these criminals Tacitus describes Nero as vilifying?

We must remember that by the year 64 CE, when the Great Fire decimated the city of Rome, the Gospels themselves had not yet been written. They would not be written until the Flavian era that followed Nero. The great majority of mainstream scholars, both Christian and non-Christian, agree on this dating.

There is simply no reason to think that many people in Rome had ever heard of this kind of Caesar-friendly Christianity only three decades or so after the Crucifixion. So few in number could such Christians have been, especially in the city of Rome, that it is exceedingly unlikely that these ostensibly peace-loving followers of New Testament ideals could have made a convincing or useful scapegoat for Nero. So who could Nero have been blaming—and who could Tacitus be describing?

The mystery is resolved if Tacitus is confusing one group of devotees of a Jewish messiah with another group who were, indeed, creating very serious trouble for the Roman government and were, in fact, quite active in Rome at that time.

Rebellion had been simmering among the Jewish population since the days of the first Roman census early in the 1st Century and the new imperial tax this census was designed to impose on them. These are events that the Gospel of Luke associates with the birth of Jesus, and they also signal the birth of the Jewish rebellion according to the ancient historian Flavius Josephus. According to all ancient sources, it was the galvanizing concept of the Messiah—a warrior who would lead the Hebrews to salvation—that most motivated the revolt against their Roman masters, however unlikely they were to succeed.

Violent disturbances among the Jewish population were an enormous concern to the Roman government. By the 1st Century CE, about 10 percent of the population of the Roman Empire was Jewish, perhaps 7 million, of which only about 2.5 million lived in the region of modern-day Israel and Palestine. The rest, known as "Diaspora" Jews, were scattered within foreign countries following the Assyrian conquest of Israel in 8th Century BCE, the Babylonian sack of Jerusalem in 6th Century BCE, and the conquests of Alexander the Great in the 4th Century BCE. These Jews comprised a significant portion of the populations of Egypt, Africa, Greece, and Italy by the 1st Century, and they had also reached Gaul and Spain. Perhaps a million Jewish people populated the Parthian Empire (in modern day Iran and Iraq). By comparison, the Jewish population of the United States in the early years of the 21st Century is between one and two percent—or about 5.4 million. (29)

In addition to their significant numbers, the proximity of the Hebrews' traditional homeland to Egypt made any potential breakaway state in the area a direct threat to the bread basket of the Mediterranean world. As its chief producer of grain, Egypt was indispensable to the Empire. Rome's leading competitor in the East, the Parthian Empire, was thus already too dangerously close for comfort to allow any instability.

Unlike any peace-loving Christians who may have existed at this time, the unrest among the Jewish population, particularly among messianic militants, was a clear and present danger to the Roman state. Nero would certainly have had a political motivation to blame them for any attack on Rome. It is far more likely that the "Christians" he blames for the Great Fire in Tacitus's history were, in fact, this hardcore group of messianic rebels.

Is there any other evidence from all of the historical record that might be the basis for the idea that Romans persecuted Christians in the 1st Century? One piece of evidence often referred to as such an example is a passage written by the 2nd Century Roman historian Suetonius, who reports that Jews in the city of Rome were causing disturbances at the instigation of a person named "Chrestus" as early as the 40s CE, and that they had to be expelled from the city by the Emperor Claudius around the year 50 CE. (30) But again, this can hardly have been the "Christ" of the New Testament since Christ never visited Rome. And the idea of Christians (by our meaning of the term) being such a problem in distant Rome only a decade or two after the Crucifixion, and long before the evangelizing missions of St. Paul and St. Peter, is simply not plausible.

In any event, Jesus's advocacy of peace with Rome in the Gospels rules him out as a possible instigator of any such disturbances in the first place. This very fact is demonstrated over and over again in the New Testament, as not just Romans but Roman governmental authorities uniformly find no problem with the Gospel of Christ. Nor is there any reason for them to. We are left to imagine Nero as a mad man unjustly accusing the kind and pacifistic Christians out of his own wanton cruelty.

Nero had good reason to fear the militant messianic Jews in Rome, however. Anticipating their Christ would arrive to deliver them, these fanatics were smoldering with resentment against the Empire. Only two years later it is they who would launch all-out war with the Romans. They make much more plausible suspects for the disturbances under Claudius and a much more likely political scapegoat for the arson under Nero that ravaged the city. These messianic Jewish rebels are in fact more believable candidates for setting the Great Fire than Nero himself, since that disaster caused calamitous financial and political challenges for the emperor. Burning for six days, the fire reduced over 70 percent of the capital city to ruins.

Nero had little reason to sing while Rome burned, though the ancient historian Suetonius reports that the emperor had exulted in the "beauty of the flames." As the capital was engulfed in fire he allegedly sang a lament about the fall of Troy. (31) "Fiddling while Rome burns" is a cliché about Nero, but contemporary historians question the objectivity of historians like Tacitus, Suetonius and Flavius Josephus, noting that their hostility to Nero reflected the political views of the emperors they worked under, as well as those with lingering republican sentiments who despised the absolute monarchy of the Julio-Claudian dynasty.

Nero sings as Rome burns, Henry Altemus (1897)

So, we have good reason to suspect that pagan Romans like Tacitus and Suetonius were confusing these two groups of messianic monotheists, making no distinction between the militant and peaceful varieties.

* * * * * * * *

During this time of civilizational conflict, the Zealots and the Sicarii were the leading groups of "messianic" Jewish rebels, according to the 1st Century historian Flavius Josephus. He describes them as religious fanatics and terrorists, readily bringing to mind today's jihadists. (32)

Josephus was writing for the Romans, of course. A Jew himself who adopted his Roman name after being captured by General Vespasian during the Jewish War, Josephus relates that even under torture one contemporary Jewish sect called "Essenes" could never declare a man (Caesar) to be their Lord. Josephus also records how the rebels at Masada committed mass suicide rather than be captured by the Romans in 73 CE. He recounts a similar event involving himself years earlier at Jotapata, where as a Jewish general he had faced defeat by the Romans and participated in his own suicide pact before arranging his own escape at the last moment. After narrowly avoiding death, Josephus turned against his countrymen and denounced them in his new role as, in essence, the Flavians' court historian.

Whatever their exact dating, the Dead Sea Scrolls confirm what Josephus relates, at least to some extent: the messianic Jews of this period were militant, xenophobic purists and strict adherents of the Mosaic Law. If the so-called "sectarian" documents of the Dead Sea Scrolls are any indication, they were not at all the peace-seeking, cheek-turning, enemy-loving, tax-paying, Roman-appeasing Christians of the sort who could possibly follow the New Testament. The Dead Sea Scrolls confirm that they constituted a religio-political powder keg about to explode—and that they would certainly have opposed Christ's central message in the Gospels.

Today, these Jewish rebels are not normally called "Christians" even though they anticipated the arrival of a "christened" or "anointed" one (the Messiah or the Christ) to lead them in their holy war against Rome. To pagan Romans like Tacitus and Suetonius, who may have been ignorant of the finer distinctions between messianic Jewish groups, the term "Christian" may well have applied to messianic Jews as a whole. Suetonius's confused mention of a Jewish "Chrestus" causing violence in Rome itself before 50 CE appears to confirm this conflation of terminology.

This confusion is important to keep in mind when reading the New Testament itself, especially when Paul clashes with a group of nominal "Apostles" who resemble militant rebels more than any idea of Christians today, as we will see.

The evidence suggests, therefore, that it was these messianic rebels and not Christians as we know them today who were martyred and persecuted by Romans during the first two centuries of the Common Era. There is ample evidence that the Romans crucified these followers of messianic Judaism by the thousands during this period. It is certain that they would refuse to acknowledge any Roman emperor as divine or in any way their master. The mystery of why Claudius and later Nero perceived these "Jewish-Christians" to be a military threat to Rome now makes perfect sense. They were not "Christians" as we understand the term today but violent insurgents.

Quite unlike these dangerous "christians," another type of

Christian seems to have immediately embraced pagan images among their first symbols, along with the dramatic modifications of traditional Jewish law this required, as well as adopting an accommodating attitude toward Romans themselves.

The troublemakers that Suetonius and Tacitus called followers of "Chrestus" or "Christians," on the other hand, are far more like the oppositional orthodox Jews in the New Testament referred to by Paul as "apostles of Christ."

The picture of Jesus's followers portrayed in the New Testament makes it impossible to understand how the Romans could feel threatened by such mild and forgiving proponents of political peace. Indeed, they seem to be the fulfillment of a Roman wish-list for what messianic Jews in Rome would comprise.

The conflation of these two groups, along with the marked contrast between them, makes it easy to see why Pliny the Younger was in a quandary over what to do with what might be called "New Testament" Christians, with whom he was dealing only a few decades after the first Jewish War.

The rebellious "Jewish Christians," as they can be designated, went to war with Rome one more time under Bar Kokhba in 132-136 CE (although violent disturbances started as early as 123 CE). They would continue to be a threat to the Roman Empire well after the first full-scale revolt. Throughout this time they were tortured and crucified in large numbers. The abundant evidence of *their* persecution by the Romans stands in stark contrast to the dearth of evidence that New Testament Christians were persecuted during Christianity's first two centuries.

This distinction between "Jewish Christians" and Gospel-adhering Christians has been convincingly argued by the scholar Robert Eisenman in his books, *James the Brother of Jesus* and *The Dead Sea Scrolls and the First Christians*. (33) Eisenman, one of the important translators of the Dead Sea Scrolls, demonstrates that the first group of messianic Jewish believers may indeed be identified as a rebel sect similar to if not identical in religion and politics with the well-known Jewish Zealot movement itself. Professor Eisenman argues that the so-called "sectarian" documents of the Dead Sea Scrolls, that is, those specific texts that detail the lifestyle and history of a purist Jewish sect normally identified as "Essenes," are likely to have been authored by the same ideological movement that instigated the revolt against Rome in the 1st Century.

Eisenman differs from the majority view of scholars here, who place the writing of some of the sectarian documents of the Scrolls as early as the 2nd Century BCE. Since the Dead Sea Scrolls were deposited in caves by messianic Jews at the time of the first rebellion even as war engulfed the region around 70 CE, however, Eisenman's argument makes more temporal and logical sense. At the very least, and whether or not his dating is correct, these documents appear to have been important enough to the Jewish rebels to hide them in caves during their first war with Rome. Coins dating to that time were found in the same cache. The authors of these documents certainly shared with the rebels both their martial zeal and fervent messianic expectations. Their documents would be preserved until discovery 19 centuries later to much controversy.

Adding to that controversy, Professor Eisenman identified in those scrolls the early Christian leaders James the Just and the Apostle Paul, connecting them to figures referred to in the sectarian Dead Sea Scroll documents by the titles "the Teacher of Righteousness" and "the Liar," respectively. (And it is curious how often Paul makes the special pleading that he is "not lying" in the New Testament, considering how often this bitter accusation appears in the Dead Sea documents recorded by the Jewish hardliners.)

However fascinating, such an identification is not required in order to see the wider point that the Scrolls community of purist messianic Jews was ideologically akin to the rebels who started the war with Rome—and to the "Apostles" Paul clashes with in the New Testament, as we shall see.

Professor Eisenman has also discovered numerous linguistic similarities between the Scrolls and the New Testament suggesting that a close and often hostile relationship existed between these two communities. This conflict appears to reflect the religious differences that erupt in the pages of the New Testament between the Apostle Paul and the early Christians led by James the Just—a conflict Paul bitterly describes in his famous letter to the Galatians.

One need not accept every conclusion that Professor Eisenman draws in order to be persuaded that the ideological dispute between the early Christian leaders James and Paul perfectly matches the differences between the militant and peaceful messianic groups of the 1st Century. In the work of Josephus, the Zealot movement is treated as a 1st Century innovation, like Christianity itself. And yet, even in the New Testament, sects with similarly sharp and strikingly similar ideological differences are both called "Apostles of Christ." One can hardly doubt that Romans like Tacitus, therefore, also counted both the hostile and messianic Zealots as "Christians."

* * * * * * * *

Paul's works are universally considered to be the oldest Christian writings even though they were penned about 20 to 30 years after Christ's death, and by a man who never personally knew Jesus. During his mission to establish the early Church, he recounts ongoing violent encounters and disagreement with Jews and, curiously, with fellow Apostles of Christ represented by James the Just.

The militancy of the Zealots' ideology resembles that of both the Dead Sea Scrolls community and, in all likelihood, the earliest so-called Christian community led by James. Both groups were focused on the messianic prophecies contained in the Jewish scripture, the main inspiration for the Jewish rebels, according to ancient sources. The Dead Sea and James groups, whether they were one and the same or not, both believed in strict adherence to the Torah—the source of conflict that made it so difficult for the Hebrews to assimilate with Romans and classical civilization, and made them the target of both Christ's scorn in the Gospels and Paul's vigorous arguments in the Epistles.

Although such practices as male circumcision limited widespread conversions, Jews of the era welcomed proselytes to some extent. A category of Jewish convert who was not circumcised but who still worshipped the Jewish God started to emerge, known as "God fearers." However, as with the worship of Roman state gods, if a man did not become circumcised, he was technically excluded from the House of Israel. He remained a mere onlooker, rather than a member among God's Chosen People.

A rising pagan interest in Judaism was another factor Romans were managing. Paul attests that his mission was to convert Gentiles in the wake of previous efforts by "Cephas" (Peter) and others who aimed only at converting Jews to the rising new messianic fervor. Since messianics were the purists with the greatest devotion to the law, Paul was probably the first messianic missionary to encounter Torah observance as a cultural obstacle. The new challenges that came with proselytizing to Gentiles, who were unaccustomed to Kosher diet and, especially, to circumcision, lead Paul to reject strict observance of Jewish law altogether in his mission.

It was this rejection that supposedly precipitated the passionate dispute between Paul and James and the controversy that would separate the Torah-rejecting and more pacifist Pauline "Christians" from the Torah-adhering Jewish "Christians" of James.

Paul Writing his Epistles, by Valentin de Boulogne
(17th Century)

Throughout his letters to his flocks, Paul emphasizes that Christ's death and resurrection liberated Christians from the constraints of Mosaic Law, thus eliminating the need for such practices as Kosher diet and circumcision. In short, he proclaimed that Christians were now "free in Christ." On the prickly issue of circumcising male converts, Paul inveighs:

> Stand fast therefore in the liberty by which Christ has made us free, and do not be entangled again with a yoke of bondage. Indeed I, Paul, say to you that *if you become circumcised, Christ will profit you nothing.* And I testify again to every man who becomes circumcised that he is a debtor to keep the whole law.

You have become estranged from Christ, *you who attempt to be justified by law; you have fallen from grace.* For we through the Spirit eagerly wait for the hope of righteousness by faith. For in Christ Jesus neither circumcision nor uncircumcision avails anything, but faith working through love. (Emphasis added.) (34)

Paul suggests this new "freedom" will break down the wall separating Jew from Gentile, thereby eliminating any reason for future conflict.

This idea is fairly summarized in a letter to the Ephesians ascribed to Paul (but more likely written by a follower of Paul's ideas a decade or two later during the Flavian era):

Therefore remember that at one time you Gentiles in the flesh, called "the uncircumcision" by what is called the circumcision, which is made in the flesh by hands—remember that you were at that time separated from Christ, alienated from the commonwealth of Israel and strangers to the covenants of promise, having no *hope* and without God in the world. But now in Christ Jesus you who once were far off have been brought near by the blood of Christ. *For he himself is our peace, who has made us both one and has broken down in his flesh the dividing wall of hostility by abolishing the law of commandments expressed in ordinances*, that he might create in himself one new man in place of the two, so making peace, and might reconcile us both to God in one body through the Cross, *thereby killing the hostility*. And he came and preached peace to you who were far off and peace to those who were near. For through him we both have access in one Spirit to the Father. So then you are no longer strangers and aliens, but you are fellow citizens with the saints and members of the household of God, built on the foundation of the apostles and prophets, Christ Jesus himself being the cornerstone... (Emphasis added.) (35)

As the Apostle Paul famously proclaims to the Christians of Corinth:

> Though I am free and belong to no one, I have made myself a slave to everyone, to win as many as possible. To the Jews I became like a Jew, to win the Jews. To those under the law I became like one under the law (though I myself am not under the law), so as to win those under the law. To those not having the law I became like one not having the law (though I am not free from God's law but am under Christ's law), so as to win those not having the law. To the weak I became weak, to win the weak. *I have become all things to all people so that by all possible means I might save some.* I do all this for the sake of the gospel that I may share in its blessings. (Emphasis added.) (36)

Paul's letter to the Galatians reveals that "Christians" said to have been Jesus's original followers somehow believe, in contrast to Paul's doctrine and only a couple of decades after the Crucifixion, that strict Torah observance is still mandatory, including Kosher diet and circumcision.

If the Gospels record history, this is impossible to understand since they quote Jesus announcing the end of Kosher dietary restrictions and his praising the faith of a presumably uncircumcised Roman soldier.

Christ's message would be extraordinary, to say the least, and *revolutionary* for a "grassroots" Jewish leader of the 1st Century. It is all the more incredible that his oldest followers could have missed it. The Gospels famously depict the disciples ignoring strict Sabbath observance, as well as Jesus arguing in favor of violating the Torah with Jewish religious authorities. How can two groups depicted as "Christians" disagree over such a fundamental message of Christ's ministry?

A closer look at Paul's letter to the faithful in Galatia reveals an interesting detail. He complains that "not even Titus, who was with me, was compelled to be circumcised, even though he was a Greek. This matter arose because some false believers had infiltrated our ranks to spy on the freedom we have in Christ Jesus and to make us slaves."

Paul wrote in Greek, but in Hebrew literature the term "Kittim" might denote not only Greeks but any foreigners from across the Mediterranean Sea, including, according to some scholars, Romans. So, intriguingly, it is possible that "Titus," Paul's Gentile convert who famously avoided circumcision was a Roman. Since Paul does not cite any other examples of converts allowed to keep their foreskins, Paul's friend "Titus" may have been a special exception for some reason we are not told.

Paul's complaint about Christian authorities "spy[ing] on the freedom" of his own community makes no sense if the "freedom" he spoke of was not generally opposed by the earlier "Christians." Again, we see the hostile division among Christians in the 1st Century.

The implication that spies could somehow make Paul's followers "slaves" suggests these spies were backed by the Christian *leadership* who could enforce their position. Paul boasts, however, that he didn't give in to them even for a minute. It is clear that he is establishing his own oppositional Christian leadership.

Indeed, Paul fearlessly belittles the existing authorities: "As for those who were held in high esteem—whatever they were makes no difference to me; God does not show favoritism—they added nothing to my message."

Paul cannot explicitly say that rival "Christians" agreed with him on the subject of circumcision, but he does write that "they recognized that I had been entrusted with the task of preaching the gospel to the uncircumcised, just as Peter had been to the circumcised." (Paul does not tell us if it was ever agreed that they be allowed to stay uncircumcised, however.)

If Paul's innovations had been acceptable, even theoretically, then his emotional objections and complex arguments would not have been necessary. Despite the fact that Paul himself boasts of his own chameleon-like behavior, he is frustrated that on the issue of Kosher diet, often put simply as "eating with Gentiles," his fellow Apostles are inconsistent. Sometimes they lapse back into Kosher ways. In his letter to the Galatians, he chastises them for this:

When Cephas came to Antioch, I opposed him to his face, because he stood condemned. For before certain men came from James, he used to eat with the Gentiles. But when they arrived, he began to draw back and separate himself from the Gentiles because he was afraid of those who belong to the circumcision group. The other Jews joined him in his hypocrisy, so that by their hypocrisy even Barnabas was led astray. (37)

Paul also admonishes Cephas for being cowed by James's men (the circumcision advocates) to give up eating with Gentiles. Cephas feared them, Paul tells us. So, it seems, did the other "Jews," including Paul's associate Barnabas (Joseph).

While Paul does claim to have "presented" the "gospel" that he preached to James and the Christian leadership while "meeting privately" with them, he does not spell out precisely what he said. Significantly, Paul does not say that Cephas and James or anyone else ever agreed with him or backed down from their own positions, even after he confronted the Apostle (Peter) "to his face," as the later Book of Acts claims.

When it comes to observing strict Jewish customs, James and Peter are clearly with the rebel Zealots' camp and the "sectarians" who preserved the Dead Sea Scrolls at the end of the first Jewish War—the very same camp that Jesus himself denounces throughout the Gospels.

Two Old Men Disputing (St. Paul and St. Peter), by Rembrandt (1628)

How could this conflict among Christians arise so soon after Christ settled all those issues, according to the Gospels?

* * * * * * * *

The writings attributed to Paul have no symbolic references to fish, as would the Gospels and other writings in the New Testament written after the Flavians' victorious prosecution of the Jewish War.

Paul was probably writing before the Flavian dynasty, during the rule of Nero and perhaps his predecessor, Claudius, suggesting that this symbolism had not yet been developed. The Gospels, written in the Flavian era, are equally filled with examples of Jesus criticizing traditional Jewish practice, however, from strict Sabbath observance to Kosher diet. Both Paul's letters and the Gospels explicitly advocate peace with Rome, as well, thus arguing for both political and cultural assimilation.

In the Gospels, Jesus displays contempt for contemporary notions of religious "purity" by publicly associating himself with "unclean" persons and objects, including prostitutes, tax collectors and Roman coins, all anathema to the Jewish people at the time. He even famously declares, in direct contradiction of Jewish Law, "Listen to me, everyone. Understand this: Nothing outside of you can make you 'unclean' by going into you. It is what comes out of you that makes you 'unclean'"—a direct challenge to Kosher laws. (38)

Jesus even commends the faith of a presumably uncircumcised Roman soldier as exceeding that of *any Jew.* (39) And, just as in Acts' accounts of Paul's ministry, Jesus's foils in the Gospels are invariably Jewish religious authorities, such as Pharisees, scribes, and priests—and never Roman authorities.

However, rather than citing any of Jesus's words or experiences to make his point, or simply reminding his "Christian" opponents of Jesus's own strong anti-Torah message (if it existed), Paul instead insists he learned his gospel from no man at all as he confronts the hardliner James, who, for his part, never seems to have heard of any of Jesus's ideas on the subject, either. Paul claims to have received his own distinct "gospel" directly from personal revelation. He even goes on to stress how little contact he has had with any Christians before preaching this new radical message. (40)

In the letter Paul writes to the Galatians describing his early travels he contradicts the account given in the Book of Acts in some important ways. As a first-person narrative from correspondence, however, the Galatians account should be given more historical weight, even if Paul's own credibility is questionable.

In any case, Acts itself, as we shall see in Part II, suggests that the apostles carried on a Kosher lifestyle well after Jesus supposedly renounced it.

* * * * * * * *

Had Jesus actually expressed the Pauline sentiments he is credited with saying in the Gospels, then James and the existing Christian community could never have disagreed with Paul in the first place.

Paul would not have needed to "oppose" Peter (Cephas) "to his face" (41) about such matters. Likewise, James, the Lord's "brother," would never have felt any need to "spy on" Paul's "freedom in Christ," as Galatians reports. (42) Paul would only have had to quote Jesus himself to settle the dispute. Yet he never does. Nor does his opponent, James, the supposed "brother" of Jesus, show any awareness of the revolutionary aspects of Jesus's gospel.

Paul's anti-Torah message is so pronounced that modern-day Protestants ascribe to the idea that faith by itself, whatever one's sins, is enough to earn salvation, citing Paul as support for this fundamental interpretation, especially passages like this:

> Where, then, is boasting? It is excluded. Because of what law? The law that requires works? No, because of the law that requires faith. For we maintain that a person is justified by faith apart from the works of the law. Or is God the God of Jews only? Is he not the God of Gentiles too? (43)

Before he converted to "Christianity," Paul says that he "persecuted the Church and tried to destroy it." (44) His zeal for traditional Judaism motivated him, he says, to attack what then must have been a "Christian" movement of observant Jews. Paul's problem with them at that point was clearly not the Kosher lifestyle, but their messianic fervor. Following his famous vision of the Risen Christ on the road to Damascus, when he claims the "scales fell from his eyes," Paul was driven to join the movement he had once fought so bitterly—something of a public relations coup for these Jewish "Christians" at the time, no doubt.

Yet, observe that his later fight with these same Jewish-Christians over the issues of circumcision and Kosher diet soon made him their enemy once more. We are left to wonder: was his conversion and association with the group he once persecuted designed from the start as a means of infiltrating them, sowing division, and undermining their devotion to the cultural hostilities that made rebellion so attractive?

We had long considered this to be the likely reality before the publication of *Operation Messiah: St. Paul, Roman Intelligence and the Birth of Christianity* by Thijs Voskuilen and Rose Mary Sheldon in 2008, and here the reader is directed to this work for the complete case. These authors go so far as to argue that Paul was himself a Roman intelligence operative, an *agent provocateur* engaged in a dangerous psy-ops campaign against the rebel "Christians." (45)

In stark contrast to Paul's message, his opponent James warns in a letter ascribed to him that the Father in Heaven "does not change like shifting shadows," (46) and emphasizes that one must not "merely listen to the word" but also "do what it says." (47)

Lacking documents known with certainty to have been written by them, it is difficult for us to know the details of the ideology or ideologies of the contemporary Jewish-Christians. However, apart from the problematic work of Josephus that we will discuss in Part II, the sectarian documents of the Dead Sea Scrolls (whatever the date of their composition) and this letter ascribed to James may be our best sources.

James seems to retain the contemporary Jewish idea of purity, urging his readers "to keep from being polluted by the world." (48) James also insists that, "whoever keeps the whole law and yet stumbles at just one point is guilty of breaking all of it." (49) In what seems to be a direct contradiction of Paul, the author asks, "What good is it, my brothers and sisters, if someone claims to have faith but has no deeds? … [F]aith by itself, if it is not accompanied by action, is dead." (50)

Icon of James the Just

James challenges less devout Jews with the notion that mere belief is not enough: "You believe that there is one God. Good! [But] even the demons believe that—and shudder." (51)

While James urges "peace," it is not at all clear that he means more than an internal peace among fellow Christians. "What causes fights and quarrels among you?" (52) James almost seems to threaten the Jewish establishment itself, which was then cooperating with Rome: "Now listen, you rich people, weep and wail because of the misery that is coming on you..." (53)

We see in the authentic letters of Paul, written before the Gospels, that the New Testament records a struggle between two types of "Christians"—well after Jesus allegedly had settled these disputes, according to the later Gospels. (54) Like Paul, James faces ideological foes within Judaism. Yet unlike Paul, James's conflicts seem to be with the "enemies" of the Scrolls community—not with the Scrolls community itself—starting with the Roman-collaborating Jewish establishment, as well as Paul and his followers.

The dispute between Paul and James as recorded in Galatians disturbed St. Augustine so much that he wrote to the respected early translator of the New Testament, St. Jerome, asking: how could the *Apostles* be in such heated disagreement? (55) Even during the reign of the Emperor Nero, decades after the supposed death of Jesus, Paul is telling us that this same conflict is still raging. Paul's group was amenable to the wider pagan world while James's group was violently opposed. *Why was this happening after the advent of Christ?*

We can now see the answer to this enigma that seemed insoluble to St. Augustine: in the 1st Century there were two different kinds of Christians. One advocated peace that flowed directly from a lax view of the Torah's requirements while accommodating Gentiles in harmony with Roman governance. The other advocated a hardline to preserve religious tradition and identity, and, in all likelihood, necessary opposition to Rome.

Now the references to troublesome "Christians" or to the followers of "Chrestus" by the ancient sources can be readily identified: they were not referring to the Christians we know today, requiring us to believe a bizarre scenario of irrationally sadistic Romans unjustly persecuting peace-loving Christians. Instead, these historical accounts refer to their religious rivals, who opposed Rome and who are shown clashing with Paul in the New Testament itself.

* * * * * * * *

The Church's solution for why this amnesia about Jesus's ministry occurred in Paul's time has been to hypothesize that after the Crucifixion the disciples must have undergone a "Judaizing" retrenchment. Those who followed Jesus's revolutionary mission reverted to previous ways. Other scholars ignore or minimize the heated quarrel between Paul and his "Christian" rivals, including Paul's outright damnation of them.

Yet, if Christians had somehow returned to traditional Jewish practice, surely Paul could have just cited Jesus himself on these disputes to settle the matter. But Paul does not. Instead, decades after Jesus's alleged ministry, he repeatedly emphasizes that he received his own gospel from no man exclusively through his own revelation.

From all of this, it is far more plausible to believe that the relevant Gospel material did not yet exist. Paul's adherents must have written it later as a demonstration of Pauline theology, giving his innovations the authority of Christ himself in order to trump Paul's contemporary "Jewish-Christian" opponents. This is the only conclusion that explains all the evidence, including the fact that the writing of the Gospels is dated to the Flavian era, *after* Paul's writings and *after* the first Jewish War. (56) As a direct result of that war, Paul's ideological foes were dead or in hiding by then, leaving only "Pauline" Christians still standing.

Now we can understand why Christians who followed the Gospels never seem to have been subjected to much persecution by the Roman government. Why would they be?

According to the early Christian apologist Tertullian, who lived in northern Africa at the turn of the 3rd Century, certain Roman governors of Africa actually intervened to secure acquittals for charged "Christians" (who were by this time almost exclusively of the Pauline varieties; surviving Jewish-Christians by then had taken the sectarian name of "Ebionites"). Sometimes these officials refused to bring any charges against Christians, at all. (57) While there were a couple of other local places and governors where we do know that New Testament Christianity was attacked, notably at Lyon and Vienne in 177 CE and later during the persecution that commenced under Diocletian in 303 CE, these appear to be brief exceptions to the Romans' rule.

Therefore, we can be reasonably certain that there was no cause for early Christian iconography to disguise itself in order to avoid persecution by Romans in the 1st and 2nd Centuries. The true purpose of using the symbols with which we started our investigation, the identical dolphin-and-anchor motif used by the Emperor Titus and the early Christians, may well have been exactly the opposite.

* * * * * * * *

Roman persecution of Christians, rare as it was, would come to an end with the "Edict" of Milan in 313 CE, when Constantine the Great began legalizing Christianity shortly before it became the official religion of the Roman Empire.

It was only at this point, as Christianity was officially instated by Rome, that the Cross finally emerged as the leading visual symbol of the faith.

We are told that the Emperor Constantine's own mother, Helena, following her son's famous vision of a "chi-ro" Cross (more akin to the ichthys wheel we observed earlier) in the sky before a decisive military victory, traveled to the Holy Land in 325-328 CE and discovered the True Cross, thus helping to institutionalize the shift from the dolphin-and-anchor motif used by both the Flavians and the Christians to a new symbol that had no connection to the Flavians.

Let us now examine those first Christian symbols that came before the Cross and how such symbolism came to be used by both the emperor of Rome and early Christians within the same generation. How common was this fish-and-anchor combination of symbols? Was it common enough to account for an overlap in its use, despite what we have been taught was total opposition between the groups using it? And, if not, what could account for this coincidence?

Apart from the fish or the Cross, at least as common and ancient a symbol of Christianity was the dolphin-and-anchor motif used by the Roman Emperor Titus. The crude image we have seen of a single fish drawn with two curved lines may strike one as the most primitive original, but at least as old, and perhaps even more widespread than the fish alone, was an anchor attended by one or more dolphins or fish. Here, for example, is a late Christian sample from an early 3rd Century catacombs with the inscription "fish of the living":

3rd Century Christian inscription

Here is a much earlier example dated to the early 2nd Century found in the very oldest Christian site in the world, the Catacombs of St. Domitilla. As mentioned earlier, Domitilla was the granddaughter of the Emperor Vespasian and the niece of the Flavian emperors Titus and Domitian:

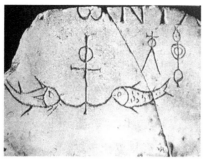

Christian inscription, 2nd Century Catacombs of St. Domitilla

Most ancients regarded the dolphin as a kind of fish, indeed, the King of Fish. Even today the dolphin is associated with Jesus Christ. This 2nd Century Christian ring shows the same variation found on Titus's coins:

2nd Century Christian ring

Here is another 2nd to 4th century example of the Christian motif:

2nd-4th Century Christian ringstone

Sometimes this symbol is surrounded by the letters that confirm its Christian nature:

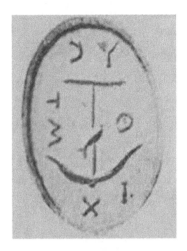

We can also note this in this 3rd-4th Century example of a Christian insignia from the British Museum:

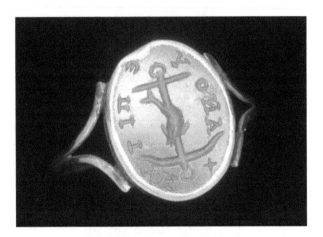

The same motif was apparently used in this artifact that predates any archeological evidence of Christianity (that has been acknowledged). It is a 1st Century cameo from the Flavian era in the Hermitage museum at St. Petersburg. Remember, no ruler had used this motif on coins since the Seleucid Empire four centuries before the Emperor Titus resurrected it for his coins:

Flavian era 1st Century cameo

Notice how the subtle rope depicted in the cameo above would later replace the dolphin entirely in this modern-day Christian version of the symbol:

In one of the very earliest examples of a Christian symbol from one of the oldest catacombs we can see that the first Christians sometimes represented themselves with two fish juxtaposed beside a trident instead of an anchor:

Early 2nd Century Christian catacombs

The Temple of Venus erected during the late 1st Century Flavian dynasty, again before all acknowledged archeological evidence of Christianity, was also decorated with a dolphin-and-trident motif repeated at the top of the pediment:

We see this motif appearing on the very pagan 2nd Century basilica of Neptune in Rome, as well:

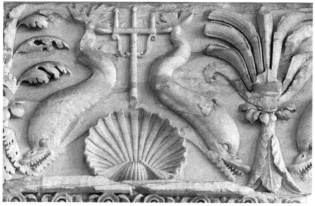

Dolphin-and-trident, Basilica of Neptune, 2nd Century

Christians sometimes juxtaposed an anchor with a fish, as here in the Catacombs of St. Sebastian at Rome:

Here is another example from the Catacombs of St. Sebastian:

From the Christian Catacombs of Priscilla, this fish is facing an anchor:

An anchor alone or juxtaposed with a fish or dolphin is commonly seen on countless early Christian rings, like these:

Here's a variation from a 3rd or 4th Century Roman Christian intaglio ring:

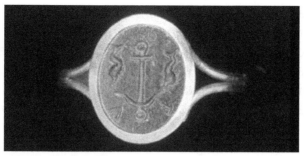

And another of the same age:

Here are details from a mosaic floor of a 2nd Century mansion at Plaza de la Corredera in Cordoba, Spain:

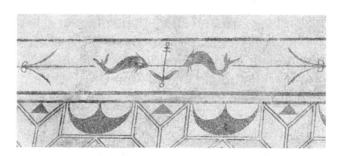

All of these images comprise a closely related family of symbols used by Christians during at least the first three centuries, almost to the total exclusion of the symbol of the Cross. While these anchor/fish Christian symbols have been found in abundance, only 20 instances of Christians using a cross as a symbol over the first four centuries have ever been discovered in Rome's famous catacombs.

The anchor had long been a universal pagan symbol of safety, security and homecoming. The New Testament itself states of Christian salvation: "We have this hope as anchor for the soul, firm and secure. It enters the inner sanctuary behind the curtain, where our forerunner, Jesus, has entered on our behalf." (58) This passage refers to the annual Yom Kippur entrance into the Holy of Holies by the Jewish High Priest in order to supplicate God for the atonement of the sins of the people—and how Christ himself had supplanted this important religious observance.

Oddly, St. Clement of Alexandria did not cite this passage from the New Testament when recommending the anchor as a Christian symbol (in the list where he also recommends the fish). Nor does he cite any previous use of the anchor by Jews, who did use an anchor on some of their coins. Instead, he mentions only pagan precedents from the Seleucid Empire as a pedigree for his recommendation.

Some have observed that the anchor forms a kind of Cross (though not all of its representations suggest this). Thus, they speculate, this makes it an appropriate symbol of both Christ and Christian hope for redemption through the Crucifixion.

However, the anchor is referenced by St. Paul as a Christian metaphor *before* the Cross itself was used as a Christian symbol, as we have seen. When employing the anchor metaphor in their earliest literature, Christians associated it with *hope*, in Latin "spes," or, *Spes in Christo; spes in Deo; spes in Deo Christo*, as rendered in the traditional Catholic formulation.

Above, we can see many examples of two fishes or dolphins facing or aiming at the anchor. This has been interpreted as the Christian's *quest* for hope and redemption and the search for knowledge of Christ. When the symbol was depicted as a dolphin entwined around an anchor, it made the anchor an alternative to a cross with the dolphin representing Christ himself, as can be seen even on this pendant that is still offered to the faithful today:

Here is a modern-day Catholic pendant with Christ himself in the place of the dolphin on an anchor:

A distinction between Christians and Christ is suggested in the variations of the symbolism. The fish (or multiple fishes) juxtaposed with or aiming *at* an anchor seems to represent the Christian follower at burial sites, while the fish or dolphin entwined or superimposed *on* the anchor seems to represent Christ, especially on rings, seals, and even modern pendants.

The anchor can also be seen as a sort of *fishhook* with the approaching fish representing converts for whom the Apostles were "fishing," while the superimposed symbol for Christ served as the *bait* on the hook, what the convert symbolically *eats*, the flesh of Christ that nourishes the spirit's hunger. This first Christian symbol, therefore, seems to represent the act of evangelism more vividly than the Cross itself, illustrating missionaries as "fishers of men."

Centuries later, the Renaissance printer from Venice, Aldus Manutius, would adopt this symbol as his own device, reputedly after observing it on an ancient coin of the Emperor Titus:

Today, this is also the logo for Doubleday Books:

According to the entry for "Anchor" in *The Catholic Encyclopedia:*

> During the second and third centuries the anchor
> occurs frequently in the epitaphs of the catacombs,
> and *particularly in the most ancient parts* of the cem-
> eteries of Sts. Priscilla, Domitilla, Calixtus, and the
> Coemetarium majus. About *seventy examples* of it
> have been found *in the cemetery of Priscilla alone,*
> prior to the 4th Century. *In the oldest of these (2nd
> Century)* the anchor is found associated with such
> expressions as *pax tecum, pax tibi, in pace,* thus
> expressing the firm *hope* of the authors of these
> inscriptions that their friends have been admitted to
> Heaven. (Emphasis added.) (59)

So, there are no fewer than 70 examples of the anchor from
just *one* of the ancient Christian catacombs. And these symbols
inhabit the oldest parts of those sites. In contrast, we have scant
few examples of the Cross, as the same entry from the *Catholic
Encyclopedia* confirms:

> The rare appearance of a cross in the Christian
> monuments of the first four centuries is a well-known
> peculiarity; not more than a score of examples belong
> to this period. Yet, though the cross is of infrequent
> occurrence in its familiar form, certain monuments
> appear to represent it *in a manner intelligible to a
> Christian but not to an outsider.* The anchor was the
> symbol best adapted for this purpose, and the one
> most frequently employed. (Emphasis added.) (60)

Curiously, the anchor was by far the more common way to depict
the Cross *than the Cross itself* during the first four centuries after
Christ.

Despite its nearly universal use among the earliest Christians,
the dolphin-and-anchor symbol was phased out in favor of the
Cross after Christianity was instated by Constantine as the Roman
religion. From the middle of the 3rd Century, the anchor's use as a

Christian symbol is found only rarely in monuments. By the early 4th Century, it virtually disappears. (61)

In Hagia Sophia in Istanbul (formerly Constantinople), which was constructed as a Christian basilica in the 6th Century, we still see panels adorned with dolphins and a trident that are strikingly similar to those we saw earlier in the oldest catacombs and in Flavian monuments:

Dolphin-and-trident motif, Hagia Sophia, 527 CE

The Catholic Encyclopedia refers to these dolphin-and-trident symbols thus: "To the same category of [dolphin-and-anchor] symbols, probably, belongs the group of representations of the dolphin and trident." (62) The same may be said of the Flavian use of both dolphin-and-anchor and dolphin-and-trident symbols.

We can certainly begin to see, therefore, compelling reasons for these earliest Christian symbols to be discontinued under Constantine.

* * * * * * * *

The dolphin-and-anchor or dolphin-and-trident motifs obviously have distinctly pagan roots and parallels, even according to some of the earliest Church fathers, to the exclusion of Jewish sources. This alone may have been reason enough for phasing them out in favor of a symbol that was unique to Christianity after Christianity had become the state religion of Rome.

This in turn only begs the question: Why would the earliest Christians represent themselves with pagan and imperial symbolism in the first place—Christians who were even closer to their imperial source?

Emphasizing their alleged persecution in Roman times, Christians often venerate their saints for being unable to worship the Romans' pagan deities. A true Christian could never sacrifice animals or even offer incense for the safety or well-being of the emperor, even on pain of martyrdom. Paganism was such anathema to early Christians, we are told, that they refused to eat food that had been sacrificed to any emperor or pagan god. It was this commitment to strictly exclusive monotheism that is said to have pitted the early Christians against Roman society and caused their alleged persecution.

By this understanding it is difficult to see why Christians would adopt a symbol directly imported not from Judaism or their own creative imaginations but straight from imperial pagan propaganda currently in circulation on Roman coins. Moreover, the fact that they chose the symbol of not just any Roman emperor but the very emperor who fulfilled Jesus's prophecy about his Second Coming is impossible to reconcile with the traditional understanding of Church history.

Since these pagan symbols predate the use of the Cross, the traditional explanations for Christians using them make little sense. As we have already observed, the reasoning that they were adopted as substitutes or disguises for the Cross presupposes that pagans were aware of the Cross as a Christian symbol and might have reacted negatively to it. But, as we have seen, the Cross was not used before the anchor or the fish as a Christian seal. Something that had not yet existed would not need to be disguised as something else. And the policy of the Roman government was tolerant toward Christians. There was no need to hide anything.

We shall now see evidence that, rather than being a ruse to cover their tracks from purported Roman oppressors, using these pagan symbols had the opposite motive. It is highly probable that Christians chose them not to hide their opposition to Roman authority but to *advertise* their affiliation with it, instead.

It's time to take a deeper look at this symbol that the Flavians and Christians shared and where it came from.

II. Religion and Propaganda

As we have seen, the symbol below was used by both a Roman emperor and early Christians. However, this is not from Christian catacombs but is a 2nd Century BCE mosaic floor of the House of the Trident on Delos, the sun-drenched island sacred to the sun god Apollo and alleged to be his birthplace:

Symbol of the god Apollo at Delos, 2nd Century BCE

So we can see that hundreds of years earlier, the dolphin-and-anchor symbol used by Christians and Titus had been used as a symbol of Apollo by the Greeks who ruled the kingdoms of the eastern Mediterranean.

This symbol was originally devised for Apollo because, according to a famous story from Homer, the sun god was once transformed into a dolphin, making the animal sacred to him.

King Seleucus I (c. 358-281 BCE), Alexander the Great's general who founded the Seleucid dynasty of Middle Eastern potentates, declared himself to be the son of the god Apollo. He adopted his divine father's symbol on inscriptions, like this one:

King Seleucus I inscription with anchor and dolphins

Like other Hellenistic monarchs, Antiochus I, the son of Seleucus I, adopted the surname "Soter," Greek for "Savior," the title later applied to Jesus. (As we have seen, St. Clement of Alexandria directly invoked Seleucus's use of the anchor symbol as a precedent for Christians using it to represent Jesus Christ.)

Here is a gold coin issue of Seleucus's son, Antiochus, with himself as "the Savior" on one side and a nude Apollo (his divine grandfather) on the other:

Antiochus the Savior, and Apollo

Seleucid symbolism was picked up in the coinage of the Jewish kingdom of the Hasmonean dynasty after the Hasmoneans successfully revolted from Seleucid oppression. Greek culture was still strong, however, especially along the new coast of their newly conquered kingdom, so it is not surprising that anchor images associated with Seleucid royalty appear on the Jewish state's first coins, like this one:

Hasmonean coin, 103-76 BCE

Of course, since graven images of the divine were proscribed under Jewish law, on Jewish coins the anchor did not symbolize Apollo, or even the Jewish god, Jehovah or Yahweh. This was forbidden. Even these anchor images probably did not appear on the Hasmoneans' coins until after their conquest of the coastal towns.

Other pagan symbolism such as the lily and the cornucopia were adopted for use on the coinage of Hasmonean kings. (1) The Herodian kings that followed them also showed the anchor on their coins as they sought to demonstrate continuity with the previous dynasty and legitimize their rule. The anchor was never, however, a Jewish *religious* symbol as it was for Christians from the start. It was used on their coins strictly for political purposes.

It is also certain that we would never find any fish or dolphins associated with the anchor image on a Jewish coin since graven images of God, whether animal or human, were forbidden by Jewish law along with any form of "idol worship." (2) No human representations of any kind are therefore present on Hebrew coin issues, and certainly no representations of an animal, an emperor, or anything symbolic of God could appear on their coins, either. Instead, we find only natural objects such as a palm tree, a pomegranate, or a star, or man-made objects associated with the Temple and its rituals, such as a trumpet, a menorah, or the Temple itself.

In contrast, Greek and Roman coin issues liberally feature the faces of gods, nude emperors, quasi-divine kings, animals representing gods, and all things anathema to Jews of that era.

The closest use of symbols found in Jewish coins to represent a person, perhaps, was a star that represented the Messiah—a very human and *not* a divine messiah since monotheistic Jews necessarily rejected the idea of human divinity. On one coin issued by the

Hasmonean Alexander Jannaeus we find the anchor on one side and the eight-pointed star of the Messiah on the other:

Jewish coin with anchor and messianic star, early 1st Century BCE

So strict were contemporary Hebrew convictions about adhering to their law against graven images that foreign coins depicting pagan deities could not even be used to purchase animals for sacrifice at the Temple. Jewish and Hellenistic pilgrims were required to exchange their currency for coins acceptable under Jewish law through the "money changers"—who were famously attacked by Jesus in the Gospels.

Although Pauline Christians clearly abandoned this strict Jewish proscription of graven images, it is still noteworthy that St. Clement of Alexandria failed to cite any Jewish precedent for using the anchor as a Christian symbol. Even though he might well have been aware that Jewish coins adopted this image from the pagan Seleucids, he cites only the Seleucids as his justification for its Christian use.

Other Roman emperors also used anchors and dolphins in their official propaganda, as we can see in this 2nd Century coin minted in the reign of Hadrian, showing the god Oceanus (whose river surrounded the entire world, according to Greek myth) carrying an anchor, much as Neptune is often depicted carrying a trident. The god is reclining on a dolphin:

However, during the precise point in time that concerns us the only source of the same dolphin-and-anchor symbolism Christians employed appears to be the coins minted by the very emperor who fulfilled Jesus's prophecy, Titus.

Titus

This Christian motif was used by the Flavian emperors Titus and—for a few months—his brother Domitian. In his own short reign, Titus released millions of coins with this symbol.

Dolphin-and-anchor motif in Titus's coins

So common is this motif on Titus's coins that it would have been impossible not to associate him with the symbol in contemporary minds.

Compare another object of Roman symbolism dated to the 1st Century—prior to any known archeological evidence of Christianity—that proves these Flavian artifacts range from bronze, silver and gold coins minted for the masses to an expensive cameo carved for the upper classes:

1st Century Titus coin and 1st Century cameo from the Hermitage

The emperor who vanquished Jerusalem was the first to use the dolphin-and-anchor symbol on Roman coins, and he did so in abundance. As we shall see, Titus used similar dolphin-and-anchor symbolism at public works, as well, decades prior to the existence of any confirmed Christian archeology. The Flavian connection to these symbols is clear; evidence of Christians using them, according to the accepted archeological view, would not exist until early in the 2nd Century.

By the time the second Jewish uprising and final war with the Romans in Judea occurred under Hadrian, a limited minting of Titus's symbol was struck by this emperor, as well, but only in the east in Alexandria. At that date, and in this part of the Empire, the symbol cannot be a reference to the Flavian Emperor Titus anymore, but to Apollo or Christ.

Hadrian coin with dolphin-and-anchor motif, Alexandria, c. 125 CE

Hadrian, who conducted an empire-wide restoration of religious culture (excluding "Jewish" Christianity with which Rome was again at war) may have aligned himself with "Roman" Christianity as a way of promoting harmony with Roman rule. At the war's conclusion Hadrian may have even sent Christians to the vanquished city of Jerusalem to replace the expelled Jews.

The 4th Century Christian historian Eusebius reports both the total expulsion of the Jewish people from their homeland following the Second Jewish Revolt and the city's complete recolonization by Romans. Of note, he also reports the appointment of the first Gentile "Bishop" of Jerusalem's "Christian" Church. Eusebius further reports the Emperor Hadrian's favorable treatment of Christians, in general—but characterizes that same emperor's ruthless slaughter of Jewish women and children ("destroying at one stroke unlimited numbers of men, women and children alike") as entirely deserved (their leader was a "bloodthirsty bandit" who as "the instigator of their crazy folly paid the penalty he deserved"). (3)

In any event, recognizably Christian archeology had already begun to emerge by Hadrian's time—and these were the symbols Christians were using. The same symbol employed by the first Roman conqueror of Judea, Titus, was employed by the next Roman conqueror of Judea, Hadrian, at a time when the symbol no longer represented Flavian rule but, at least in part, may well have publicly represented Christianity.

* * * * * * * *

Currency was a powerful aqueduct by which the Roman Empire circulated its propaganda far and wide. Because they were produced in the billions, coins are one form of artifact employed in that effort that can never be entirely lost to history. Mini-billboards and bumper stickers jingling in the pockets of the populace from one end of the Empire to the other while transacting the very business of life, coins allowed Romans to advertise the prosperity and peace they brought to the world—the *Pax Romana*—by proclaiming it right on their money.

Mediterranean rulers had used coinage as propaganda for centuries before the Romans, and the Romans were close students of the methods employed by previous rulers. They advanced the use of coins to new heights as a medium for transmitting the self-image and ideology Rome wished to sell to the world. With the advent of empire, Roman propaganda asserted imperial divinity or divine approval for their rule, a project that often entailed affiliating the emperor with official Roman state deities and gods local to certain territories, as well as encouraging the worship of some deceased emperors as gods—precisely the kind of graven images forbidden by Jewish law. In an age when there was no division between politics and religion, the success of Rome was depicted as the result of divine favor and the sanction of the gods made manifest. Coins were a direct way to spread that message.

Not only Rome's legendary founder Romulus, but also the later founders of Rome's first imperial dynasty, Julius and Augustus Caesar, were officially deified (made gods), complete with their own cults, temples, and highly organized priesthoods. This deification was proudly celebrated on Roman coins. Soon, an emperor, Caligula, would even seek deification during his lifetime, although this stimulated a degree of resistance (though not in the farther-flung parts of the Empire). Caligula even attempted to place a statue of himself as a god in the Jewish Temple itself—setting off such a violent reaction among the Hebrews that he was forced to scuttle the project. (4)

After an emperor's death, however, it was so commonplace for them to be deified by the time of the Flavians that on his deathbed Vespasian supposedly quipped: "Dear me! I must be turning into a god." (5)

Outside the city of Rome, especially in the east where many people were used to worshipping rulers as divine, Roman emperors were worshipped as gods while they were still alive as early as the reign of Augustus. Inside the city of Rome, however, where that was still a brick too far, emperors commonly associated themselves with favored divinities believed to bring order and good fortune to the world.

In the 1st Century, Greek and Roman Stoic philosophies were a major influence on the ideology that was associated with Rome's state deities. Stoics saw history as a continuous cycle of death and renewal that was driven by "Fortuna" (destiny) and "Logos" (the divine). Benevolently, these forces always provided humanity with a "Soter" (a savior) who could turn chaos and struggle into a new order of *pax* and *salus* (peace and health or safety).

The ancient idea of a "Soter" came to be identified with the god Apollo, a solar deity connected with healing, and, later also with another sun god, Sol Invictus. (6) In this context, the first emperor, Augustus, was seen as a *messianic* figure who had established a new "golden age"—the *Pax Augusta*—from the chaos of the civil wars preceding his rule after Julius Caesar's assassination. (7)

Augustus's great-uncle and adoptive father, the dictator Julius Caesar, was officially deified by the Senate shortly after his murder. This made Augustus a "son of the divine" or "Son of God." Augustus's coinage links his imperial cult with this divine imagery, as on this coin where we find the legend "DiviF", an abbreviation of *divi filius*, which means "son of god":

Augustus, "Son of God"

The dolphin, as we have seen, had long been a divine pagan symbol. It was sacred to at least three pagan divinities: Apollo, Venus (Aphrodite), and Neptune (Poseidon), who governed the seas. All three deities made good symbols for a Roman emperor. Venus was said to be the legendary ancestress of the founders of the first imperial dynasty, the deified Julius Caesar and his heir, Augustus. Neptune, of course, "ruled the seas," and Romans had conquered the Mediterranean and made it their own private lake. Like Seleucus, Augustus's cult also claimed him to be a son of Apollo, by a niece of the Divine Julius. (8)

Later emperors such as Vitellius imitated Augustus by adopting Apollo's symbols. Apollo made a good affiliation for the Flavian emperors, as well, since he was linked to previous dynastic emperors like Augustus. As founders of the dynasty that followed the

Julio-Claudian dynasty, the Flavians quite naturally used them as a model—just as Augustus found a model in the Hellenistic precedents of rulers who followed Alexander the Great, like the Seleucids and the Ptolemys of Egypt, and as Hadrian would find a model in the first Roman conqueror of Judea, Titus.

Since the Flavians, like Augustus, also ended a destructive civil war (68-69 CE), they, too, were eager to represent themselves as healers—like the healer god Apollo. The Roman civil war and the Jewish War provided Vespasian with a compelling reason to be seen as a new Divine Augustus and a new Divine Julius, both pacifier and healer and a patron of a new Roman era of peace and prosperity after violent upheaval.

In addition, the Flavian dynasty had gained empire through their victories in the east. Vespasian was even named emperor while he was still commanding the legions in Judea. This provides yet a further explanation for why the Flavians would adopt solar god symbols on their coins. Hailing from the east, like the sun that rises in the east, the Flavians could naturally be associated with solar deities like Apollo. One omen portending Vespasian's future imperial rule was a statue of the deified Julius Caesar that supposedly swiveled on its base and faced east, where Vespasian waged war in Judea. (9) Tacitus mentions the same event as foretelling the fall of Vitellius, Vespasian's rival for the throne back home in Italy, whose death paved Vespasian's way to the throne. (10)

Here is an example of a coin issued by Vespasian's son, Titus, with himself on one side and a statue of the sun god Sol or Helios on the other:

Titus and the Sun God

Titus, Vespasian's son, had practically become co-emperor after prosecuting the Jewish War with his father. Titus is reported to have been born on December 30. (11) Solar deities usually celebrated their "births" at the end of December. The Winter Solstice is the shortest day of the year and the longest night. A year is measured by the movements of the sun, and the sun may be said to reach "maturity" at the Summer Solstice only to be reborn during the Winter Solstice at the end of December when the days begin to grow longer again. So Titus's birth date provides another link to sun gods like Apollo or the Persian god Mithra, who was born on December 25, just as western Christian tradition celebrates the birth of Christ. In the eastern side of the Empire, Christmas is still celebrated on January 6. Thus, the birth of Titus occurred right in the middle of the famous "Twelve Days of Christmas."

"Christmas" celebrations may have begun only centuries later, but the relatively early association of Jesus's birth with solar deities like Apollo and the earlier Christian choice of dolphin symbols associated with Apollo are worth noting as we continue.

* * * * * * * *

The Flavian Amphitheater

The most famous construction of the Flavians, the one everyone associates with ancient Rome itself, is the Flavian Amphitheater. Today it is known as the "Colosseum."

The original inscription over its entrance read, "The Emperor Vespasian ordered this new amphitheater to be erected from his general's share of the booty [from the Jewish War]."

The Colosseum derived its popular name from the gigantic statue that had been erected in front of it:

Colossus Neronis: a colossal bronze statue of Nero, 120 feet high, the work of Zenodorus, a Greek, erected by Nero himself in the vestibule of the Domus Aurea [Golden House] on the summit of the Velia [citation], but after the death of that emperor changed by Vespasian into a statue of the Sun… (12)

A trident flanked by two dolphins, like that seen in one of the earliest Christian catacombs and on pagan temples (including one built by the Flavians), also appears on one of the Colosseum's few surviving marble architectural details:

Marble fragments from the Flavian Amphitheater,
including a keystone with dolphin-and-trident motif

Such nautical imagery adorning the Colosseum, a reference to Neptune, is unsurprising considering the mock naval battles per-formed in that notorious amphitheater. However, one must wonder: if Christians were being fed to the lions *in the Colosseum*, how is it that a pagan symbol *from the Colosseum* is being employed to represent Christians in their oldest catacombs only a few miles away?

Fish-and-Trident symbol, 2nd Century Christian catacombs

Meanwhile, the long-lost colossus of the sun god that gave the Colosseum its name towered over that section of the city during the Flavians' rule. It must have looked something like this:

Sol/Helios/Apollo

We have already seen that the dolphin-and-anchor motif was first used to represent Apollo. One of the earliest depictions of Jesus Christ made by Christians, one that predates most portraits showing him with a beard, is this 3rd Century mosaic in which a beardless Jesus resembles the sun god, Sol or Helios or Apollo, with a radiant crown:

Jesus, 3rd Century mosaic

For comparison, here is an ancient Hellenistic representation of Alexander the Great as the sun god:

Alexander as Helios, 2nd Century BCE

In the Gospel of John, Jesus famously describes himself with the title of the Sun god, "the Light of the World." (13) And, like the sun itself, his resurrection is at dawn, according to all four Gospels. (The placing of halos around the heads of saints in Christian art probably originates from the light-rays artistically depicted around the heads of solar deities like Apollo, Helios and Sol Invictus.)

In addition to using dolphin-and-anchor and dolphin-and-trident symbols, Roman emperors also employed dolphin-over-tripod symbols. The tripod was closely associated with the Oracle at Delphi, Apollo's oracle, in which the priestess, the Pythia, sat upon a tripod to deliver her prophecies. Here are examples of both a Vitellius and a Titus coin depicting a dolphin over a tripod:

Pre-Flavian Vitellius coin

Titus coin

According to one old source on Roman coinage:

> The dolphin was consecrated to Apollo, who, according to Homer, had transformed himself into one. Hence we see a Delphic tripod with a dolphin upon it, on a silver coin of Vitellius, that emperor having, as the inscription teaches us, been one of the [officials] appointed to the care of sacrificial ceremonies. A similar type appears on a denarius of Titus, but not with the same legend. (14)

This same source also claims that "[t]he Dolphin, entwined round an *anchor*, was at one time a symbol of Augustus—it is also seen on coins struck by princes of the Flavia family, sons of Vespasian." (15) However, one contemporary editor of a numismatic forum corrects this:

> The emblem of a dolphin wrapped around an anchor appears on the reverse of silver denarii produced by the Rome mint during the reigns of the Flavian emperors Titus and Domitian between AD 79 and the early 80s. (*So far as I am aware, it does not appear on the coins of Augustus, pace* the Dictionary of Roman Coins text above [though there is an Augustus denarius with the reverse showing a dolphin wrapped around *a trident...*]) (16)

Here is that Augustus coin with the dolphin-and-trident motif:

Augustus coin with dolphin-and-trident motif

So, it seems that while dolphin and even anchor imagery had been used by other emperors, the only Roman emperors to ever use the dolphin-entwined-anchor motif on coins were the Flavian emperors Titus and Domitian, although the latter seems to have dropped the image very quickly after Titus's death, and Hadrian, who would finish Titus's war 35 years later, in a limited edition after Christians had publicly adopted it.

One can see many advantages for Titus employing the dolphin-and-anchor symbolism. Since the anchor had been commonly stamped on coins of Seleucid and Jewish kings for centuries, its use by Titus further associated him with both Hellenistic and Jewish monarchs of the east. This would not have been lost upon Titus's propagandists after he had conquered Judea, as this triumph was one of his family's chief claims to the throne. However, to depict fish or dolphin figures with an anchor would have been blasphemy to the Hebrews. So the pairing of these figures in Flavian symbology—as Christians would also do—is therefore exclusively pagan.

Of course, the purely political use of the anchor on Jewish coins surprisingly becomes a religious symbol for early Christians, as it is on the coins of Titus—something Hebrews expressly forbade. And the same family of symbols so often used by the Flavians—fish, anchors and tridents—was also Christianity's predominant symbology for its first three centuries.

A symbol from Roman imperial political propaganda used in the late 1st Century was adopted by Christians within three or four decades, even at their gravesites, in the city of Rome itself. We must ask again: why do we have such a paradoxical coincidence of symbols from supposedly antagonistic groups almost perfectly overlapping each other in both time and place?

The dolphin-and-anchor motif is one of the most commonly used on the coins of the Emperor Titus. This makes it awkward enough as an appropriate Christian symbol by the conventional understanding. Adding to the paradox, Titus happens to have sacked Jerusalem and destroyed its famous Temple, just as Jesus predicted would happen within the time frame of his Second Coming.

In the oldest archeological evidence of Christians in the catacombs, as we have seen, Christians depicted fish and anchors juxtaposing each other to represent their affiliation. Let us now consider this mosaic, which was once at the bottom of an Olympic-sized pool in a public works in the city of Herculaneum buried in 79 CE by the eruption of Mt. Vesuvius during the reign of the Emperor Titus. And remember that it predates by more than two decades any accepted archeological evidence of Christianity (17):

Herculaneum, pre-80 CE

Both dolphins and people are swimming toward a cruciform anchor, the universal symbol of safety. Fish are directly equated with people. What deity the anchor represents is not clear, but what is striking about this mosaic is that the devotees of Apollo, Titus, or Jesus Christ could all have designed it with equal plausibility. The family of symbols, and their meaning, is identical to that employed by Christians in the earliest catacombs. Yet this mosaic predates all accepted archeological evidence for Christianity.

This image was captured in a time capsule by the eruption of Vesuvius during the brief reign of Titus. Titus ruled for two years, two months and twenty days. Exactly two months after he succeeded his father as Emperor, Vesuvius erupted. Since recent earthquakes rocking the area prior to the eruption damaged much of Herculaneum, and the other pool in the same gymnasium was under repair at the time, the fact that this pool had been filled and working when Vesuvius erupted implies it had been recently restored. As this public works was originally built by Augustus and numerous violent quakes had preceded the eruption in the previous months, it is probable that the restoration necessary to repair this pool had been commissioned by the Flavian emperors themselves.

Here is another 1st Century "pre-Christian" Flavian artifact. It is an intaglio that predates any accepted archeological evidence of Christianity. It is a hand-carved opposite and indented image (suggesting that it may have been used by a wealthy Flavian or a Flavian official as a seal):

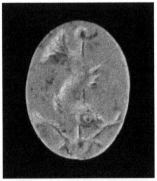

Hand-carved reverse of dolphin-and-anchor motif, 1st Century

* * * * * * * *

When we look deeper into why the Emperor Titus would choose nautical imagery, especially considering that his campaign in Judea took place mostly in the desert, yet another extraordinary correlation with Jesus Christ becomes apparent.

Titus was a talented general whose signal achievements as a military leader were his deeds during the Jewish Revolt of 66-73 CE, which earned him a Roman Triumph and ultimately the imperial chair in Rome. The Judean conflict was not a naval affair, with one notable exception: the reduction of the Jewish towns and cities around a certain very small landlocked body of water: the Sea of Galilee.

After a minor engagement with Titus's forces, the city of Tiberias on the shore of Galilee surrendered, but the rebel leader, Jesus ben Saphat (Saphias), fled with his insurgents to a town called Tarichaeae, also on the lake's shore. Leading an elite cavalry unit, Titus bravely gave them chase to the plain outside that city's walls.

Badly outnumbered there, Titus sent for reinforcements of 400 horses and 2,000 archers. Yet, after a rousing harangue from General Titus, the Roman forces rallied even before help could arrive. Titus took Tarichaeae in a creative and bold assault, crossing over the Sea of Galilee on a hastily constructed fleet of rafts and striking the town's unfortified waterfront. Thousands of rebels from the town were driven into the sea, where the Romans mercilessly wiped them out.

Writer Joseph Atwill has observed that the Roman army that day was literally "fishing for men" on the Sea of Galilee after the future Emperor Titus had figuratively driven the "demons" into its waters. Atwill has noted other parallels between Jesus's and Titus's activities, as well, that seem more than coincidental. (18)

According to Roman historian Barbara Levick:

> The importance of the engagement [at Tarichaeae] in Roman eyes, and perhaps its importance for Titus' glory, may be indicated by the number of ships in the joint triumphal procession of 71, and allusions to it on the coinage... (19)

So the use of nautical symbols by Titus on his coins, Levick argues, was inspired in part by his heroic deeds on the Sea of Galilee—just as we have seen Christians adopted the same symbols in part to celebrate Jesus's miracles on the same small body of water.

Christian use of this symbol and its near-simultaneous use in Roman imperial propaganda is simply inexplicable by any conventional understanding of Christianity's origins. The correlation between the deeds of Jesus and those of Titus only adds more improbability to the already incredible coincidence. And, of course, the dating of the Gospels themselves coincides with the reign of the Flavians, after their victory over Judea.

Detail from the Arch of Titus as Romans plunder the Temple, c. 81 CE

Since the dolphin-and-anchor motif was still circulating on Flavian coins while Christians used this iconography in their earliest catacombs, we are compelled to take a closer look at the cults of the deified Flavian emperors, Vespasian and Titus. (Their successor, Domitian, was never deified.)

* * * * * * * *

Rome's first dynasty of emperors, the Julio-Claudians, boasted an exalted ancestry with family trees extending well back into the days of the Roman republic. As previously noted, the Julii even claimed one of their ancestors was the Goddess of Love herself, Venus, via the legendary Trojan prince Aeneas. Aeneas was reported to have fled to the coast of Italy following the fall of Troy, a journey celebrated in the contemporary poet Virgil's masterwork, *The Aeneid*.

We also know that Augustus's own imperial cult claimed him to be a son of the Greek god Apollo. Caligula later associated himself with a wide variety of deities, including, perhaps, both Jupiter and Venus.

The first imperial dynasty did such a thorough job of exterminating itself through real and imagined plots, a string of executions, murders, purges and forced suicides, that by the collapse of Nero's reign in 68 CE there were very few left who could claim descent from Augustus, whether by birth or by adoption. Consequently, a nasty civil war broke out after Nero's fall, with leading generals and political figures vying for the suddenly open imperial seat, even as the unrest in Judea was still being subdued by Vespasian and Titus.

In the space of a year-and-a-half, Rome went through four successive new emperors as the armies of the contending princes faced off against each other and the population of the ruptured empire nervously anticipated the outcome. The Empire's survival hung in the balance during this period that came to be known as "The Year of Four Emperors."

Meanwhile, Vespasian had been entrusted by Nero with the considerable force of three legions and significant auxiliaries to prosecute the Jewish War. Therefore, when Nero died, Vespasian suddenly found himself to be one of the leading contenders for the throne, despite the fact that he was a man of relatively humble background. (Although Vespasian and his older brother had both achieved consulships, they had been the first of the Flavians to enter the Senate.)

So, when Vespasian made his bid for power, he faced a serious problem of legitimacy. At this point in Roman history few considerations apart from military prowess mattered in the contest for the top spot, but conservative opinion still resisted the notion that might alone could make right. Romans required divine support and providential sanction for their emperors, as well.

The ancient Romans undertook no major action without consulting the auspices, entreating the gods for their support, and asking them whether a successful outcome could be expected. The goddess of destiny, Fortuna, indicated her divine favor through success on the battlefield. Yet supernatural sanction could be revealed in many other ways.

Vespasian

Given his humble origins, Vespasian would require every "legitimizing" prop he could employ. To found a new *dynasty* of emperors, he would need to show divine favor that included not only himself but his sons, as well. To achieve this, he seems to have undertaken unprecedented and extraordinary steps for any Roman ruler. For example, Vespasian is the only Roman emperor who is reported to have actually performed *miracles* during his earthly existence.

Vespasian performed these feats at the Temple of Serapis in Alexandria. (20) Moreover, they were healing miracles. And they happened to be exactly the same healing miracles that Jesus performs in the New Testament.

Before we take a closer look at this astonishing coincidence, a little context is necessary.

* * * * * * * *

On his way back to Rome from Judea as his son Titus continued to prosecute the Judean campaign, Vespasian visited the Egyptian city of Alexandria, where he would perform these miracles.

In the three centuries prior to the arrival of the Romans, Egypt had been ruled from that city by a dynasty of Macedonian Greek rulers descended from Ptolemy I, who, like Seleucus, had been one of Alexander the Great's generals. As Egypt's new rulers, Ptolemy and his successors tried to create a new fusion of Greek and Egyptian culture and religion in order to legitimize their own rule and unify their conquered subjects.

Ptolemy I, the Savior

In this process of religious fusion, which is known as *syncretism*, Ptolemy actually created a new god called "Serapis" for the city of Alexandria out of elements of previous deities taken from the cultures of both the conqueror and the conquered. On their own coins, Flavian emperors would subsequently affiliate themselves with this deliberately invented god, who resembles Jesus Christ in many striking ways. Vespasian himself performed his miracles at the Serapian temple in Alexandria, the Serapian equivalent of the Vatican.

One of our best sources for Ptolemy creating Serapis is the Roman historian Tacitus himself:

> The origin of this God Serapis has not hitherto been made generally known by our writers. The Egyptian priests give this account: While Ptolemy, the first Macedonian king who consolidated the power of Egypt, was setting up in the newly-built city of Alexandria fortifications, temples, and rites of worship, there appeared to him in his sleep a youth of singular beauty and more than human stature, who counseled the monarch to send his most trusty friends to Pontus, and fetch his effigy from that country. This, he said, would bring prosperity to the realm, and great and illustrious would be the city which gave it a reception. At the same moment he saw the youth *ascend to heaven* in a blaze of fire. Roused by so significant and strange an appearance, Ptolemy disclosed the

vision of the night to the Egyptian priests, whose business it is to understand such matters. As they knew but little of Pontus or of foreign countries, he enquired of Timotheus, an Athenian, one of the family of the Eumolpids, whom he had invited *from Eleusis* to preside over the sacred rites, what this worship was, and who was the deity. Timotheus, questioning persons who had found their way to Pontus, learnt that there was there a city Sinope, and near it a temple, which, according to an old tradition of the neighborhood, was sacred to the *infernal Jupiter*, for there also stood close at hand a female figure, to which many gave the name of *Proserpine*. Ptolemy, however, with the true disposition of a despot, though prone to alarm, was, when the feeling of security returned, more intent on pleasures than on religious matters; and he began by degrees to neglect the affair, and to turn his thoughts to other concerns, till at length the same apparition, but now more terrible and peremptory, denounced ruin against the king and his realm, unless his bidding were performed. Ptolemy then gave directions that an embassy should be dispatched with presents to king Scydrothemis, who at that time ruled the people of Sinope, and instructed them, when they were on the point of sailing, to *consult the Pythian Apollo [i.e., the Oracle at Delphi]*. Their voyage was prosperous, and the response of the oracle was clear. The God bade them go and carry back with them the image of his father, but leave that of his sister behind.

On their arrival at Sinope, they delivered to Scydrothemis the presents from their king, with his request and message. He wavered in purpose, dreading at one moment the anger of the God, terrified at another by the threats and opposition of the people. Often he was wrought upon by the gifts and promises of the ambassadors. And so three years passed away, while Ptolemy did not cease to urge his zealous solicitations. He continued to increase the dignity of his embassies, the number of his ships, and the weight of his gold. A terrible vision then appeared to Scydrothemis, warning him to thwart no longer the purposes of the God. As he yet hesitated, various disasters, pestilence, and the unmistakable anger of heaven, which grew heavier from day to day, continued to harass him. He summoned an assembly, and explained to them the bidding of the God, the visions of Ptolemy and himself, and the miseries that were gathering about them. The people turned away angrily from their king, were jealous of Egypt, and, fearing for themselves, thronged around the temple. The story becomes at this point more marvelous, and relates that the God of his own will conveyed himself on board the fleet, which had been brought close to shore, and, wonderful to say, vast as was the extent of sea that they traversed, they arrived at Alexandria *on the third day.* A temple, proportioned to the grandeur of the city, was erected in a place called Rhacotis, where there had stood a chapel consecrated in old times to *Serapis and Isis.* Such is the most popular account of the origin and introduction of the God Serapis. I am aware indeed that there are some who say that he was brought from Seleucia, a city of Syria, in the reign of Ptolemy III, while others assert that it was the act of the same king, but that the place from which he was brought was Memphis, once a famous city and the strength of ancient Egypt. The God himself, *because he heals the sick, many identified with Æsculapius; others with Osiris,* the deity of the highest antiquity among these nations; not a few with *Jupiter, as being supreme ruler of all things;* but most people with *Pluto,* arguing from the emblems which may be seen on his statues, or from conjectures of their own. (Emphasis added.) (21)

Thus, according to Tacitus, Ptolemy's newly-minted god "Serapis" was appointed the patron deity of Alexandria, the cosmopolitan city founded by the Greeks at the Nile's delta after conquering Egypt. Serapis was a deity concerned with the afterlife, as is made clear through a number of allusions: he is to be associated with the "Infernal Jupiter" (i.e., Zeus of the Netherworld) and the Queen of Hades, Proserpine (Persephone), as well as Pluto, the Lord of the Dead himself, and Osiris, whom the Egyptians regarded as the Lord of the Dead.

Linked to this same aspect of the afterlife, Serapis was also a fertility and regenerative god. The annual death and re-birth of nature as reflected in the seasons is a major theme in the religions of the ancients, for example in the famous story of Proserpine (or Persephone, as she is also called) who, along with her mother, the Harvest Goddess Demeter (or *Ceres*), was worshipped at Eleusis. She had been kidnapped and taken to the Underworld by Hades, who wanted her for his bride. The girl's grief-stricken mother no longer made things grow, and a desolate winter fell upon the earth. Jupiter/Zeus commanded a resolution to the matter, and a compromise was reached. Having eaten a certain number of pomegranate seeds there, Proserpine/ Persephone was required to spend a period of time in Hades each year before returning to the World of the Living, where she was reunited with her mother. Religion being the science of the ancient world, thus did the ancient Greeks explain the seasons and the renewal of life each spring.

Greeks worshipped Demeter/Ceres and her daughter, Proserpine/ Persephone, near Athens, with their most important religious festival, the celebration of the "Mysteries" at Eleusis. To the cult's initiates, *secret knowledge* is there revealed, assuring them of a *happier afterlife,* for Persephone was both the Renewer of Life and the Queen of the Underworld. (22) Notably, Ptolemy consulted a religious authority from the family of priests at Eleusis, according to Tacitus, when he was establishing his new "Serapian" cult of the afterlife in Alexandria.

The Greek qualities of Serapis were combined with Egyptian ideas, reflecting the military marriage of Ptolemy and the Egyptians. The regenerative or "resurrection" aspects of Serapis's cult were linked with Osiris, the Egyptian god of the underworld and the afterlife. In addition to his title as "Lord of the Dead," Osiris was also the

"Lord of Living." According to his mythology, after he was killed and dismembered, he was physically reassembled and resurrected by his wife, Isis, except for his penis, which she was unable to find. His resurrection and apotheosis mirrored the annual flooding of the Nile and the vernal renewal of life.

Thus, out of two diverse cultures, a new god was born. "Serapis" combined the religion of Greek conquerors and that of their new Egyptian subjects, all in accordance with the accepted political statecraft of the day.

*Isis, the wife of Osiris/Serapis,
with the baby Horus*

To both Greeks and Egyptians, the seasonal renewal of life by their new fertility deity Serapis represented resurrection after death and a happier afterlife. And the Serapis cult's close association with Aesclepius/Aesculapius, the Greek god of healing and medicine, credited Serapis as a healer god, like Apollo.

So, we can now see why it is no accident that the extraordinary healing miracles performed by Vespasian were staged at the Serapian temple in Alexandria.

Aesclepius, directly identified with Serapis, was the son of Apollo. He shared with his father the title *Paean* (the Healer), but he was also the child of a mortal mother, Coronis, who died before delivering him. Apollo saved the infant Aesclepius by cutting him from his mother's womb on her funeral pyre (explaining the name "Aesclepius," meaning "to cut open"). Apollo took the demigod child to Chiron the Centaur, who then instructed him in the art of medicine.

Aesclepius, it seems, became so talented at healing that he was soon able to *raise the dead*. He proceeded to bring a number of figures from Greek mythology back from the dead: Lycurgus, Capaneus, the prophet Tyndareus, Glaucus, Orion and the hero Hippolytus (who enjoyed his own apotheosis to become a god). At some point, the gods became vexed by all of these resurrections. According to one source, Hades was annoyed that his subjects, the souls of the dead, were being "stolen" from him by Aesclepius.

So, according to myth, Zeus struck the demigod healer Aesclepius dead with a thunderbolt. Afterwards, however, Zeus reconsidered, restoring him to life and making him a god, thus fulfilling a prophecy that Aesclepius would become a god only to be killed and return to divine status, "twice renewing" his fate. (23)

Observe that Aesclepius was in this way like Jesus Christ: a child of both god and mortal, a healer who resurrected the dead and who suffered death only to be resurrected and experience his own apotheosis and transmutation into a god.

Like a number of other figures from pagan myth, Aesclepius was a *suffering savior god*, specifically one who was worshipped for his powers to heal and, it seems, to help his devotees obtain a better afterlife.

Christians who find it implausible that a person who suffered the ignominious death of crucifixion could ever be thought of as a god by the ancients, and from this proceed to argue the historical veracity of the Gospels, ignore this crucial reality. Many gods in the ancient world were said to have suffered on earth, to have been martyred and then resurrected, prior to Jesus. The devotee could better identify with his god for this very reason. Heracles (Hercules) provides yet one more example of this recurrent classical theme. Resembling the youth in Ptolemy's vision of Serapis, and like Romulus and Moses, Jesus was also "taken up" into heaven.

Here is an image of the god Serapis, created by Ptolemy to unite his newly-conquered kingdom:

Serapis, 3rd Century BCE bronze

On his head is a "modius" or grain measure, showing that he is a fertility god with roots in Eleusis, and, as a symbol also worn by Hades (or Pluto), it also associates him with the afterlife. Sometimes he's represented without a modius on his head, such as in this silver 2nd Century bust from Egypt:

Serapis, Egypt, 2nd Century CE

The name "Serapis" is partially derived from the Egyptian bull god "Apis," whose fertility was linked to Osiris. Thus Ptolemy's god, "Osiris-Apis," in time, became "Sir-Apis."

The Greeks and Romans, of course, disliked animal gods, preferring human-shaped deities, instead. The emperor Augustus famously refused to pay respects to Apis when he was in Egypt, saying, "I am used to worshipping gods, not cattle." Therefore, under the Ptolemys and later the Romans, Serapis is almost invariably represented as a benevolent human and loving father figure, like this:

Serapis

Serapis was also a prophetic or oracular deity, like Apollo. And, since Serapis is closely associated with—even identified with—Aesclepius, he is also linked to Apollo and healing.

This tradition of combining gods continued into Rome as evinced by this curious 1st Century bronze statue of a "pantheistic deity," which syncretizes Zeus carrying his thunder in one hand and Apollo's bow in another while wearing an Egyptian solar crown and the symbols of other gods. Just as Christianity is taking shape, Rome, at the confluence of all rivers, was already conjuring a universalized image of God:

1st Century pantheistic deity, Rome

It is interesting that as we have just done, Tacitus found it necessary to explain the origins of Ptolemy's god, Serapis, to provide the necessary historical context before describing the miracles of Vespasian.

What were these miracles performed by Rome's future emperor at the temple of Serapis? Let us take a look at them now in their historical context.

* * * * * * * *

Vespasian

From Tacitus's *Histories*, Book IV:

> In the months during which Vespasian was waiting at Alexandria for the periodical return of the summer gales and settled weather at sea, many wonders occurred which seemed to point him out as the object of the favor of heaven and of the partiality of the Gods. One of the common people of Alexandria, well-known for his *blindness*, threw himself at the Emperor's knees, and implored him with groans to heal his infirmity. This he did by the advice of the God Serapis, whom this nation, devoted as it is to many superstitions, worships more than any other divinity. He begged Vespasian that he would deign to *moisten*

his cheeks and eyeballs with his spittle. Another with a *diseased hand*, at the counsel of the same God, prayed *that the limb might feel the print of a Cæsar's foot.* At first Vespasian ridiculed and repulsed them. They persisted; and he, though on the one hand he feared the scandal of a fruitless attempt, yet, on the other, was induced by the entreaties of the men and by the language of his flatterers to hope for success. At last he ordered that the opinion of physicians should be taken, as to whether such blindness and infirmity were within the reach of human skill. They discussed the matter from different points of view. "In the one case," they said, "the faculty of sight was not wholly destroyed, and might return, if the obstacles were removed; in the other case, the limb, which had fallen into a diseased condition might be restored, if a healing influence were applied; such, perhaps, might be the pleasure of the Gods, and the Emperor might be chosen to be the minister of the divine will; at any rate, all the glory of a successful remedy would be Cæsar's, while the ridicule of failure would fall on the sufferers." And so Vespasian, supposing that *all things were possible to his good fortune* [Destiny], and that nothing was any longer past belief, with a joyful countenance, amid the intense expectation of the multitude of bystanders, accomplished what was required. *The hand was instantly restored to its use, and the light of day again shone upon the blind.* Persons actually present attest both facts, even now when nothing is to be gained by falsehood. (Emphasis added.) (24)

Vespasian's miracles turn out to be: exactly the same healing miracles performed by Jesus Christ in the Gospels.

Jesus is said to have cured a man with a diseased or *withered hand.* (25) And in the Gospel of Mark, Jesus is said to have cured a blind man by *spitting into his eyes.* Just like Vespasian.

In the Roman historian Suetonius's account of Vespasian's healings at Alexandria, Vespasian cures a lame man by touching him with his heel and cures a blind man by spitting into his eyes. (26) In this slightly different account, Vespasian is still shown performing miracles identical to those of Jesus Christ in the Gospels, which were—again—*written during the Flavians' reign.*

Ruins of the Serapeum at Alexandria where Vespasian performed his healing miracles

Vespasian biographer Barbara Levick denies that this humble new emperor was a "cynical" manipulator of religion and was, perhaps, just a victim of the flattery of others (27). However, this is obviously contradicted by the facts.

Indeed, when Vespasian captured the priest and rebel general, Josephus, during the Jewish War we are told that his Jewish captive predicted he would become emperor. Josephus records that he declared this to Vespasian himself while Nero was still alive. As Levick concedes, this isn't credible. The Roman general would have surely executed the man on the spot for saying such a thing if only to protect himself from being associated with such a dangerous lunatic. (28)

However, if this was a lie concocted later, as it must have been, then Vespasian was a party to that lie. After all, by then Josephus had become, in effect, the Flavians' own court historian, in which capacity he unblinkingly records this tale.

And, of course, Vespasian himself had to have been aware of the true nature of his own "miraculous" healings. He could not have taken the chance of failing at the temple of Serapis. So he must have been pre-assured of success, which required a considerable degree of religious and political cynicism.

According to Mark's Gospel (29), Jesus cured a blind man by spitting into his eyes and healed a crippled man by laying his hands upon him. In the Gospel of John (30), Jesus cured a blind man by mixing his spittle with some earth and applying it to the blind man's eyes. Both the saliva of Jesus and the saliva of Vespasian are reported to have cured the blind. Likewise, the touches of both are said to have restored the lame. And both Jesus and Vespasian were regarded as *Jewish messiahs* by their respective devotees.

According to Flavius Josephus, Vespasian *was* the Jewish Messiah:

> But now, what did the most to elevate them [the Jews] in undertaking this war, was an ambiguous oracle that was also found in their sacred writings, how about that time, one from their country should become governor of the habitable earth. The Jews took this prediction to belong to themselves in particular, and many of the wise men were thereby deceived in their determination. Now this oracle certainly denoted the government of Vespasian, who was appointed emperor in Judea. However, it is not possible for men to avoid fate, although they see it beforehand. But these men interpreted some of these signals according to their own pleasure, and some of them they utterly despised, until their madness was demonstrated, both by the taking of their city and their own destruction. (Emphasis added.) (31)

The 2nd Century Roman historian Suetonius agreed completely (32), as does his contemporary, Tacitus, who wrote:

> The majority [of the Jews] were convinced that the ancient scriptures of their priests alluded to the present as the very time when the Orient would triumph and from Judaea would go forth men destined to rule the world. *This mysterious prophecy really referred*

to Vespasian and Titus, but the common people, true to the selfish ambitions of mankind, thought that this exalted destiny was reserved for them, and not even their calamities opened their eyes to the truth. (Emphasis added.) (33)

Jewish prophecies of a coming messiah were a fundamental motivation behind the Jewish revolt. As it turned out, the Emperor Vespasian (along with his son Titus) fulfilled the messianic prophecy of the "Christ" predicted by Hebrew scripture, according to both contemporary Roman *and* Jewish sources. Even the Rabbi Johanan ben Zakkai, a father of modern Rabbinic Judaism, declared at the time that Vespasian was the messiah of Hebrew prophecy, according to the Talmud. (34) It is doubtful that the famous rabbi was sincere and this is likely to have been required of him by the Roman state. However, like Jesus, Vespasian could claim both Gentiles *and* Jews among those who, at least formally, believed he was the Messiah of Hebrew prophecy.

For his part, the Jewish historian Josephus finds the idea of the "Messiah" to be both the cause and the cure of the Jewish revolt. Like Christianity, he, too, converts the politically explosive concept of the Messiah into a pro-Roman one—in his case by simply naming Vespasian himself the Messiah.

Because they were reported by both Tacitus and Suetonius, we know that Vespasian's healing miracles at Alexandria were a propaganda coup for the Flavian imperial cult. Their coins inform us that both Vespasian and his son, Titus, celebrated Serapis and associated themselves with that fake deity. Here is an example with Titus on one side and the bearded god Serapis on the other:

Titus and Serapis

Many students of ancient history have observed the numerous elements of Christianity that are apparently pagan in origin, but the wider questions that this observation implies have largely gone unanswered: why were those elements introduced, at all? And more: how could those pagan elements—especially the idea of worshipping a man-god born of a mortal—be interwoven into a religion born of a fiercely monotheistic faith?

In light of the Jewish purity laws then practiced—whether at the Temple or within groups like the Qumran sectarians or the suicidally violent rebels of the 1st and 2nd Centuries—how could a pious Jewish sect so modify their faith as to centrally feature the worship of a man who had walked the earth in the flesh at such a time?

The Jews were willing to fight the mighty Roman war machine, and to die and be tortured in vast numbers, precisely in order to protect their strictly monotheistic tradition from foreign "pollution" and the blasphemy of emperor worship. In a period when so many were willing to commit mass suicide rather than submit to foreign domination, we are hard-pressed to explain how a form of Judaism could actually blend the most objectionable elements of the paganism they were fighting against into the very heart of its identity: the worship of a man-god who suffered, died, and was resurrected during his earthly life as a pagan suffering savior god. The religious use of graven images that are forbidden representations of the divine even add a form of "idol worship" that quotes the pagan symbology of a *Roman emperor.*

While Pauline Christians in the 1st Century rejected Kosher dietary restrictions, circumcision and the like, the most revolutionary aspects of their "Christianity" are the identification of the Messiah with God himself and the use of divine symbols as early as the first decades of the 2nd Century. And the symbols they were using were far more than abstract personifications of divine features like "Wisdom," something already underway within Jewish thought—this was the worship and depiction of a man *as God.*

A philosophical merging of Judaism with Platonism and Stoicism is readily understandable as a natural outgrowth of Judaism, and that project was already under way by such philosophers as Philo, as we will see. The sweeping scope of such sudden changes to Judaism in the earliest Christian tradition, however, is something far harder to account for. In addition, we should expect to find this ideological blending within the more moderate or overtly pro-Roman elements of Judaism rather than among orthodox messianics or strict adherents of the Torah. If indeed emperor worship itself was one of their chief grievances with Rome, then any group of contemporary messianic Jews embracing man-god worship is inexplicable.

Apart from the emerging picture of an imperial Roman origin for Christianity, the simultaneous introduction of all of these radical Rome-centric innovations requires a much better eexplanation than has ever been offered.

* * * * * * * *

Much can be learned by their coins about the values promoted by the Roman Empire under the Flavians.

The coins of Domitian, Titus's younger brother, who did not participate in the glorious triumph over Judea with his father and brother, also depict Serapian temples and Serapis, such as on this coin:

Domitian and a Serapeum

It is understandable why Serapis, so closely associated with Isis, would be venerated by Domitian. He had hidden inside the Temple of Isis and escaped, disguised as an Egyptian priest, when Vitellius's war with the Flavians for the imperial seat raged in Rome itself. Domitian was forever grateful to Isis, therefore, and on one of his monuments he is even depicted wearing Egyptian garb. Serapis, being associated with Osiris, the husband of Isis, often shares a temple with her. Domitian also associated the mother goddess Isis with the Roman goddess Minerva, the virgin, as we can see from three adjoining temples that he built to both goddesses and to Serapis.

Noticeably, Domitian's coins change the subject from the gods and symbols advertised on his father's and brother's coins. To an extent still argued about among scholars, Domitian seems to have favored more traditional Roman gods like Minerva and Jupiter, instead, at least more than did his immediate predecessors, Vespasian and Titus. Domitian even depicts himself hurling Jovian thunderbolts at his enemies on his coins and architecture, a striking departure from the iconography of his father and brother.

Titus and Vespasian wanted to be seen as "healing" the Roman world both through their victory in Judea and through Vespasian's ending of the civil wars of succession after Nero's death. (Domitian played no part in those triumphs.) So Vespasian's identification with both Apollo and Serapis, like Titus's, served this political purpose. Vespasian's own propaganda presented him as "the New Serapis," and other coin issues struck during Vespasian's reign celebrate this identification, as we can see from this coin featuring Vespasian and Serapis:

Vespasian and Serapis

Vespasian's identification with Serapis suggests that his cult's devotees prayed to him for health or the health of loved ones. Also, because of Serapis's connections to the gods of the afterlife, they would have probably prayed to Vespasian for a happy afterlife, as well.

When a deadly plague broke out during the reign of Vespasian's eldest son, Titus, the new emperor issued coins that honored both Apollo and Serapis to supplicate the gods for relief and healing.

"Salus," meaning safety or health (and the Latin root for the English word "salvation"), was herself a divine daughter of Aesclepius. At one time Salus was worshipped in her own temple on Rome's Quirinal Hill, and, according to Pliny the Elder, with a statue in the Temple of Concordia (the goddess of "Harmony"). Salus, who came to be associated with the health, safety, and welfare of the people, was celebrated on Roman coins, like this Titus issue:

Titus and Health

The salutary benefits brought by the Caesars had been celebrated on coins at least as early as Tiberius's "Salus Augusta" coins. "Harmony" herself was also a regular on Roman coins, as in this Titus issue:

Titus and Harmony

"Faith, hope and charity," in Latin, "Fides, Spes et Caritas," are regarded as three primary virtues of Christianity. This is based on the famous passage from St. Paul in 1 Corinthians: "And now these three remain: faith, hope and love. But the greatest of these is love." (35) (Love is usually understood in the sense of *giving* in this context; the word "charity" is sometimes substituted for the word "love," as in the King James Bible translation.)

Each of these cardinal virtues is celebrated in Flavian currency, as well. For example, the New Testament famously defines faith: "Now faith is the assurance of things hoped for, the conviction of things not seen." (36) The goddess "Spes," or Hope, commonly appears on Roman coins. In the following she is on the reverse of a Titus issue:

Titus and Hope

Some Christians may believe that compassion, including Christian altruism and charity, were articulated for the first time by Jesus Christ against a backdrop of Roman brutality. However, this is clearly not the case. For evidence of this, we may look to Pliny the Elder, who was an intimate friend of both Vespasian and Titus.

Gaius Plinius Secundus, better known as "Pliny the Elder," was a highly educated Roman general and statesman who had served with and befriended Titus in the Roman army stationed in Germania during Nero's reign. He was also uncle and adopted father to Pliny the Younger, who would later write the famous letter to Trajan asking clarification on the policy regarding Christians, which we previously examined.

In fact, the Emperor Trajan himself, on the other side of that historic correspondence, was the son of one of Vespasian's generals in Judea. (These relationships may help explain the tolerance and delicacy with which both Trajan and Pliny the Younger handled the Christian question some 20 years after the religion's popularity had peaked and begun to wane.)

Pliny the Elder later dedicated his monumental collection of ancient science, *The Natural History*, to Titus. While Pliny the Elder did not live to see Titus's full reign, since he died tragically during the eruption of Vesuvius in 79 CE exactly two months after Titus assumed imperial office, his adulation of the Flavian dynasty, including his arguments for its divine status, had already been recorded in his compendium of ancient science published during the reign of Vespasian. According to Pliny:

> For mortal to help mortal, that is God, and this is the way to everlasting glory. This is the road that Roman leaders have taken, and it is this road that the greatest

ruler of all time is treading, at a pace favored by heaven, along with his offspring, as he brings relief to an exhausted world. This was the ancient way of rewarding those who deserved it, to regard them as Gods. (37)

Pliny the Elder thus credits the Flavians with a fair expression of Christian love in the context of "charity," the idea that true glory and Godliness comes from helping others. God *is* love, he argues. Pliny is also directly associating such compassion with both the Roman Empire itself and the Emperor Vespasian personally. Although none of the Flavian emperors had yet died when Pliny wrote this, Pliny is already associating their compassion with their divinity.

For other praise of Titus's love and charity in action we need only turn to the historian Suetonius's biography of Titus. It begins with this extraordinary assertion:

Titus… had such winning ways—perhaps inborn, perhaps cultivated subsequently, or conferred on him by fortune—that he became the object of universal love and adoration. (38)

Born on December 30, in "a small, dingy, slum bedroom," (39) according to Suetonius, Titus is said to have been remarkable for his beauty, grace and dignity, his phenomenal memory, his talent on the lyre (like Apollo), his ability to compose verse in both Greek and Latin with equal ease, even extemporaneously, and his abilities in almost all of "the arts of war and peace." (40) As emperor, Titus "never took anything away from any citizen, but showed the greatest respect for private property, and would not even accept the gifts that were permissible and customary." None of his predecessors, it seems, had "ever displayed such generosity." (41)

Suetonius also tells us that Titus was "naturally kind-hearted," having as a personal rule "never to dismiss any petitioner without leaving him some *hope* that his request would be favorably considered." (Emphasis added.) When a day passed without his helping someone he is quoted as complaining, "My friends, I have wasted a day." Titus, we are told, made a virtue of his humble background and freely used the public baths "in the company of the common people." (42)

Titus's short reign was characterized by a series of disasters: the eruption of Vesuvius that buried Herculaneum and Pompeii, yet another fire that burned through Rome for three days and nights, and an outbreak of disease that was described by Suetonius as one of the worst "that had ever been known." Titus's reaction to these crises he describes as follows:

> Throughout this assortment of disasters, he showed far more than an Emperor's concern, it resembled the *deep love* of a father for his children, which he con-veyed not only in a series of comforting edicts but by helping the victims *to the utmost extent of his purse.* (Emphasis added.) (43)

Suetonius tells us Titus "stripped his own country mansions of their decorations" in order to help restoration efforts after the fire, and that he "attempted to cure the plague and limit its ravages by every imaginable means, human as well as divine—resorting to all sorts of sacrifices and medicinal remedies." (44) Here, we can clearly see why Titus associated himself with Apollo the "Paean" and the healer Serapis, with whom his father identified, as his coins issued during this period reflect.

The untimely death of Titus, Suetonius asserts without a hint of irony, was "a far greater loss to the world than to Titus himself." (45) When news of Titus's death was released, only two years, two months and 20 days into his reign, "the entire population went into mourning as though they had suffered a personal loss." (46)

Although Suetonius says that Titus died of a fever, the 3rd Century Greek writer Lucius Flavius Philostratus preserves a tra-dition that Titus was killed by "his own kith and kin" (presumably his brother Domitian) "through eating the *fish* called the sea-hare." (Emphasis added.) (47) Philostratus adds that Nero also used this "fish" to murder his enemies.

Even if the factual status of this account is fishy, the metaphori-cal association of Titus's death by *fish* is pungent considering its potential symbolism.

* * * * * * * *

It should be noted that previous Roman leaders were also extolled for their benevolence, especially Julius Caesar and his successor Augustus. The Divine Julius, in particular, was celebrated for his mercy, or "clementia." Julius Caesar famously pardoned many of his political enemies only to be assassinated by them. Indeed, the deification of Clementia (mercy) may have begun with the cult of the Divine Julius, who symbolized and was worshipped for this virtue by the Romans.

In this sense, as historian Francesco Carotta has keenly observed, Caesar, like Jesus, "loved his enemies," "blessed those who cursed him," and "did good" to those who had "done him evil." Carotta has also observed a number of other similarities between the man-gods Jesus Christ and Julius Caesar, just as Atwill has noted certain other parallels between Christ and the Emperor Titus.

As we can see from how liberally emperors swapped divine affiliations, the work of these two writers, Carotta and Atwill, is not necessarily irreconcilable.

Since the Flavians were the second imperial dynasty, they necessarily modeled their own cult on that of the Julians, their only precedent. They even represented themselves as new "Caesars," whose very name they assumed for themselves while incorporating their own archetype, or *topos*, into Flavian propaganda. (48)

Moderns will sometimes assume that the cults of Roman leaders represented something less than a serious religion. But, as Carotta usefully reminds us, Julius Caesar became a very real god to ordinary Romans after his death. Julius Caesar's official deification by the Senate required the clearing of the makeshift altar that the people had already spontaneously erected to him so that his official temple could be built in its place.

A priesthood sanctioned by law in Caesar's cult officiated over solemn ceremonies from one side of the Roman Empire to the other, as the maps provided by Carotta illustrate. Lasting for more than a hundred years, Caesar's religion was finally supplanted only by the cult of the Flavians, and, according to Carotta, by Christianity itself.

Roman priest, 2nd Century marble bust

Not every ruler deified by the Roman Senate enjoyed the same level of genuine devotion as Julius Caesar. But Augustus and, later, the first two Flavian emperors, appear to have been among those who did. They were all deified by the people.

Remains of the temple of Vespasian and Titus, Rome

* * * * * * * *

As we have seen, far from being Christian antagonists, the gods who were venerated by Roman emperors on their coins symbolize what we would today recognize as Christian virtues.

Here is another coin, for example, struck in the year 44 BCE, the year of Julius Caesar's assassination and deification. The coin celebrates Caesar's forgiveness and "clementia":

Julius Caesar and Mercy

Clementia herself was not depicted on Flavian coin issues. However, the related concept of fairness, equity or "justice"—divinely personified by "Aequitas"—was readily promoted to the whole world on Flavian coinage, as in this Titus issue:

Titus and Justice

Happiness, too, the joy that the Roman peace and prosperity brought the world, was celebrated on Flavian coins, as in this Vespasian issue of "Felicitas":

Vespasian and Happiness

"Peace" was a major theme on Flavian coins as well, of course, both the "coming of peace" (*Pacis Eventus*), the cause of the new prosperity, and the fact that it had been brought about by the emperors of Rome (*Pax Augusta*), a theme celebrated in similar fashion since the days of Augustus himself. Here is Vespasian associated with *Pax*:

Vespasian and Peace

There in one coin we see celebrated both the end of the Roman civil war and the end of the Jewish War. Soon, the Goddess of Peace herself, and the new "Temple of Peace" erected in Rome and dedicated by Vespasian, were also advertised on Flavian coins.

One of their most important credentials as peacemakers was the Flavians' victory over Judea, and one of the most common issues of coins under both Vespasian and Titus is the "Judea Capta" series, usually symbolized by a palm tree and a mourning woman or enslaved "Jewess." Sometimes, the triumphant Titus stands opposite the palm tree, as in this example:

Judea Capta

Even Otho, one of the Flavian predecessors during the chaotic Year of Four Emperors between Nero and the Flavians, prematurely proclaimed a new *Pax Orbis Terrarum*, or "peace on earth," which Flavian coinage would later, with more legitimacy, dub *Pacis Orbis Terrarum*. The emperors of Rome, in bringing "peace on earth," were saviors not just of Rome but of all nations, and of the whole world.

Otho and Pax Orbis Terrarum

Vespasian and Pacis Orbis Terrarum

This Roman peace was seen as eternal. And the eternity of Rome, or "Aeternitas," was duly celebrated on their coinage:

Vespasian and Eternity

The Romans never forgot that these benefits were divinely bestowed, the result of both Destiny and Providence (personified by the deity *Fortuna*), also celebrated by the Flavian mints.

Titus and Providence

Titus honored his father Vespasian's deification and used it for his own purposes, just as Augustus did Julius Caesar's, by declaring himself to be the "Son of God":

Titus Son of God and Judea Capta

While the coincidence of moral concepts regularly depicted by Romans, especially Flavians, with key Christian ideas and values is stunning, their commonality might be ascribed to the fact that Roman propagandists and the first Christian apologists were operating in the same cultural context. After all, the earliest Gospels were written during Flavian rule.

On the other hand, we should not expect any specific sectarian sentiments, especially monotheistic ones, to be expressed on Roman coins since they were cast with an aim of appealing to the widest possible cross-section of a sprawling and diverse empire.

According to one historian of the period:

> The ideology [of the Emperor Vespasian] found expression in every medium, notably in buildings restored or freshly constructed in Rome. Coinage was banal. Types were borrowed from past reigns, allusions reassuringly predictable. (49)

So, given their empire-wide purpose, the similarity of themes between Roman propaganda and Christian ideology is all the more remarkable. Far from the cultural clash between Imperial Rome and Christianity that has been promulgated in popular tradition, the truth is that they extolled largely identical virtues.

So, although quasi-divine Hellenistic monarchs of the east had used similar imagery in the distant past, and other emperors had used some dolphin-and-trident motifs, the clear intersection of

Christian symbolism with Titus's dolphin-and-anchor motif during this time is doubly challenging to the traditional idea of Christian and Roman conflict.

How could a symbol so specifically derived from the pagan god Apollo and associated with pagan emperors who had just conquered Judea and destroyed the Jewish Temple become the most prominent symbol adopted by Christians in the city of Rome itself?

Christians were supposed to have regarded all things pagan as corrupt and, during this time, were allegedly persecuted by imperial Roman authorities to such a degree that they had to disguise their symbols. Christians are said to have been willing to die rather than surrender to pagan worship in any form—especially any kind of emperor worship.

As we have seen, it is easy to understand why Emperor Titus would adopt the dolphin-and-anchor motif for himself. Other emperors had used similar images to associate themselves with Apollo. Ancient monarchs from the Hellenistic east used similar images for the same reason. The gods Apollo and Serapis (and in part Aesclepius, Apollo's son) also made an especially good "fit" for the Flavians, who billed themselves as healers who had "arisen in the east," like solar deities. And, although it never became a religious symbol for the Jewish people, their monarchs had also used an anchor on their coins frequently enough for it to be associated with Jewish monarchy. This could also be a useful element for the coinage of the Flavian conquerors of Judea.

The anchor may have become a recognizable symbol of Jewish monarchy at this time, and, as we have seen, the fish became a representation of Jesus and a common symbol used in Christianity's earliest stories and literature. So, it may be argued, these factors led the first Christians to *independently* come upon the combination of the two as an appropriate way to represent Christianity. That the combined image was previously associated with Apollo, a healing god, would only further associate it with the healing miracles of Jesus. Being a pagan image, it was also "safe," a form of symbolism that was unlikely to offend the sensibilities of Roman officials.

However tempting this interpretation might be, however, it fails to reckon with the problems we have been considering: only decades after the Crucifixion, Christians in Rome must have already abandoned all Jewish inhibitions against violating the Ten

Commandments' prohibition of graven images and Jewish laws forbidding any representation of the divine. As we have seen, if the earliest Christians were authentically pious Jews, they would never have combined the image of an anchor with any animal, and certainly not one associated with a pagan god or a Roman emperor. Moreover, the pagan symbol they chose was the exact same symbol adopted by a Roman emperor on coins widely circulated at the time. And that emperor's imperial cult coincidentally advertised him as the Jewish Messiah.

It was Jews, not Christians, who forbade graven images, it might be countered. If so, in addition to Kosher diet and circumcision, we may now add this to the list of the aspects of Mosaic Law that Pauline Christians abandoned. If, therefore, Christians were free to choose whatever symbols they wished to represent themselves, including symbols unlikely to be recognized by outsiders, if that was their concern, they had a virtually limitless catalog to choose from without specifically affiliating themselves with a Roman emperor.

Why are Christians using readily identified imperial propaganda—including trident-and-dolphin symbols engraved on the Colosseum, of all places, which was only a couple of miles from their catacombs—despite their alleged hostility to and persecution by the Roman government?

Why should Jesus himself have so many characteristics in common with a pagan god, e.g. a resurrected suffering savior/healing man-god? Indeed, why should he share so many historical parallels with the Roman emperors Vespasian and Titus, especially Jewish messianic claims paradoxically combined with the characteristics of a pagan "Mystery Cult" healer man-god with identical miracles, parallel accomplishments on the Sea of Galilee, and the same visual iconography—unless it was deliberate?

That they used the same unique symbol at that time cannot be random synchronicity in light of all of these other parallels.

We know that the first Christians did not create their own distinctive and unique symbol. They had an unlimited catalog to choose from at a time rich with visual iconography. Yet they chose the symbolism of pagan imperial propaganda prominently depicted on current coinage and public architecture.

Though visual representations of the divine are forbidden under

Jewish law, the Hebrews did employ definite symbols associated with their faith. If the movement originated in Judea, why didn't the first Christians mine *Judaic* traditions instead of turning to pagan and imperial references?

Equating the anchor with the Cross, as those who espouse the standard *crux dissimulata* theory, is an artificial stretch, since anchors associated with early Christian symbolism often do not even have a stock, eliminating their similarity to a cross altogether. A cross, however, could easily be grafted *onto* a pre-existing anchor symbol at a later date.

If they feared persecution by the Roman state, why didn't the earliest Christians simply choose a unique but innocuous non-pagan symbol that did not directly reference Imperial Rome? Even if it were just a cynical disguise for Roman eyes, why would Christians go so far as to mark it conspicuously on the graves of their loved ones?

* * * * * * * *

As St. Clement of Alexandria demonstrates in the 3rd Century, early Christians were well aware of the pagan king Seleucus's prior use of the anchor image. The Christians who first adopted the symbol in the early 2nd Century so soon after the reign of Domitian surely knew it was a symbol favored by his brother, the beloved Titus, since his coins were still in wide circulation.

A century later, St. Clement of Alexandria does not even mention the anchor symbol used by Jewish rulers when he recommends Christians use an anchor, along with fish and doves (the latter symbols being blasphemous to Jewish religious sensibilities). While Clemens does not specifically mention the use of the dolphin-and-anchor motif by the Roman dynasty with which he shares the names "Titus Flavius," it is clear from archeological evidence that the dolphin-and-anchor motif was already commonly used by Christians during St. Clement of Alexandria's time. His list was therefore in part a retrospective inventory of already accepted Christian symbols.

It is quite possible that Clemens assumed the dolphin-and-anchor association with his own "Flavian" ancestors. Given the symbol's connection to a long-defunct imperial dynasty, however, Clemens might have sought a broader justification for the symbol in his time by invoking earlier pagan sources. In any case, the unique Flavian/Christian symbol has ancient *pagan* roots stretching back to Seleucus, as St. Clement himself confirms.

Many scholars have observed similarities between Jesus and the gods of the so-called pagan "Mystery Cults," as we have noted. Now that similarity can also be seen in their shared use of symbols. But if paganism had been anathema to the first Christians—*if Christianity's roots are really Jewish*—why are such pagan symbols the first to appear in Christian history?

Observe that the Emperor Titus himself took his dolphin-and-anchor symbol from Seleucus—the very same precedent cited by his possible relative, Titus Flavius Clemens, as an appropriate source for *Christian* use of the symbol. The Emperor Titus and the later Christian Titus Flavius Clemens of Alexandria derive this symbolism from the same source.

The dolphin-and-anchor motif is not so empty and common that it could have referred to just about anything, like a smiley face or a peace sign. If it was, the symbol would not have been useful as a distinctive motif for Titus on his coinage—or for the Christians. And, though emperors often recycled iconography from other emperors, we know that Titus was the first Roman to use it. Except for a few early issues by his younger brother, only Hadrian, who fought the second Jewish War, would also briefly employ it—at a time when it was already publicly used to identify Christians. Seleucus, who had used a variation of it, had lived almost four centuries earlier. Its use at Apollo's temple at Delos predates even that.

As a symbol of the god Apollo, a healing and solar deity associated with Serapis, it was almost certainly a religious symbol of Titus's imperial cult, and therefore Christians adopting it is especially difficult to explain.

To add to the extraordinary mosaic floor preserved by the eruption of Vesuvius at Herculaneum during the reign of Titus, which mirrors the early Christian iconography in the catacombs so perfectly, we find this mosaic from its sister city, Pompeii, also frozen in time in 79 CE by the eruption. This mosaic gives the "House of the Black Anchor," an archeological site at Pompeii, its name. This anchor has a stock (notice the cruciform top of the anchor) in this purely pagan and pre-Christian use of the image:

Pagan cruciform anchor

The popularity of the images of the anchor or the trident combined with one or two fish by supposed pagans seems to have reached its height during the Flavians' rule. This gladiatorial shoulder-guard, for example, was discovered at Pompeii:

Flavian era Roman shoulder guard

Notice the broad syncretism represented by the symbols in this pre-Christian artifact. (Again, no Christian artifact anywhere dating before the 2nd Century has ever been confirmed.) The trident has the ribbons (sometimes shown as serpents) of the "caduceus" indicating the staff of Mercury, who guided the souls of the dead to the afterlife. The dolphin is wrapped around a trident here, Neptune's symbol, rather than an anchor, but it is flanked by a stockless anchor and a rudder.

Far from avoiding paganism, with the adoption of anchors, tridents and fish Christians were employing the most fashionable pagan images of the late 1st and early 2nd Centuries that were linked to healing and a happy afterlife. A Jewish provenance for Christianity is becoming harder and harder to believe.

* * * * * * * *

Any similarity of anchors or tridents to crosses was, surely, a *later* super-imposition onto the pre-existing symbols. If it was the pagan origins of these images that made later Christians uncomfortable and motivated their discontinuation of them, then the adoption of the Cross was the actual "disguise." Instead of the anchor/fish symbols being a *crux dissimulata*, the crucifix itself is probably more accurately understood as an *anchora dissimulata*. At that later time, any pagan symbolism, especially any reference to the Flavians, would have been viewed as awkward and obsolete by Constantine's imperial administration.

Before that time, however, anchors and fish had been the dominant symbols of Christianity. Here, from the 4th Century, is a mosaic from a Christian catacombs in Tunisia where all of the early Christian iconography now familiar to us comes together:

From the Christian Catacombs of Hermes,
4th Century, Sousse, Tunisia

III. Roman Messiahs

The parallels between early Christianity and the imperial cult of the Flavians already seem undeniable.

In the case of Christians, fish-and-anchor symbology was in part chosen to celebrate Jesus's deeds and miracles on the Sea of Galilee.

In the case of the Roman Emperor Titus, the dolphin-and-anchor motif appears to have been chosen, in part, to celebrate his miraculous naval victories on the same body of water.

Fishers on the Sea of Galilee

Like Jesus, Titus drove "demons" (his Jewish rebel enemies) into the Sea at Galilee.

Both Jesus and Titus descended from Galilee to "triumphal" entries into Jerusalem at the age of 33. And Titus fulfilled Jesus's apocalyptic prophecy within the predicted timeframe.

Titus and Jesus both held the title "Son of God." Both were that distinctly Roman, un-Jewish and un-monotheistic thing that caused such friction with Jewish culture: a man-god.

Titus and his father, Vespasian, were associated with another man-god, the benevolent and bearded Serapis. Serapis is represented by his dual identity, Aesclepius, the son of a god and a mortal woman who suffered on earth only to be martyred for resurrecting the dead and experience his own apotheosis.

Like Jesus, Serapis also ascended into heaven, according to Ptolemy's vision of his state-crafted god. As generals of Alexander the Great, both Ptolemy in his conquest of Egypt and Seleucus in his conquest of his territory were doubtlessly models for the Romans on how to manage newly-conquered foreign territories. Like Jesus and Serapis, Titus had his own apotheosis after his death, as depicted in this architectural detail from his triumphal arch in Rome:

Apotheosis of Titus, the deified Titus carried to heaven on the wings of an eagle, Arch of Titus, Rome

Both 2nd Century Roman historians Tacitus and Suetonius identify Titus and his father Vespasian as the "messiahs" of Jewish prophecy. In a work composed before the ascension of Titus, the historian Josephus specifically acknowledges Vespasian to be the Jewish Messiah. According to the Talmud, even a contemporary *rabbi* agreed that Vespasian was the prophesied Jewish Messiah. And he fits the description: a ruler of the world who hailed from Judea. This aspect of Vespasian's imperial cult should not be dismissed today as merely an amusing example of ancient quackery. These were the claims of the Emperor of Rome. As such, propaganda of this sort carried great weight across the Empire.

This, then, was the cultural climate and the political reality when the Gospels were being written—in Greek and, quite possibly, in Rome.

In those Gospels, Jesus is a healer, like the first Flavian emperors and the gods and man-gods with whom they associated themselves—even though this is not a feature normally associated with Jewish messiahs. And Jesus's healing miracles exactly mirror Vespasian's healing miracles.

Representations of Serapis, the god Ptolemy created, strikingly resemble Jesus Christ. Simultaneously, some of the first portraits of Jesus from the 3rd Century show him as a beardless solar deity like Sol Invictus or Apollo. All were pagan gods that Vespasian and Titus associated with themselves.

In the New Testament, Jesus is proclaimed to be "the light of the world" and was resurrected at dawn, a seeming parallel to solar deities, like his date of birth. Notice that only from a Roman perspective could there be a rising Jewish "deity" linked to the east or the dawn. Only to Rome is Judea "east." In Judea there would be no reason to associate Jesus with the east, or the dawn, at all.

And, of course, Titus's siege of Jerusalem and its famous Temple are precisely what Jesus describes as he enters the city and predicts the Temple's destruction within the lifetime of some listening to him. Astonishingly, Jesus connects this act of destruction with his triumphant Second Coming and the final arrival of the Christian millennium. From the Gospel of Mark, chapter 13:

> As he [Jesus] came out of the Temple, one of his disciples said to him, "Look, Teacher, what large stones and what large buildings!" Then Jesus asked him, "Do you see these great buildings? Not one stone will be left here upon another; all will be thrown down."
>
> When he was sitting on the Mount of Olives opposite the Temple, Peter, James, John, and Andrew asked him privately, "Tell us, when will this be, and what will be the sign that all these things are about to be accomplished?" Then Jesus began to say to them, "Beware that no one leads you astray. Many will come in my name and say, 'I am he!' and they will lead many

astray. When you hear of wars and rumors of wars, do not be alarmed; this must take place, but the end is still to come. For nation will rise against nation, and kingdom against kingdom; there will be earthquakes in various places; there will be famines. This is but the beginning of the birth pangs.

"As for yourselves, beware; for they will hand you over to councils; and you will be beaten in synagogues; and you will stand before governors and kings because of me, as a testimony to them. And the good news must first be proclaimed to all nations. When they bring you to trial and hand you over, do not worry beforehand about what you are to say; but say whatever is given you at that time, for it is not you who speak, but the Holy Spirit. Brother will betray brother to death, and a father his child, and children will rise against parents and have them put to death; and you will be hated by all because of my name. But the one who endures to the end will be saved.

"But when you see the desolating sacrilege set up where it ought not to be (let the reader understand), then those in Judea must flee to the mountains; the one on the housetop must not go down or enter the house to take anything away; the one in the field must not turn back to get a coat. Woe to those who are pregnant and to those who are nursing infants in those days! Pray that it may not be in winter. For in those days there will be suffering, such as has not been from the beginning of the creation that God created until now, no, and never will be. And if the Lord had not cut short those days, no one would be saved; but for the sake of the elect, whom he chose, he has cut short those days. And if anyone says to you at that time, 'Look! Here is the Messiah!' or 'Look! There he is!'—do not believe it. False messiahs and false prophets will appear and produce signs and omens, to lead astray, if possible, the elect. But be alert; I have already told you everything.

"But in those days, after that suffering, the sun will be darkened, and the moon will not give its light, and the stars will be falling from heaven, and the powers in the heavens will be shaken.

Then they will see 'the Son of Man coming in clouds' with great power and glory. Then he will send out the angels, and gather his elect from the four winds, from the ends of the earth to the ends of heaven.

"From the fig tree learn its lesson: as soon as its branch becomes tender and puts forth its leaves, you know that summer is near. So also, when you see these things taking place, you know that he is near, *at the very gates*. Truly I tell you, *this generation will not pass away until all these things have taken place*. Heaven and earth will pass away, but my words will not pass away.

"But about that day or hour no one knows, neither the angels in heaven, nor the Son, but only the Father. Beware, keep alert; for you do not know when the time will come. It is like a man going on a journey, when he leaves home and puts his slaves in charge, each with his work, and commands the doorkeeper to be on the watch. Therefore, keep awake—for you do not know when the master of the house will come, in the evening, or at midnight, or at cockcrow, or at dawn, or else he may find you asleep when he comes suddenly. And what I say to you I say to all: Keep awake." (Emphasis added.) (1)

The urgency of Jesus's warning is unmistakable. The meaning is clear. The "coming" of the "Son of Man" in his "power and glory" will be accomplished before the current generation "passes away." This event will coincide with the destruction of the Temple and, indeed, the Jewish Revolt itself, which is fairly well described in Jesus's apocalyptic prophecy, including the calamitous misery, hardships, famine and tribulations that war would bring.

All of these events happened within the lifetime of people from Jesus's time just as predicted. The Flavian historian Josephus was

recording his history of those same events, which he had personally witnessed at Titus's side, during approximately the same time
Jesus's prophecies were being written down in the Gospels.

The plain meaning of what Jesus is quoted as saying, especially
given that it was written after the war, is that his glorious Second
Coming would transpire *with the victory of Titus.*

Either that or Jesus made a big mistake.

And it increasingly appears that he did not.

* * * * * * * *

Was Jesus's prediction meant to apply to the current events at the
time it was written instead of the current events of our time? Could
the bloody campaign of a future Roman emperor have been the
fulfillment, and the explanation, of Jesus Christ's prophecy?

In the Gospel of Mark, Jesus himself is accused of threatening
to destroy the Temple:

> Those who passed by hurled insults at him, shaking
> their heads and saying, "So! You who are going to
> destroy the Temple and build it in three days, come
> down from the cross and save yourself!" (2)

This is yet another reason why references to Vespasian as the
messiah of Jewish prophesy—even by Jewish priestly figures such
as Josephus and the rabbi Johanan ben Zakkai—are so striking.
The Flavian father and his son *were* "messiahs" who *did* destroy
the Temple in a "glorious" triumph. They did rise in Judea to rule the
world exactly when Jesus predicted his return.

Model of the Jerusalem Temple in the 1st Century at the Israel Museum

Allegedly predicted some 40 years before the event, though written down only afterwards, Christ's prophecy of the Temple's destruction would certainly be miraculous if true, even though predicting the rebellion, and the Jewish people's defeat at the hands of the Roman military machine, might have been possible for a truly foresighted individual in Christ's time. Even then, events were pointing, at least, in that inevitable direction.

But there is a problem. Jesus describes the war with details so remarkably similar to Flavius Josephus's contemporaneous historical account—including the appearance of "false messiahs" and a portentous vision of a battle seen in the clouds before the siege—that one must conclude that Jesus's prophecy was probably composed after the event with the benefit of hindsight, unless Jesus had genuinely divine foresight of this event and his words were simply not written down until 40 years later, by pure coincidence, when Josephus was writing his historical account.

For these obvious reasons, most scholars point to Jesus's prophecy as the primary evidence (though by no means the only evidence) that the Gospels must have been written after (or perhaps even during) the Jewish War, since the actual events as recorded by historians mirror what Jesus predicted in such precise factual and literary detail.

In either case, through his prophecy Jesus is put on record as warning Jews in the 1st Century against rebelling from Rome. His divine proscription against war is not only consistent with his own teachings concerning peace, obedience to Roman authority, paying taxes, and even his extravagant praise of a Roman centurion, it is also consistent with the teachings of the earliest contributor to the New Testament itself, St. Paul. We have already noted that Christ's rejection of the Jewish purity laws that alienated the Jewish population from the wider Hellenistic world, along with his rejection of key aspects of the Mosaic Law, are perfectly consistent with Paul's rejection of the Kosher lifestyle.

Notably, Jesus predicts a total Jewish defeat—one that will entail the destruction of Jerusalem and the Temple. Even so, paradoxically, he proposes that this military catastrophe will signal the Glorious Second Coming of the Son of Man. Simultaneously, Jesus identifies the leaders of the coming Jewish rebellion as "false messiahs."

The historian Flavius Josephus's description of the cultural ferment before the war dovetails with Jesus's predictions that these "false messiahs" were to blame for leading the Jewish people astray. Josephus's own writings suggest that these Jewish rebel leaders presented themselves as the prophesied messiah, and he describes how they led their people to disaster. Knowing they were written concurrently, one must wonder whether Josephus's history is supporting Jesus's prophecy or Jesus's prophecy is supporting Josephus's history.

Most Jews would naturally see these rebel leaders as far more credible Jewish messiahs than the Jesus of the Gospels. What a Jewish "messiah" meant to the Jewish people at that time was a warrior and a champion, something completely different from the Jesus depicted in the Gospels. They were anticipating the arrival of a *military* leader, like Joshua (*Yeshu'a,* itself meaning "God saves," rendered via the Greek as "Jesus"). They were awaiting a new King, like David, or a rebel priest, like Judas Maccabeus—in other words, a perfectly *human* and never a divine political leader who would lead them to military victory and national and cultural independence. This did not preclude divine assistance, but it certainly precluded the messiah himself being divine.

Here is how the Flavians' court historian, Flavius Josephus, describes one of the "false messiahs" who inspired the Jewish rebellion against Rome:

> It came to pass, while Cuspius Fadus was [Roman] procurator of Judea, that a certain charlatan, whose name was Theudas, persuaded a great part of the people to take their effects with them, and follow him to the Jordan River: for he told them he was a prophet, and that he would, by his own command, divide the river, and afford them an easy passage over it. Many were deluded by his words. However, Fadus did not permit them to make any advantage of his wild attempt, but sent a troop of horsemen out against them. After falling upon them unexpectedly, they slew many of them, and took many of them alive. They also took Theudas alive, cut off his head, and carried it to Jerusalem. (3)

Parting the Jordan River would mirror the miracle performed when the original Joshua/Jesus led the Israelites across that river to the Promised Land. (4)

False though these messiahs Josephus mentions invariably turn out to be, each leading the Jewish people to apocalypse at the hands of the Romans, they at least fulfilled the expectations of monotheistic Hebrews, like those so vividly expressed in the Dead Sea Scrolls.

Josephus, the Jewish priest, general and scholar who became the Flavian court historian after he was captured by the Romans, confirms that the main motivations for Jewish revolt against Rome were the same messianic prophecies that led to their ruin. Exactly as Jesus warned.

We will take a much closer look at Flavius Josephus, and at the astonishing cast of characters who link the Flavians directly to Christianity, in Part II.

* * * * * * * *

There is no reason in Jewish prophecy for the messiah to be a healer god, much less a god, at all.

Quite the reverse: in the first place, messianic Jewish rebels were expecting a warrior; in the second, such a man-god is blasphemous to the very concept of monotheism.

For some time, Christians also wrestled with the polytheistic implications of Jesus's divinity. The "solution" they ultimately came up with, the Trinity, is just another paradoxical "mystery" that has been inherited by the faith.

There was no reason for the Jewish people to have expected a divine man, a kind of demigod, in any of their messiahs. It was a *pagan* idea. They had already experienced a number of messiahs— and they had rigid religious reasons to strenuously deny the very possibility of their divinity. As one might expect, the early Jewish response to Pauline Christianity was to parody the Gospel narratives, especially accounts of Jesus's virgin birth, healing miracles, and the claims of Jesus's divinity. (5)

According to the Christian Gospels, the messiah who actually came was a surprise to his contemporary Jews. He was neither a military nor a political leader of any kind, but a humble peace lover and an advocate not of Jewish exceptionalism (almost the entire job description of the messiah up to that point) but a proponent of *transnationalism*. Indeed, he was a passionate ambassador of the same universal peace desired by the Roman Empire.

Insofar as the messiah anticipated by the Jews was a *world* leader, it was in connection with the sectarian triumph of Israel over its foreign enemies, i.e. the restoration of Jewish independence or the establishment of Jewish domination over the whole earth. The prophetic victory of the messiah over "the nations" never entailed including Gentiles and embracing their Torah-violating practices.

As the Romans had done with respect to Hellenism, it was their standing policy to plunder, absorb and adopt what they saw as the best parts of the foreign cultures they conquered. Politically, they followed a complementary policy of slowly expanding citizenship and potential senate membership to eventually include those from once-conquered alien nations. This promise of inclusion was an important key to Rome's success, stability, and longevity as an empire.

In contrast, the 1st Century Jewish rebels' outright xenophobia, the violent extremes to which many contemporary Hebrews were willing to take their purity laws, and the sharp contrast revealed in the Dead Sea Scrolls to the Gospels' and the Romans' ideology of peace and pluralism, all suggest that a radically different approach would have been followed by Jews had they succeeded in their revolt against Rome—that is, had the Jewish messiah they anticipated actually arrived.

Instead, in this era of virulent Jewish rebellion against Rome, Jesus Christ is portrayed declaring a Roman centurion's faith in the God of Abraham as exceeding that of any Jew. Such a statement is tantamount to a Muslim claiming that an infidel American GI exceeds the faith in Allah of any contemporary Muslim. It is, quite frankly, unbelievable, and it is no wonder that such a thing was not published until *after* the Romans had won the Jewish War.

At the time in which he allegedly made it, consider how confidently Jesus utters such a shockingly controversial claim in the Gospels. Never mind the fear of Roman authorities—saying such a thing in Jewish company would be unthinkably provocative. It could be argued, therefore, that such confidence could only come after the Romans' had utterly defeated and enslaved the Jewish rebels.

Here is a Gospel account of Jesus's encounter with the centurion who asked him to heal a paralyzed servant:

> "... Lord, I do not deserve to have you come under my roof. But just say the word, and my servant will be healed. For I myself am a man under authority, with soldiers under me. I tell this one, 'Go,' and he goes; and that one, 'Come,' and he comes. I say to my servant, 'Do this,' and he does it."
>
> When Jesus heard this, he was amazed and said to those following him, "Truly I tell you, I have not found anyone in Israel with such great faith. I say to you that many will come from the east and the west, and will take their places at the feast with Abraham, Isaac and Jacob in the kingdom of heaven. But the subjects of the kingdom will be thrown outside, into the darkness, where there will be weeping and gnashing of teeth." (Emphasis added.) (6)

Jesus is genuinely impressed by the Roman's *military* position in this passage. This is simply extraordinary. Again we must remember that the two Gospels in which we find this story were written during the Flavians' reign following their brutal military conquest of Judea.

In this, and so many other ways, Jesus could not be more "pro-Roman" even as he opposes Jewish exceptionalism in any form. His final entreaty to the disciples before ascending into heaven at the end of Matthew's Gospel is to "go and make disciples of all the nations." (7)

All of this seems to indicate that Jesus was not advocating peace as a form of "passive" or "nonviolent resistance" to the Romans in order to subversively overthrow their brutal empire, like an ancient-world Gandhi—but in order to accept and even accommodate Rome's imperialist ambitions over the Jews and all the nations.

* * * * * * * *

The Roman Empire required locals to support its army within the marked boundaries of the "milestones" within which they lived. Milestones set along Roman roads served the dual purpose of measuring these taxes. Jesus instructs Christians to "go the extra mile," thus providing the Romans additional assistance. (8)

Jesus praises the blessings of meekness (9), of making peace (10), and of "loving one's enemies." (11) In contrast, the Qumran sectarians who authored the Dead Sea Scrolls required "everlasting hatred" for their enemies, whom they branded the "Sons of the Pit." (12)

To his followers, Jesus commanded "turning the other cheek" to aggression (13) and explicitly child-like acceptance, in general. (14) In the Gospels, Jesus advocates universal peace and his very birth is heralded by angels presaging *peace on earth* (15)—the same hope churned out on Roman coins as the Gospels were being composed. Meanwhile, Jewish hardliners were committed to an "eye for an eye," rebellion against foreign pollution, and national sovereignty brought about by a warrior messiah.

The transnational scope of Jesus's words is in perfect harmony with the imperial agenda of Rome at the time they were written. Jesus shares the same "political theology" Paul expresses in his letter to the Romans, which is probably one of the three or four oldest parts of the New Testament and one of seven letters attributed to Paul that are considered by most scholars to have been authentically composed by him:

> Let everyone be subject to the governing authorities, for there is no authority except that which God has established. *The authorities that exist have been established by God.* Consequently, *whoever rebels against the authority is rebelling against what God has instituted, and those who do so will bring judgment on themselves.* For rulers hold no terror for those who do right, but for those who do wrong. Do you want to be free from fear of the one in authority? Then do what is right and you will be commended. *For the one in authority is God's servant for your good.* But if you do wrong, be afraid, for rulers do not bear the sword for

no reason. They are God's servants, agents of wrath to bring punishment on the wrongdoer. Therefore, it is necessary to submit to the authorities, not only because of possible punishment but also as a matter of conscience. This is also why you pay taxes, for *the authorities are God's servants*, who give their full time to governing. Give to everyone what you owe them: If you owe taxes, pay taxes; if revenue, then revenue; if respect, then respect; if honor, then honor. (Emphasis added.) (16)

Many Christians today do not realize that according to the New Testament obedience to the state is a moral and religious obligation—or that the government, even the Roman government that enforced slavery, crucified tens of thousands, and fed slaves and criminals to lions in their infamous arenas, must be recognized as God's appointed agent on earth. The New Testament makes political rebellion a sin. Commandments and proclamations to this effect are repeated for emphasis in several places in the New Testament.

As an example, we see these sentiments expressed by the author of the first epistle that is (dubiously) ascribed to St. Peter:

Submit yourselves for the Lord's sake to every human authority: whether to the emperor, as the supreme authority, or to governors, who are sent by him to punish those who do wrong and to commend those who do right. For it is God's will that by doing good you should silence the ignorant talk of foolish people. Live as free people, but do not use your freedom as a cover-up for evil; live as God's slaves. Show proper respect to everyone, love the family of believers, fear God, honor the emperor.

Slaves, in reverent fear of God submit yourselves to your masters, not only to those who are good and considerate, but *also to those who are harsh.* For it is commendable if someone bears up under the pain of unjust suffering because they are conscious of God. But how is it to your credit if you receive a beating for doing good and you endure it, this is commendable before God. (Emphasis added.) (17)

The writer here repeatedly stresses that a Christian should "honor the emperor." Deference to authority, indeed to the absolute monarch *Caesar*, is an obligation for all Christians, according to scripture itself.

Slavery was another Roman institution, as Jews would soon experience firsthand in the aftermath of the Jewish War when tens of thousands of them were enslaved, as the Judea Capta coins of Vespasian and Titus amply bear witness. The New Testament provides instructions to the slaves of early slave-owning Christians, some of whom were no doubt high-ranking or aristocratic Romans. In 1 Timothy 6:1-2, slaves are advised thusly:

All who are under the yoke of slavery should consider their masters worthy of full respect, so that God's name and our teaching may not be slandered. Those who have believing masters should not show them disrespect just because they are fellow believers. Instead, they should serve them even better because their masters are dear to them as fellow believers and are devoted to the welfare of their slaves.

On at least four occasions, the New Testament commands compliant obedience from slaves, such as in this passage from the Epistle to the Colossians:

Slaves, obey your earthly masters in everything; and do it, not only when their eye is on you and to curry their favor, but with sincerity of heart and reverence for the Lord. Whatever you do, work at it with all your heart, as working for the Lord, not for human masters, since you know that you will receive an inheritance from the Lord as a reward. It is the Lord Christ you are serving. (18)

Slaves are addressed directly here. Tens of thousands of Jews at the time this was written had suddenly become slaves of the Romans at the end of the war. Many were former messianic rebels.

Slaves pour wine, Roman mosaic, 2nd Century, Tunisia

Many Jews who were not enslaved must have been dispossessed of their property following the conquest. In this context, Christ's famous congratulations of the poor, assuring them that they are the "blessed" or the fortunate ones, is alarming when stripped of modern embellishments. (19) In the Kingdom of Heaven, Jesus states, "Many who are the first will be last, and the last first." (20) In order to emphasize this idea, in the Gospel of John the Jewish Messiah himself, Jesus, washes the disciples' feet at the Last Supper—like a slave. (21)

A means of conditioning the newly-enslaved Jews to accept their situation of abject servitude in the aftermath of the first Jewish War could not have been better devised:

> When he had finished washing their feet, he put on his clothes and returned to his place. "Do you understand what I have done for you?" he asked them. "You call me 'Teacher' and 'Lord,' and rightly so, for that is what I am. Now that I, your Lord and Teacher, have washed your feet, you also should wash one another's feet. I have set you an example that you should do as I have done for you. Very truly I tell you, no servant is greater than his master, nor is a messenger greater than the one who sent him. Now that you know these things, you will be blessed if you do them. (22)

The master, curiously, is still "greater" than the servant, yet Jesus is modeling the role he wants to see his Jewish disciples accept. In Matthew, Jesus is explicitly asked by his disciples, "Who, then, is the greatest in the kingdom of heaven?" Jesus straightforwardly tells the disciples that they must dramatically change their current expectations:

> He called a little child to him, and placed the child among them. And he said, "Truly I tell you, unless you *change* and become like children, you will never enter the kingdom of heaven. Therefore, whoever takes the lowly position of this child is the greatest in the kingdom of heaven." (Emphasis added) (23)

The messianic prophecies found in Hebrew literature unmistakably promise that a savior will come to lead the Israelites to victory and even rule over their oppressors. The conquests of Joshua, the later elimination of their regional rivals, the famous victories of David over the Philistines, the Maccabean revolt—all are events in their history and heritage that confirm the nature of what we might call "Jewish exceptionalism" throughout their ancient literature. All such anticipations of the Messiah express the same martial values and political hopes that inspired the Jewish revolts under the Romans in the 1st and 2nd Centuries.

What Jesus represents is nothing short of a radical redefinition of this concept of exceptionalism and the very nature of the Messiah. An argument among the disciples in the Gospel of Luke gives Jesus an opportunity to express his *anti-messianic* mission:

> A dispute also arose among them as to which of them was considered to be greatest. Jesus said to them, "The kings of the Gentiles lord it over them; and those who exercise authority over them call themselves Benefactors. But you are not to be like that. Instead, the greatest among you should be like the youngest, and the one who rules like the one who serves. For who is greater, the one who is at the table or the one who serves? Is it not the one who is at the table? But I am among you as one who serves. (24)

In light of the praise Jesus lavished on the Roman centurion, and the regard he has for his own authority, it is not clear that Jesus is condemning the Gentiles, or even disputing that their rulers can be "benefactors," and he readily concedes that the one sitting "at the table" is greater than the one "who serves." Jesus merely asserts that his followers must embrace not just service, but servitude and humility. Like the Jewish priests and Levites of old, they have a distinct assignment, and like the Messiah himself they are to be the servants, not the served, but this will result in a special reward for them in the afterlife. They must let go of any expectation of earthly rule or reward.

So the Messiah is no longer a King David or a conquering military leader who will lead the Jewish people to victory in this world—instead, he is a humble slave. And Matthew's version further defines his messianic mission as sacrifice and not rule:

> Jesus called them together and said, "You know that the rulers of the Gentiles lord it over them, and their officials exercise authority over them. Not so with you. Instead, whoever wants to become great among you must be your servant, and whoever want to be first must be your slave—just as the Son of Man did not come to be served, but to serve, and to give his life as a ransom for many." (25)

Nothing could have been more amenable to the 1st Century Roman state in the aftermath of the war with Judea than to redefine the mission of the Jewish Messiah as one of servitude and sacrifice rather than conquest and rule—or, indeed, to redefine the special role of the Chosen People themselves as one of humble subjugation. The message could not be more ironic if George Orwell had written it himself: the voice of totalitarian power invokes surrender as the ultimate victory for the conquered. Meanwhile, Vespasian was constructing the Colosseum as a not-so-subtle alternative to the newly offered "salvation."

Questioned about paying taxes to Romans, Jesus himself explicitly endorses "rendering unto Caesar" the things that are Caesar's, implying that there exists no conflict between the dictates of God and the requirements of Rome's ruler. It is sometimes asserted that this is an ambiguous instruction on the part of Jesus, but, in fact, the meaning could not be more plain: "And Jesus said to them, 'Render to Caesar the things that are Caesar's, and to God the things that are God's.' And they were amazed at him." (26)

The accusation later brought against Jesus, that he refused to pay the Roman tax (27), is pointedly untrue. It is shown to be something concocted by his conniving accusers, who know it to be false. According to Matthew, the accusations against Jesus were "false witness." We are thus assured that Jesus pays his taxes. (28) Notice, too, that Christ's earthly parents dutifully show up to be counted for the Roman census in the Gospel of Luke's nativity account. Jesus obeys Roman law.

Not only is the Roman governor Pilate unable to find any fault in Jesus but, in all four Gospels, Pilate officially pronounces Christ's innocence. The Roman governor is elaborately portrayed, again, in all four of the Gospels, as being compelled by the Jewish crowd to order Jesus's crucifixion. (29) Famously, no less than three times must the crowd demand Jesus's death before Pilate reluctantly yields, according to all four of the Gospels. In Matthew's rendering of the notorious scene, which is often credited among the origins of the tradition known as the "blood libel" against the Jewish people and a source for Christian anti-Semitism generally, the Jewish crowd assumes full responsibility for the Crucifixion and shouts in unison: "His blood is on us and on our children." (30)

Even without the assumption of collective guilt by the crowd in Matthew, the original intention of the story is explicit. It is meant to exonerate the Roman government of any responsibility for the death of Jesus so that the responsibility and cataclysmic consequences may be assigned exclusively to the Jews.

Just as Jesus is quoted warning against rebellion, predicting complete destruction of Jerusalem and the famous Temple at the heart of the Jewish religion, the Gospels also depict the Jews rejecting their true savior and killing him. And the Jewish crowd takes full responsibility, even including their own children—the very generation who would suffer ignominious defeat at the hands of the Flavians, just as Christ foresees.

This was certainly how the first Christian writers who discussed the Jewish War, such as Origen and Eusebius, would subsequently regard that defeat—as the deserved punishment of the Jewish people for the murder of Christ.

To fix blame on the Jews it was not really necessary to exonerate Pilate. The Roman governor could have also been shown to be culpable even as he admitted the charges to be false, thus indicting all mankind in a universal and broadly philosophical statement. Pilate could have even consulted the crowd as a means of helping to cravenly cover his own shared guilt in the terrible deed.

Instead, Pilate is specifically depicted as remarkably hesitant to order the death of Jesus, and it is only the crowd's repeated demands that finally compel him to relent to their bloodlust. He immediately orders a basin of water to melodramatically wash his hands of the deed in a gratuitous illustration of his innocence that is as exaggerated as a political cartoon.

The exoneration of Pilate himself was not necessary even to appease Rome. The 1st Century historian Josephus, almost certainly reflecting the official imperial position of his Flavian patrons, was a critic of Pontius Pilate's administration of Judea, repeatedly describing how he provoked Jewish anger and near-insurrection by an insensitivity to Jewish customs that was even greater than that of contemporary Roman governors.

Yet, the exoneration of Pilate that is presented in the Gospels is not just an exculpation of Pilate himself but also of the Roman state. And if Pilate's declaration of Jesus's innocence, and the crowd's thrice-stated demand that he be crucified, are part of an artificial exoneration of the Romans for his crucifixion, then we must ask two questions:

1. How did these stories become woven into the basic narrative of the life of Jesus in the Gospels?
2. Who would want to exonerate the Roman government so emphatically—other than the Roman government?

As in the story of the centurion whose faith Jesus praises above any Jew, Rome's official fingerprints are now becoming impossible to ignore. (31)

* * * * * * * *

When the Apostle Peter (Cephas), according to the Book of Acts, addresses his "fellow Israelites," as he puts it, he summarizes the death of Jesus thusly: "You handed him over to be killed, and you disowned him before Pilate, though he [Pilate] had decided to let him go. You disowned the Holy and Righteous One and asked that a murderer be released to you." (32)

St. Peter, we are being told, is against the Israelites. He is accusing them and blaming them—and in the same breath, curiously, he is clearing the Roman governor of any blame.

With similarly broad political symbolism, in all of the Gospels, Jesus is betrayed by his own disciple, "Judas," who shares the name of the patriarch who gave his name to the whole nation of "Judea" and the whole tribe of "Jews."

Again, the metaphor is as glaring as any propaganda poster.

According to Josephus, the first author of the rebel "philosophy" early in the 1st Century was named "Judas the Galilean." It was this Judas who founded the "Zealot" sect of insurrectionists. In the Gospels, Jesus and many of his disciples in the early 1st Century are explicitly referred to as "Galileans."

Curiously, "Iscariot," the title of this same Judas, also suggests that he was a rebel and possibly a member of the militant sect known as the "Sicarii," who were notorious for causing much trouble for Rome. "Judas Iscariot" practically means "Jewish Rebel." (33)

Simon (not Peter, we are reassured, but another one of Jesus's disciples who is called by that same name) is referred to as "the Zealot." Another disciple is named "Thaddeus," a name resembling that of a person called "Theudas" (which itself may be a corruption of the name "Judas"), who is also described by Flavius Josephus as a troublesome Jewish rebel figure. (34)

There are 12 disciples—the number of Jewish tribes. This is no accident. Jesus himself tells the disciples at the Last Supper that they will "sit on thrones judging the Twelve Tribes of Israel." (35) Their number is symbolic of Israel itself.

The Gospels show these disciples, who seem to echo notorious figures of the Jewish rebellion, repeatedly failing to grasp their messiah's message, lacking sufficient faith, denying their relationship with Jesus, doubting his resurrection, betraying him with a kiss, and exchanging his life for the amount of silver the Temple charged for a sacrificial lamb. (36) The very name of Christ's betrayer is, at least in part, symbolic of his whole people.

*6th Century mosaic in Basilica of
Sant'Apollinare Nuova, Last Supper*

The Gospels inform us that Jesus was rejected by his home-town and his own family. (37) This may be referencing an older tra-dition, since those who joined militant or separatist Jewish sects may also have faced rejection by their own families. In John, this tradition seems to extend even to Jesus's own disciples, some of whom abandoned him, suggesting the conflicts that could arise even among messianic Jews. (38)

Although executed by the Romans in a manner common to them, crucifixion, Jesus is actually convicted by Jewish officials for violat-ing Jewish law, according to the Gospels. His trial and execution are the climax of Jesus's rhetorical jousts with Jewish authorities, from the scribes to the priests to the Pharisees, and is punishment for his own attack on the Jewish Temple as a "den of thieves." (39) The charges that condemn him confound the Roman governor, Pontius Pilate.

In attacking the "money changers" at the Temple, Jesus enacts another criticism of Mosaic Law. To Gentiles, the merchants who exchanged pagan coins displaying forbidden graven images of gods and emperors for currency that was religiously acceptable to the Jews must have seemed like "thieves" charging the poor money in the name of an empty symbolism, even as Romans might have taken offense to images of their gods and rulers being condemned as blasphemous.

And, of course, with his attack on the Temple that is related in the Gospels, Jesus morally justifies, prophetically foreshadows, and, perhaps, even *commences* Titus's own subsequent razing of the Temple, which Jesus correlates with his return.

There is only one moment in the New Testament where the stridently anti-Jewish tone of the Gospels is matched by a seemingly anti-Gentile message. Since this might be raised as an objection to our thesis, let us consider that passage now, in detail.

* * * * * * * *

The lone possible exception to the pro-Gentile message in the New Testament is the story of the Canaanite woman, as told in the Gospel of Matthew:

> Leaving that place, Jesus withdrew to the region of Tyre and Sidon. A Canaanite woman from that vicinity came to him, crying out, "Lord, Son of David, have mercy on me! My daughter is demon-possessed and suffering terribly."
>
> Jesus did not answer a word. So his disciples came to him and urged him, "Send her away, for she keeps crying out after us."
>
> He answered, "I was sent only to the lost sheep of Israel."
>
> The woman came and knelt before him. "Lord, help me!" she said.
>
> He replied, "It is not right to take the children's bread and toss it to the dogs."
>
> "Ye it is, Lord," she said. "Even the dogs eat the crumbs that fall from their master's table."
>
> Then Jesus said to her, "Woman, you have great faith! Your request is granted." And her daughter was healed at that moment. (40)

Here in this cryptic passage Jesus seems to imply that Gentiles, any who are not among "the lost sheep of Israel," are all "dogs" that are not the concern of his mission.

So, how are we to square this one line with Jesus's otherwise consistent calls for a transnational Christian mission in the New Testament?

First, if it is interpreted in this way, this assertion does stand out against all of Jesus's other pleas for universal peace and brotherhood. However, Jesus also refers to some Israelites as "lost sheep." Also, Jesus's definition of his own mission here seems to anticipate Paul's later claim to being the first missionary to convert the Gentiles. And finally, we see that after Jesus's objections he nevertheless agrees to heal the woman's daughter anyway, even in the face of his disciples' opposition.

This passage implies that Jewish opposition to Gentiles was so undeniable in the 1st Century that even the Gospels could not avoid acknowledging it. The best a Roman innovator of Jewish religion could do and still be somewhat credible was to "soften" this xenophobia and then countermand it by example.

Jesus's assertion also resembles what could have been a well-known adage within the Jewish-Christian movement: "It is not right to take the children's bread and toss it to the dogs."

In any event, the entire point of the story seems to be Jesus's correction of his disciples' opposition to healing a Gentile's daughter. One can only surmise that the Jewish-Christian rebel leaders, like James, so prominently exhibited this kind of anti-Gentile attitude that it required addressing it with a demonstration of why it was "un-Christian." This "teachable moment," therefore, shows the very process by which Jewish-Christian ideology, or messianic Jewish rebellion, was being systematically turned upside-down in the writing of the Gospels.

* * * * * * * *

As a divine being, Jesus Christ is sacrilegious to the Jewish nation and tradition. As early as the authentic Pauline epistles, Christianity would celebrate a man-god who brings to all humanity the Hope of Resurrection and Eternal Happiness in the Afterlife—just like a

Mystery Cult demigod of the Suffering Savior archetype so common in Hellenistic paganism.

The Sadducees, one of the three great sects of the Jews of the 1st Century, denied the existence of an afterlife or an immortal soul altogether. (41) And while the Pharisees and the Qumran sectarians both seem to have shared a belief in the Resurrection of the Dead and a Final Judgment, their conception of the messiah could never be equated with God himself.

Meanwhile, Jesus himself suggests that Christianity contains a "secret knowledge" revealed only to initiates—a signature of so many pagan "mystery" cults. When teaching the crowd by the Sea of Galilee, according to Mark, Jesus uses parables, "but when he was alone with his own disciples, he explained everything." (42) And the first epistle to Timothy explicitly refers to "the Mystery of Faith." Many others have observed Christianity's plentiful parallels with the pagan mystery cults. (43)

As we restore the mosaic of evidence, tile by tile, we are getting closer to a complete picture; but there are still many pieces left to fill in.

* * * * * * * *

In the 2nd Century, the pagan Celsus wrote a scathing satire depicting Jesus Christ as the illegitimate son of a Roman soldier. (44)

Celsus was a famous critic of Christianity, and he was surely mocking the notion of a virgin birth, but he added the coded insinuation that the true "lineage" of this messiah was Roman—indeed, that he was born of the Roman war effort. Fascinatingly, this same caricature of Jesus is repeated in the Jewish Talmud, as well. (45)

Obviously, Pauline Christianity is more than a form of Judaism— it is a blend of Jewish and pagan elements. The transreligious and transnational nature of the New Testament that stands in stark contrast to Jewish exceptionalism is visible in its holy scriptures in many ways that we have not yet addressed.

For example, there is the famous Christmas visit of three "Magi" (46), who are said to have observed the astrological portent of a rising star that leads them to the very spot where the baby Jesus is born. Magi, of course, are priests of the religion of Zoroastrianism.

Although popularly referred to as either "wise men" or "kings," Matthew calls them *magi*, which identifies them as Zoroastrian. They came "from the East" according to standard translations, though that phrase (ἀπὸ ἀνατολῶν) may literally mean "from the rising [of the sun]," a synonym for the east. Zoroastrians lived to the east of Israel. They invented the Zodiac familiar to us today and their famous reputation for interpreting the stars is being invoked here—something that no Jewish scripture would ever do.

Adoration of the Magi, Roman sarcophagus, 4th Century CE, St. Agnes Cemetery, Rome, coming from the east.

Relating a pagan, Zoroastrian source for one of its star symbols, the Gospels here do something impossible in the Jewish religion. The religion of the Hebrews was itself deeply influenced by the religious ideas of their neighbors, but it never credited those polytheistic, idol-worshipping faiths directly, for obvious reasons.

The Jews had, however, represented the messiah with a star in Hebrew literature and coins, as in the name given to the 2nd Century messianic rebel leader Bar Kokhba (whose name literally means "son of the Star"). And, alone among Roman emperors, Vespasian and Titus employed this same distinctive eight-pointed star on coins commemorating their eastern navy.

Just as Jesus's birth is heralded by a star, one of the portents of Vespasian's death was a comet, according to the ancient historian Suetonius. Indeed, the ancient historian Tacitus tells us that Vespasian's ascension to the throne was prefigured *in the stars*. (47)

One Vespasian coin depicts both a ship's prow symbolic of the 10th Legion, which helped quell the Jewish revolt—and a star. This remarkable star on Vespasian's coin is the same kind of messianic star used on Jewish coins to represent their messiah. Notice how the unique eight-pointed star also forms an *Ichthys Wheel* of the type used as an early Christian symbol that we have previously noted:

Vespasian coin with 10th Legion galley and a "Flavian star"

Ancient Jewish coin with Seleucid anchor and Messianic Star

Mark Anthony issue also honoring Judean 10th Legion symbolized by galley (but with no star)

Titus coin with 10th Legion galley and Flavian/messianic star

Eight-pointed Ichthys wheel

The Flavian star is at least similar to the star (which is actually a comet) that was used on Roman coins to celebrate the deification of Julius Caesar:

Divine Julius Caesar coin with star (comet)

Though somewhat related to the comet-symbol of Julius Caesar, the specific star on the Flavian coins of Vespasian and Titus is obviously more like the Jewish messianic star, complete with the points in between its eight rays. Such a star does not appear on any other Roman emperors' coins.

Since the Flavians were the only Jewish messiahs to ever become Roman emperors and the only Roman emperors to become Jewish messiahs, this should not, perhaps, be surprising.

* * * * * * * *

As we have seen, Jesus's similarities to Serapis and Aesclepius, and his very nature as a man-god, were as alien to Judaism as Roman emperor worship, indicating a profound influence of Hellenistic and Roman ideas on Christianity.

While it is certainly true that radical Jewish sectarians like those in the Dead Sea Scrolls community believed in the righteousness of personal poverty—and the poor and disaffected were no doubt drawn to the rebel cause—scholars widely agree that Jesus's advocacy of storing one's "treasures" in the Kingdom of Heaven rather than on the perishable earth (48) is more readily founded in the Greek philosopher Plato. That ancient philosopher's dualism had in the pagan mind already ideologically severed the universe into two opposed dimensions: the spiritual and material. In declaring that the Kingdom of God is not of this earth, Jesus uses Platonic dualism to religiously invalidate any earthly military ambitions of the Jews, literally sequestering their political ambitions in a separate dimension.

All of the transnational and transreligious elements in the New Testament suggest a universalized agenda—i.e., an imperial one. The very phrase in the New Testament, "Kingdom of Heaven," as properly translated from the Greek by the Jesus Seminar, should read: "God's imperial rule."

God's earthly agent was the emperor, as Paul claims in his letter to the Romans, and rebellion is therefore a sin. According to the Flavians' own propaganda, their first two emperors were actual messiahs of Jewish prophecy. And, according to the Romans, the emperor, a man, could certainly become a god.

* * * * * * * *

Religions before Rome (and, to some extent, before Alexander) were largely matters of one's ethnicity and nationality in an age when the distinction between religion, politics and science was blurry and parochialism was sharply defined. Following the conquests of Alexander the Great, however, imperialistic motives began to inspire transnational religious syncretism like that which we have seen by the Seleucids and the Ptolemys to melt down regional and sectarian divisions into a durable imperial alloy.

The remarkably blatant example of this kind of syncretism in the political creation of the god Serapis by Ptolemy I "the Savior" was certainly appreciated and personally utilized by Vespasian.

Seleucus, another of Alexander's generals who referred to himself as "the Savior" while linking himself to Apollo by employing a dolphin-and-anchor symbol, clearly provided inspiration for Vespasian's son, Titus.

The Romans shared the same methods and motives of these

first Hellenistic imperialists. Indeed, they were avid students of their methods. Over time, Romans developed this kind of statecraft into an elaborately sophisticated adjunct of their warfare. They employed the Greeks' own tactics against them when they conquered Greek territories, incorporating Greek religion and matching Greek gods to their own gods almost one-for-one. When it came to politicization of religion, the Romans proved themselves to be unparalleled in their pragmatism, ambition and opportunism.

With the political propaganda employed by the Emperor Vespasian, however, the exploitation of foreign religion for political purposes would soar to new heights, as we shall now see.

Aesclepius, the Healer

We have already noted that Vespasian's Jewish supporters acknowledged him as the Messiah of prophecy and seen how he performed healing miracles at the Serapeum in Alexandria in perhaps the most cynical show of political propaganda by any Roman emperor ever recorded. However, our ancient sources also tell us that Vespasian received portents by traditional Roman gods back in his Italian homeland, as well, even as his son Titus received favorable prophecies from the priests of the Greek goddess of Love, Aphrodite, on the island of Cyprus.

Titus and Venus, the goddess of love

It seems the deities of almost every ethnic group in the East were eager to endorse Vespasian and his family as the next dynasty of Rome while the dire uncertainty of imperial succession roiled the world during what would be called the "Year of Four Emperors."

The manufactured god Serapis, who had long outlived the Ptolemys for whom he was originally assembled, made his contribution to the propaganda of the Flavians.

Titus and Serapis

Could what the god Serapis was for Ptolemy the Savior have been the model for what Jesus would be for the Flavian messiahs?

It was, after all, the *Roman* government that was striving, quite brutally, to unify all nations under one emperor—a mission that would, arguably, culminate in the official unification of their empire under the Roman-friendly monotheism of Christianity by the 4th Century.

Jesus challenges the entire Mosaic purity code that helped ignite the Jewish people's conflict with Rome. He obviates the need for strict Sabbath observance by letting his disciples work on the Sabbath. In the Gospels written during Flavian rule, Jesus rejects or transforms nearly everything that is distinctively Jewish in the Jewish religion. (49)

Unlike traditional Jewish messiahs (and so like pagan gods), Jesus performs healing miracles even on the Sabbath, offending the Jewish authorities while mimicking pagan deities with resurrections and other wonders. (50)

While most Christians today retain some form of Sabbath observance, the Christian "Sabbath" is no longer even celebrated on the seventh day, as God commanded the Jews. Except for a small minority of Christians, their Sabbath is observed on the first day of the week: the day of the Sun (Sunday), in accordance with the worship of the pagan god, Sol Invictus, as decreed by Emperor Constantine, who was originally a devotee of Sol Invictus.

Jesus's disciples also ignore the contemporary Jewish practice of fasting, or so we are told at Mark 2:18. And, as if following up on Jesus's suggestion that a presumably uncircumcised centurion could exceed every Jew in his faith, St. Paul explicitly does away with the need for circumcision altogether, which is a Jewish practice dating back to Abraham himself and, as the symbol of the Covenant with God's Chosen People, is one of God's earliest commands. Unsurprisingly, circumcision was also one of the chief obstacles for eager Roman initiates wishing to adopt Jewish ways. (51)

It seems that "Gospel" Christians of the Pauline variety had no use for any of the traditional Jewish holy days, either, from Yom Kippur to Passover or any of the others. Christian holy days such as Christmas and Easter are not even calculated on a Hebrew calendar but on a Roman one. Even where the events that inspired them can be lined up with the Gospels' narrative, as in the case of the Crucifixion and Resurrection that should properly coincide with Passover, the celebration of the Resurrection coincides with pagan spring fertility festivals, instead. And the birth of Jesus is celebrated at around the same time as the birth of pagan solar deities (and the birth of Emperor Titus).

While it is true that over time Christianity would grow increasingly un-Jewish and even anti-Jewish, the Gospels themselves—even the earliest, along with the letters of St. Paul—embody a fierce ongoing argument with the Jews. The "heavies" in the New Testament are invariably the Jews. It is impossible to deny that this is partially responsible for the last two millennia of anti-Semitism. The origins of this "blood libel" against Jewish people began in the text of the most printed book on Earth.

The New Testament *is* anti-Semitic, not incidentally, not implicitly, but fundamentally and thematically. Anti-Semitism is its purpose. From its very origins, the New Testament is quite literally "anti-Semitism." The "New Testament" is a rebuttal to the "Old Testament" written at a time of holy war between the Romans and the Jews.

Once it is highlighted, the New Testament's overtly Roman perspective explains an entire host of otherwise completely inexplicable issues. One of them is Paul's reference to personal contacts inside the house of the emperor and also to a powerful secretary of Emperor Nero himself. Suddenly, such offhand mentions by St. Paul, puzzling, braggadocios, and usually overlooked for these reasons, become suddenly meaningful simply by taking them literally. (51)

We will shortly see that this person, Epaphroditus, one of the highest-ranking secretaries of the Emperor Nero, may actually be the confidant Paul is referring to in his letter to the Philippians, which he concluded with: "All God's people here send you greetings, especially those who belong to Caesar's household." (52) Paul's reference to being in custody (53) in that same letter suggests that he wrote this letter while in Rome.

We shall return to Paul's relationships with this Roman official named "Epaphroditus," and other high-ranking Romans, when we focus on the people who are so deeply interwoven into this story, in Part II.

* * * * * * * *

Already we have seen that the religious and political goals in the Gospels track perfectly with the agenda of contemporary Romans while also clashing with popular Jewish attitudes on the very grounds that had instigated the Jewish War—a war that was won by the Romans just prior to the Gospels' writing.

In the Gospels, Jesus condemns the things that brought Jews into conflict with the Romans even as he expresses themes of hope, peace, charity, eternal salvation, joy, universal brotherhood, and the proclamation of world peace to the whole of the human race. All of these are distinctly Roman political ideals, which they were actively disseminating far and wide at this time, as evidenced in their coinage. Indeed, Jesus virtually personified all of the social virtues that were the currency of Roman imperialism in the wake of the Jewish War.

* * * * * * * *

One might object to naming the New Testament "anti-Semitic" on these grounds: that it, especially the Book of Matthew, bases Jesus Christ's claim to be the Jewish Messiah on Hebrew prophecies and that Jesus was, after all, himself Jewish.

However, while it is certainly true that Jesus is said by the Gospels to have fulfilled some of the basic Jewish messianic prophecies, such as being born of the line of King David, the authors of the Gospels themselves seem to employ the whole of Hebrew Scriptures, including parts that have nothing to do with the messiah, to a haphazard variety of literary ends that hardly seem Jewish.

For example, in order to depict Jesus as the new lawgiver, or a new "Moses," Jesus is shown delivering his sermon on a "mount" (just as Moses received the Torah atop Mount Sinai).

Another example is that just as Pharaoh ordered male babies slaughtered at the time of Moses's birth, so Herod orders the "Slaughter of the Innocents" in Bethlehem at the time of Jesus's birth, according to Matthew (though this is not backed up by the record of any contemporary historians or archeological evidence of any kind).

Detail from Vatican tapestry, Slaughter of the Innocents

And there are other instances of this kind of holistic and theologically curious sourcing to the Old Testament in many New Testament details regarding Christ.

In another instance, just as the "Joseph" of Genesis interpreted prophetic dreams in Egypt so, too, does *Joseph*, the husband of Mary, have prophetic dreams that compel him to take his family to Egypt. Though the text of the original Joseph story seems to have no necessary relation to the coming of the messiah, the story is recycled anyway in the New Testament, which seems to treat the entire Old Testament as prophetic of Jesus as if to give the Gospels a generalized "Jewish" patina. St. Paul himself describes his own experiences reading the holy words from a sacred scripture as sending him (and presumably other interpreters) into a state of religious ecstasy, prompting new visions of the messiah.

As the focus of centuries of the Jewish people's prophetic hopes, the concept of the messiah would come to be seen as the embodiment and physical manifestation of the Word of God. Yet, so dramatically did the Gospels' Jesus seem to reverse the traditional expectations of the messiah, Jesus is liberally shown to embody the whole of Hebrew scripture itself as prophetic of him, including material that had little or nothing to do with the messianic concept.

Scholars have long observed many more examples of Hebrew literature being oddly recapitulated in the New Testament in this "prophecy-fulfilling" fashion. We can be sure, for this reason, that one of the primary sources for the late 1st Century Gospel authors who depicted Christ was ancient Hebrew scripture.

However, Jesus does not fulfill the predictions of glory and rule that traditionally qualified one as a Jewish messiah. Instead, he only predicts that such glory and rule will be fulfilled during his imminent and decisive *second* coming in yet another jarring innovation to the messianic concept that markedly deviates from Hebrew religion— even while seemingly basing itself on the Old Testament prophecy of Isaiah.

Innovatively, in order to support the departure from the messianic archetype of a delivering warrior, Gospel authors seem to have used the prophecies of Isaiah as a basis for their accounts of Jesus—specifically, the prophecy of the "expiation" that was required before the messiah could arrive and which must include, as Isaiah claims, a human sacrifice.

In the Old Testament, the prophet Isaiah envisions a time when the people's sins have accumulated to such a point that the messiah's arrival will be impossible. To become worthy of the messianic advent, Isaiah warns that a propitiation of human blood will have to be made. An animal sacrifice, such as a mere "lamb," will no longer suffice. According to Isaiah:

> Who has believed our message and to whom has the arm of the Lord been revealed?
>
> He grew up before him like a tender shoot, and like a root out of dry ground. He had no beauty or majesty to attract us to him, nothing in his appearance that we should desire him.
>
> He was *despised and rejected by mankind*, a man of suffering, and familiar with pain. Like one from whom people hide their faces he was despised, and we held him in low esteem.
>
> Surely he took up our pain and bore our suffering, *yet we considered him punished by God*, stricken by him, and afflicted.
>
> But *he was pierced for our transgressions*, he was crushed for our iniquities; the punishment that brought us peace was on him, and *by his wounds we are healed.*

We all, like sheep, have gone astray, each of us has turned to our own way; and the Lord has laid on him the iniquity of us all.

He was oppressed and afflicted, yet *he did not open his mouth; he was led like a lamb to the slaughter*, and as a sheep before its shearers is silent, so *he did not open his mouth*.

By oppression and judgment he was taken away. *Yet who of his generation protested?* For he was cut off from the land of the living; for the transgression of my people he was punished.

He was assigned a grave with the wicked, and with the rich in his death, though *he had done no violence*, nor was any deceit in his mouth.

Yet it was the Lord's will to crush him and cause him to suffer, and though the Lord makes his life an offering for sin, he will see his offspring and prolong his days, and the will of the Lord will prosper in his hand.

After he has *suffered*, he will see the *light of life* and be satisfied; by his knowledge my righteous servant will *justify many*, and *he will bear their iniquities*.

Therefore I will give him a portion among the great, and he will divide the spoils with the strong, because he *poured out his life unto death*, and was *numbered with the transgressors*. For he *bore the sin of many*, and made intercession for the transgressors. (Emphasis added.) (54)

Notice how closely this Old Testament prophecy coincides with the account of Jesus's life in the Gospels—especially the stories of his trial and execution. So closely, in fact, that most scholars now acknowledge that *Isaiah* must be a primary source for the Gospels' narrative about Jesus.

There can be no doubt that many contemporary Jews also believed that some form of human sacrifice was also required to achieve the expiation and purification required for the People of Israel to be worthy of the Messianic Advent, and martyred figures such as John the Baptist and James the Just may have been seen by rebellious Jews in just this way.

In order to flesh out the biography of Jesus, therefore, Gospel authors liberally mined ancient Hebrew scripture as a source of material for the life of Jesus rather than simply relating actual recent history. One might reasonably be entitled to ask why, if Jesus existed, did they feel free to do this?

Even if a historical Jesus really existed, so little was known about him at the end of the 1st Century that the authors of the Gospels felt free to creatively insert material centuries older into his biography in order to serve their very current political purposes.

(How this happened, and exactly who might have been involved in employing such tactics to compose the New Testament, will be addressed in Part II.)

Even if Isaiah's prophecy may have shaped the story of Jesus, there remain important differences between Isaiah's so-called "Suffering Servant" story and the story of Jesus in the Gospels. Jesus did not "prolong his days" nor did he "see his offspring," for example, like Isaiah's martyr. Most importantly, Isaiah's "Suffering Servant" is *not* a messiah.

Nevertheless, the one whose coming is predicted in Isaiah's passage would certainly be a convenient reference for writers who wished to use Jewish texts for propaganda, especially in a war whose *casus belli* was the Jewish religion. Notice how Isaiah is predicting a generation of Jews who have gone astray—and who need redemption. He goes on to mention a messianic precursor who will be rejected by Jews. He will be peaceful, and he will be misunderstood by Jews and even despised by them. He will be martyred, as a result. Never mind that Isaiah does not predict that he will be a healer, his poetry is still an elegant foreshadowing of Jesus that complements the pagan idea of a healer God: "*by his wounds we are healed.*" (55)

Again, neither this "Suffering Servant" nor the prophecy of the messiah whose glorious coming and world rule was also predicted by Isaiah suggest the arrival of a pagan man-god, healer god, or mystery cult god. Yet such a prophecy of a sacrificial precursor to the conquering messiah could quite easily be seen as extremely convenient to Roman emperors who had just conquered Judea in a holy war; especially to a Roman government that was already adept at using religion as a tool of cultural conquest.

The Jewish messiah of prophecy is converted by Paul and the Gospel authors into a "suffering" mystery cult savior modeled after healer gods like Aesclepius and Serapis while retaining parts of Isaiah's "Suffering Servant" that serve perfectly as a premonition of the Flavians. It is hard to imagine what could have accommodated the Romans more in their conflict with fundamentalist Jews than the kind of cultural syncretism personified in Jesus Christ.

*Jesus Christ depicted as a Roman Emperor,
c. 500 CE, Ravenna, Italy*

* * * * * * * *

The New Testament does not present an anti-Roman message and then give the Roman government a couple of perfunctory nods of appeasement to gain security in treacherous times. Rather, the central, overriding and consistent theme propounded in the New Testament is one of peace, meekness, submission, obedience, mercy, and getting along with all of the people of the earth—and especially with Roman authority. In other words, it embodies the Romans' central objectives in regards to rebellious Jews and their wider empire.

In a time of Jewish rebellion, 1st Century Christian literature commands its adherents to pay their taxes, honor the emperor and go the extra mile for Romans. It argues that existing governmental authorities are nothing less than the agents of God, appointed *by* God, and that all virtuous people have nothing to fear from Roman authority. Submission to them is itself a virtue, and the more subservient the submission, the greater that virtue. All this the New Testament instructs us.

Our inherited idea of the earliest Christians being driven underground by hostile Roman authorities because of their incompatible codes of ethics simply is not true. Christians were apparently devotees of precisely the same virtues embodied by the Flavians' imperial cult even as their very Gospels were being composed.

Not only Romans, but even Roman *centurions* are awarded highest praise in the New Testament in the immediate aftermath of the bloody conquest of Judea. The greatest story ever told takes pains to completely exonerate Romans while theatrically blaming Jews for Christ's death, three times, with a cartoonishly heavy hand. This theme is further confirmed in the betrayal of Judas and the accusations of the Jewish authorities as the Roman Governor Pontius Pilate washes his hands of any blame.

These melodramatic flourishes, illustrating political biases we can now clearly see, are so exaggerated and strange outside their historical context that they continue to fuel a mindless anti-Semitism even after two millennia.

* * * * * * * *

If, as a thought experiment, one were to imagine what a sophisticated Roman propaganda war aimed at rebellious Hebrews in the 1st Century during their conflict with Nero and the Flavians might theoretically have looked like, the New Testament would match such a model in every imaginable respect.

The overtly Roman politics, the religious shape of its political propaganda, the commanded servile worship of a Caesar-like man-god in the place of a liberating Jewish Messiah, the sweeping rejection of the Kosher lifestyle and denial of Jewish exceptionalism, all of it leaves nothing off the Roman government's check-list of 1st Century "corrections" to Jewish religion and culture. Christianity contains all of the revisions to Judaism that the Romans who conquered Judea could have possibly desired as the spoils of their victory.

Where Jewish morality and Roman morality overlap, we can find Jewish doctrines quite favorably featured in the New Testament, such as Jesus's adoption of the early rabbis' Golden Rule. Obviously, the "mortal helping mortal" benevolence of the Flavians praised by the Emperor Titus's personal friend, Pliny the Elder, parallels this concept of charity. Even more famously, the altruism of Jesus is mirrored in the philosophical work of the 1st Century Roman Stoic writer Seneca, who was a tutor and assistant of the Emperor Nero.

Titus was educated along with the Emperor Claudius's son, Britannicus, in the imperial palace, where Nero, who was only two years Titus's senior, was being instructed by Seneca. It is therefore certainly possible that Titus himself knew that famous philosopher personally, as his father Vespasian must have known the man who Nero later named as an imperial advisor. St. Paul lived and wrote at precisely the same time as Seneca. Both were writing in Rome during the same years, and the two may have died at about the same time, as well. Seneca's enduring influence as a philosopher can be felt even today.

This passage of Seneca is relevant to us now:

> Let us consider, most excellent Liberalis, what still remains of the earlier part of the subject; in what way a benefit should be bestowed. I think that I can point out the shortest way to this; let us give in the way in which we ourselves should like to receive. Above all we should give willingly, quickly, and without any hesitation; a benefit commands no gratitude if it has hung for a long time in the hands of the giver, if he seems unwilling to part with it, and gives it as though he were being robbed of it. (56)

So Seneca was clearly a Roman advocate of the "golden rule." In addition, Nero's teacher was also an early critic of Roman slavery:

> I do not wish to involve myself in too large a question, and to discuss the treatment of slaves, towards whom we Romans are excessively haughty, cruel, and insulting. But this is the kernel of my advice: Treat

your inferiors as you would be treated by your betters. And as often as you reflect how much power you have over a slave, remember that your master has just as much power over you. (57)

Seneca the Younger

Statements like these from Seneca make it easy to see why later Christians would invent (as they did) a correspondence between St. Paul and Seneca, which is now rejected as an obvious forgery created at a later date. (58)

Although we have already seen that the New Testament repeatedly commands slaves to obey their masters—even when their master isn't looking, and even *happily*—the New Testament is also famous for a doctrine of benevolent treatment of slaves by their masters that echoes this policy of Seneca. Consider this New Testament passage from the Epistle to the Ephesians that reflects Seneca's view:

Slaves, obey your earthly masters with respect and fear, and with sincerity of heart, just as you would obey Christ. Obey them not only to win their favor when their eye is on you, but as slaves of Christ, doing the will of God from your heart. Serve wholeheartedly, as if you know that the Lord will reward each one for whatever good they do, whether they are slave or free.

And masters, treat your slaves in the *same way*. Do not threaten them, since you know that he who is both their Master and yours is in heaven, and there is no favoritism with him. (Emphasis added.) (59)

This Seneca-like compassion resembles the paternalistic love and concern of Emperor Titus, as we have previously seen Suetonius describe it.

At their circuses, the Romans, like Jesus, fed the multitudes with bread. The Emperor Titus would take the practice to new heights himself during the opening of the Colosseum.

Roman emperors, especially the Flavians, were keen to advertise themselves as bringers of peace and saviors of the world. One might think there is a paradoxical element in these Roman generals associating themselves with peace given their brutal war with Judea. Yet Jesus, too, commanded peace even as he launched a physical attack on the Temple in Jerusalem. While advocating peace, Jesus states: "Think not that I am come to send peace on earth: I came not to send peace, but a sword." (60)

Therefore calling the Jesus of the Gospels a "pacifist" and therefore incompatible with the Romans' agenda is mistaken. His commands for pacifism appear to have been directed specifically at the Jewish rebels of the 1st Century.

Jesus himself went so far as to command his disciples to carry weapons. As we might expect by now, however, the specified context of his instruction is revealing:

> He said to them, "But now if you have a purse, take it, and also a bag; and if you don't have a sword, sell your cloak and buy one. It is written: "'*And he was numbered with the transgressors*'; and I tell you that this must be fulfilled in me, Yes, what is written about me is reaching its fulfillment."
> The disciples said, "See, Lord, here are two swords."
> "That's enough!" he replied. (Emphasis added) (61)

This is, of course, none other than Isaiah's "Suffering Servant" prophecy. Here, Jesus draws a connection between himself and this passage from Hebrew prophecy—which was not a prophecy about the messiah himself but only about the sacrificial precursor to the messiah.

Also, Jesus tells his followers to carry swords in order to be "numbered with the transgressors." They are to have swords, it seems, for the express purpose of getting Jesus into trouble, thus checking off another prophetic requirement from the Old Testament's Isaiah prophecy of the suffering servant.

The same passage from Isaiah also implies that the accusations will be false and that the Suffering Servant is really a man of peace. So, far from justifying the use of weapons in self-defense, as some have interpreted it today, this instruction by Jesus seems to rationalize the fact that the first (pre-Pauline) "Christians" were known for carrying weapons and were therefore "transgressors." Notice how Jesus also stresses *limiting* their weapons.

Finally, while justifying the prophetic consequences of taking up the sword, none of this alters Jesus's perfectly clear instructions to submit to aggressors, love one's enemies, obey authorities, turn the other cheek, and foster peace. Indeed, Jesus reproves Peter on the only occasion where the disciples actually use their swords in the Gospels. "'Put your sword back in its place,'" Jesus said to him, "for all who draw the sword will die by the sword.'" (62)

If we take "all who draw the sword" to mean anyone who initiates violence, then Jesus's prediction is obviously wrong. Everyone knows that many violent killers die natural deaths long after their crimes, including a lot of Roman centurions who had killed Jews during the war. In its historical context during the late 1st Century post-war period, therefore, the phrase would have been heard as a warning against rebellion, a dire prophecy aimed at those who "took up the sword" against the Roman Empire.

Those who rebelled against Rome would, indeed, pay dearly, as we know, so Jesus's prediction is again absolutely correct. Those who weren't slain on the battlefield were captured—and many thousands of them were crucified even as their families were enslaved.

Christ's ideas did not represent any pre-existing "pacifist" branch of 1st Century messianic Jews—no evidence for such a sect exists before the 1st Century. Instead, he simply personifies the Roman Empire's opposition to messianic Jews. If Christianity is not Roman propaganda, it must be an extremely strange coincidence that Christ's story of Jewish guilt and message of transnational peace was written down during the Flavians' reign in the years immediately after those emperors had crushed the Jewish rebellion.

Just like Serapis, Christ seems to be a pacifying combination-god perfectly designed to bridge the fractious cultural divide between the conquered Jews and the victorious Romans in the aftermath of their epical religious war.

* * * * * * * *

In addition to all of their overlapping imperial and Christian values, the Flavian dynasty also appears to have introduced a more conservative sexual morality to Roman society that markedly contrasts with the notorious licentiousness of the Julio-Claudians and rings more true to Christian doctrine in this respect. We generally equate ancient Romans with the famous debauchery of the previous dynasty and, undoubtedly, most of the early Roman emperors are renowned for their orgiastic indulgences. There is evidence, of course, of sexual decadence after the Flavians ruled Rome. Yet during the reign of the Flavians some of Pompeii's pornographic murals were painted over, suggesting a more modest approach by Vespasian or possibly by Titus, who had taken the throne only two months before the eruption of Vesuvius. (63)

For his part, after Titus's death, his younger brother Domitian would restore the traditional penalty of being buried alive for all Vestal Virgins who broke their vows of chastity. This may be attributed to the fact that Domitian took a more conservative approach to traditional Roman religion, in general, than either his father or brother. But it also illustrates the more conservative sexual mores instituted by the Flavians after the wanton sexual excesses of the Julio-Claudians. (64)

So it seems that even the sexual modesty and chastity preached in the New Testament does not conflict with the theory of its Roman provenance. Although the ancient historian Suetonius preserved both reports and rumors of sexual excesses in the youth of Titus and Domitian throughout his life, the Flavian dynasty as a whole frowned on the decadence of their dynastic predecessors' even more extreme behavior—a change in direction, at least—representing another coincidence of Flavian and Jewish morality that is preserved in Christianity.

The New Testament famously depicts Jesus as associating with prostitutes and saving a woman about to be stoned to death for adultery, the required penalty under Mosaic Law, in what seems to be an effort to moderate the severe sexual ethics that was then dominant in certain sects of orthodox Judaism.

Despite the remarkable overlap that we have been observing, the New Testament is not a perfect reflection of contemporary Roman ethics, of course. Most notably, the ancient Romans had rather liberal laws regarding divorce while the New Testament seems to forbid divorce entirely. And both Jesus and St. Paul appear to recommend (but not require) celibacy. (65)

However, the doctrines expressed by Paul and the Gospel writers were not aimed at a general Roman audience but at those (both Jew and Gentile) who had been—or were "at risk" of being—influenced by messianic Judaism. The Gospels were not written for a general Jewish audience, either, since Mosaic Law itself permitted divorce. (66) Instead, the sexual morality in the New Testament seems to both reflect and respond to the far stricter regulations and mores of the radical Jewish groups of the era, such as the Essenes and the militant Dead Sea scrolls sectarians. In other words, these ideas were a reflection of the preexisting sexual morality of the very Jewish-Christian rebel groups to whom the Romans were appealing. Rather than selling them yet another massive alteration of their ethics, in this respect their own tradition was simply carried straight into Christianity in a way that augmented its authenticity, with little practical downside.

Asceticism and chastity were not unknown to the ancient Roman religion, either, as the very existence of Vestal Virgins shows, and both Platonic and Stoic thought increasingly emphasized the virtue of sexual discipline. But Christian monasticism, surely, traces its roots back to the celibate ways of the Jewish radicals reflected in the New Testament.

* * * * * * * *

Adding to their own parallels with the New Testament's Jesus, and their unique departures from previous emperors, Vespasian and Titus took special pride in their *humble origins*—something that scholar Barbara Levick calls Vespasian's "ostentatious modesty."

In fact, the small, dingy bedroom where the Nativity of Titus took place was actually opened to the viewing public, and it continued to be a tourist destination throughout the reign of Trajan, if not much longer. (67) The Flavians were eager to advertise their beginnings in relative poverty, just as the Gospels emphasize the humble origins of Christ.

Both father and son, Vespasian and Titus were Jewish messiahs heralded to come from modest origins, just like the ghost who preceded and predicted them, *Jesus*. As well as being healer gods like Serapis and Jesus, these Roman emperors were *deified* men.

The benevolence of the first two Flavian emperors was legendary. Their "common touch," fostering of peace, and the loving compassion of Titus through Rome's tribulations, made them models for future emperors. In fact, nearly every Christian Roman emperor following Constantine the Great would adopt the name "Flavius" among his imperial appellations. Even though none of the 2nd or 3rd Century pagan emperors of Rome would use this name, from the family of the first Christian Emperor Constantine all the way to the dynasty of Justinian only two out of 38 emperors did *not* adopt the name "Flavius." (And one of these did not need to, since his mother was already named "Flavia." The other holdout, Avitus, himself a Christian bishop, ruled only 15 months before he was removed by a coup.)

No emperors subsequent to the Flavians were actual members of the Flavian family. But these later Christian emperors did not utilize the family names "Julius," "Claudius," or "Aurelius" with anything like the same consistency. The name almost all of them chose, indeed their common denominator, was "Flavius." Whether these Christian emperors were aware of a foundational connection between the Flavian family and Christianity we do not know. But it is a fact that nearly all of them selected the Flavians as both a moral model and a namesake.

It is remarkable how many prominent early Christians also bear the names of Flavian family members, close associates, or servants: names like Titus, Epaphroditus, Tertulla/Tertullian, Stephanus, Domitilla, and Clemens or Clement. There is the St. Clement of Alexandria, whose full name is "Titus Flavius Clemens" and whose recommendations for Christian symbols include Titus's dolphin and anchor symbols. No fewer than 14 popes and three antipopes are named "Clement."

There is no doubt that Christians greatly admired the emperors Vespasian and Titus. St. Augustine, the most important Christian philosopher before Thomas Aquinas, described Vespasian as "a most agreeable emperor" in his famous work *City of God*, while to many medievals such as the poet Dante, author of *The Divine Comedy*, they enjoyed a "high" reputation as "scourges of the Jews." (68) The mercy and compassion of Titus is the subject of one of Mozart's last composed operas, which was one of the first to reach London, *La Clemenza di Tito* (The Mercy of Titus).

We have still only begun to outline the many links that connect the Flavians to Christianity. As we will see in Part II, their political and familial relationships are stunningly intertwined. Remember, the coin was the *last* thing we found, which dropped perfectly into place after decades of research had left only that space curiously unfilled. In Part II we will look behind these symbols at the personal connections forged by the Flavians and the very first Christians and other historical figures, some of whom even appear in the New Testament itself.

Even before we get to that astonishing evidence, however, the strength of the connection between early Christianity and the imperial cult of the Flavians that we have seen suggests a relationship vital to understanding the history of Western Civilization that has been lost along with its forbidden and forgotten historical context. In the case of the dolphin-and-anchor motif, that connection is now literally visible.

The discovery of that final physical evidence alone reveals that, almost simultaneously with the Flavian dynasty, the earliest Christians in Rome were using a deified Flavian emperor's symbol to represent their own deity and religion. This iconographic overlap occurred while this symbol was circulating on Roman coins across the Empire even as the Gospels were being written and well after the first Christians began marking their oldest burial sites with the same iconography. Even at a public works in Herculaneum, buried by the eruption of Mt. Vesuvius during the reign of Titus, a mosaic at their imperial baths displays identical symbolism to that found in the very first catacombs.

This legacy of shared symbols between Flavians and Christians would persist until Christianity became the official state religion of the Roman Empire two centuries later, at which point Christians, around the time of Constantine the Great, would replace that Flavian-Christian symbol with the symbol of the Cross.

If we look at a Venn diagram of the worldviews of Flavian emperors and the earliest Christians, we see they substantially overlap in time, place, ideology, politics and even in the specific symbols they used to identify themselves. The meaning of those symbols could not have been lost on these Christians who nevertheless used them in the city of Rome itself. The ideology and symbology of the first Christians and imperial Romans at this moment in time share too much to be mere coincidence. They are, indeed, two sides of the same coin. (69)

Coin of Emperor Titus (left and middle); and the symbol of Jesus Christ (right)

Meanwhile, a group of contemporary Jews connected to the imperial court and all of its vast resources were acknowledging Vespasian and Titus as the messiahs who had risen from Judea to fulfill Jewish prophecies and become "rulers of the world."

It is time to introduce ourselves to this group of people, as well as others historically acknowledged to have much in common with Christianity—who were all, as it turns out, friends of the Flavians.

Part II

Jews and Christians
at the Flavian Court

I. Jews—or Christians?

The many historical, ideological and iconographic connections between the propaganda of the Flavian emperors and early Christianity demand that we take a closer look at the people who were associated with this imperial dynasty. Who were they? And, if the Gospels are a form of Roman propaganda, were any of these associates of the Flavians connected to early Christianity?

First among the close relatives of the Flavian emperors we must take note of is Vespasian's nephew and Titus's cousin, a man named Titus Flavius Clemens. As we have already seen, his name was shared by the later Titus Flavius Clemens, the Christian father known today as St. Clement of Alexandria, who lived in the 3rd Century. The latter Clemens suggested that both anchors and dolphins be adopted as Christian symbols a century after the death of this possible ancestor.

This earlier Titus Flavius Clemens, who lived during the imperial rule of his Flavian relatives, was known as St. Clement of Rome— one of the first *popes*.

According to Church tradition, one of the first popes (either the third or fourth depending on the ancient list used) was the 1st Century "St. Clement of Rome." However, Tertullian names him as the successor of St. Peter himself, and St. Jerome reports a tradition that Clement was the "second after the apostle" (Peter) himself. (1)

Of course, there really was no such office as "pope" (Bishop of Rome) yet, although there already may well have been an elaborate Church hierarchy. Lists of the early Church's actual leadership are the sketchiest of evidence since they are based on an orally transmitted tradition. The tradition that places this 1st Century pope as the second or third after Christ's own appointed "rock," Peter, can only be as certain as the authority of St. Jerome, who claimed Clement to have been the successor of the famous "fisherman" himself. However, Clement's high place on these lists is astounding.

How could such a close relative of the Flavian emperors be the second, third or fourth *pope*, or any such high-ranking figure in the early Church?

The historical reality of this early Church leader is supported by the ascription of a body of literature to him. Only his first letter or "epistle" is regarded as genuine by most scholars today, or at least it is thought to be a collection of material by a single author that may date to the late 1st Century. Yet there is ample reason to believe that St. Clement was a member of the imperial Flavian dynasty.

Remember that Titus's younger brother, Domitian, who inherited the throne after his brother's untimely death, quickly discontinued Titus's dolphin-and-anchor motif on his coins. He also immediately rebuilt and rededicated the fire-ravaged Pantheon in order to honor the traditional Roman gods. And, toward the end of his reign, in 95 CE, according to the 3rd Century Roman historian Cassius Dio:

> ...Domitian slew, along with many others, Flavius Clemens the consul, although he was a cousin and had to wife Flavia Domitilla, who was also a relative of the emperor's. The charge brought against them both was that of atheism, a charge on which many others who drifted into Jewish ways were condemned. Some of these were put to death, and the rest were at least deprived of their property. Domitilla was merely banished to Pandateria. (2)

Cassius Dio tells us that Titus Flavius Clemens was a consul and great-nephew of Vespasian himself. Cassius Dio also reports that this Clemens was executed by his cousin, the Emperor Domitian, in 95 CE.

The capital crimes of "atheism" and "drifting into Jewish ways" cited for his death sentence have been variously interpreted by scholars to mean that Clemens had become either a "soft" convert to Judaism (a "God fearer") or had been, himself, a Christian. To a polytheist, any monotheist is, after all, almost an atheist simply by denying the existence of almost every god. Therefore the charge of "atheism" could be reasonably leveled at monotheists and those who had adopted "Jewish ways."

Since this Clemens executed by Domitian was an uncircumcised

Roman, and unlikely to have ever adopted a Kosher diet, it is far easier to think of him as a kind of Christian than a "Judaizer." This would fit his description of "adopting Jewish ways" better than if he were actually practicing Judaism. Domitian was going after a wider group among whom Clemens and his wife had been the leading figures, for Cassius tells us that "many others" were slain or banished along with them, apparently on the same charges.

If what our theory implies is correct and the Flavians were intimately involved with the creation of Christianity, then the timing of Clemens's involvement would perfectly coincide with Pliny the Younger's claim that Christianity was in vogue around 20 years prior to his letter to Trajan—that is, in the very middle of the Flavian era when Clemens must have been flourishing. Clemens's status as a Christian leader would also support Pliny's description of Christians as reaching across "all classes" of Romans. Moreover, since Clemens's near relatives, Vespasian and Titus, claimed to be Jewish messiahs, Clemens no doubt acknowledged them as such—making him potentially messianic in his "Jewish ways."

The 2nd Century historian Suetonius confirms the execution of Titus Flavius Clemens but does not specify a charge, saying only that it was "a trivial pretext." (3) He does reveal, however, that the childless Domitian named the young sons of Clemens as his own heirs—suggesting that Clemens may have been a *political* rival who could have presented a threat to Domitian's own position.

Since Domitian was assassinated the year following these executions by a plot within his own family and court, Suetonius was likely correct in describing the charge of "atheism" against Clemens as a mere pretext to get rid of him. Such a plot by close members of the imperial family in this instance was probably more than mere paranoia on the emperor's part. Still, it is an unusual charge for the time and indicates a unique religious matter that Domitian may have considered threatening.

Plots against Domitian's life had become very real by this time in his reign. It is not too fantastic to imagine, given what we now know, that Clemens's possible adoption of the mantel of Jewish Messiah after the death of Vespasian and Titus—or his adoption of any leadership position that tradition might recognize as a primordial "pope"— would have been perceived by Domitian as a political challenge.

Domitian had not taken part in the "heroic" Jewish War through which his father and brother both gained a triumph and their imperial seat, as well as their title of Jewish messiah. On the other hand, because Titus Flavius Clemens was a member of the Flavian family and a *consularis* in rank, he would most certainly have been a priest of their imperial cults, as well as a "pontiff," although not the Pontifex Maximus. That title was then reserved for the emperor, though today it is reserved for the pope.

Vespasian, "Pontifex Maximus"

Eusebius, the Church historian who wrote in the early 4th Century, also mentions "Clement" as a 1st Century pope. Usefully, he adds to the picture that a "niece" of the consul Flavius Clemens named "Flavia Domitilla" was banished "to Pontus" because of her "testimony to Christ." (4) Since this is the same name as Titus Flavius Clemens's own banished wife, and since the post-Domitian period was characterized by tolerance of Christians, it is probable that Eusebius is confused here, if not intentionally throwing us off the track. Were there really two ladies of that family named "Flavia Domitilla"—both banished for their quasi-Jewish religious beliefs at around the same time? Or just one? If they are the same, then "Flavia Domitilla" was the wife of the consul Clemens, not his niece. She *was* a niece of the emperors Titus and Domitian, and she was the granddaughter of the Emperor Vespasian himself. And she hadn't just adopted Jewish ways—she was a Christian, according to Eusebius. With all of the confusion surrounding the identification of 1st Century Jewish and Christian sectarians, errors of this sort are familiar. However, the name "Domitilla" implies that Eusebius's Christian was a descendant of Vespasian's own wife (just as Flavius Clemens's wife was) rather than a Flavian niece from his own branch of the family. If she was a "niece" only by marriage, then she would be a descendant of Vespasian unknown to history.

Flavia Domitilla the Younger

In all likelihood, these two "Flavia Domitillas," both banished for either "drifting into Jewish ways" or making a "testimony to Christ," are in fact the *same person*.

Revealingly, the Christian historian Eusebius directly follows his account of Domitilla's banishment with Domitian ordering the execution of all of the relatives of Christ's own family, and all those of King David's royal line, i.e., all potential "messianic" claimants to his throne. (5) If we may safely identify the two "Flavia Domitillas" as one person, then the 1st Century Pope, St. Clement, is our Titus Flavius Clemens (her husband). After his cousin Titus's death, Clemens was probably the highest-ranking Christian of his time.

In addition to the various similarities between Titus Flavius Clemens and St. Clement in name, time, place, "Judaizing ways," and fate—as well as having the same wife—the Church of St. Clement of Rome, built during the 5th Century, once contained an inscription dedicating it to "Flavius Clemens, martyr," according to a 1725 report by Cardinal Annibal Albani that has survived. (6)

The later St. Clement (of Alexandria) also bore the name "Titus Flavius Clemens." Since there may well have been a real family relationship between these two sainted Christians, the latter might provide us with yet another Flavian Christian. Freed Roman slaves also normally took the name of their patrons, so, at the least, this man is a descendant of someone who had a Flavian patron, probably

Clemens himself. This could explain why he promoted both fish and anchors as Christian symbols, and why he understood them to first come from Seleucus, the pagan Hellenistic king.

As it turns out, the symbol associated with St. Clement of Rome just happens to be an *anchor.* The later tradition that St. Clement of Rome was martyred early in the reign of Trajan (c. 99 CE) by being attached to an anchor and drowned may be a thinly veiled reference to the crucifixion and, for that reason, untrustworthy. However, the Titus Flavius Clemens put to death by Domitian can safely be said to have expired in the year 95 CE, not in the time of Trajan.

Whether it is true or not, the symbolism of St. Clement being killed by an anchor resembles the tradition that Titus died by eating a fish. That Titus and Clement died by fish and by anchor, respectively, could be satiric echoes of early Christian symbolism. Or, however unlikely, perhaps Domitian possessed such a black streak of irony that he personally selected these methods to eliminate his Judaizing rivals to the throne.

The fact that the anchor is a symbol of both the Flavian Emperor Titus *and* the pope, St. Clement of Rome, appears to confirm again that Titus's nephew Clemens and Christianity's St. Clement of Rome are the same person. It was certainly natural that Clemens would share the symbolic anchor image of his imperial relatives, whatever the actual manner of his death.

Here, St. Clement is shown in stained glass holding an anchor:

St. Clement

And, here, again, we see him martyred with an anchor:

The Martyrdom of St. Clement of Rome

* * * * * * * *

About the same time that Domitian executed Clemens he also executed a man named Epaphroditus. Epaphroditus was the imperial secretary of Nero that we mentioned earlier as a possible associate of St. Paul, who gave such warm greetings to "Epaphroditus" in his letter.

We will learn more about Epaphroditus shortly, but the coincidence of his execution along with Clemens suggests that the high-ranking freedman Epaphroditus who served Nero, Vespasian, and Titus may have been involved with Clemens in some kind of conspiracy suspected by Domitian, in addition to associating with St. Paul decades earlier. This alone is noteworthy. (7)

What is more, in the same letter in which Paul praises "Epaphroditus" he also mentions a "Clement" among his "co-workers, whose names are in the book of life." (8)

Of course, if Paul's friend Clement was an adult around 60-63 CE, when Paul is thought to have written this letter, then this Clement could not be the same person. The Titus Flavius Clemens we are talking about would have been a child at that time.

However, as with nearly all Roman family names, his family name was freely given out among his relatives. The naming conventions of ancient Rome were rigid, but not perfectly so. The eldest son typically bore the exact same name as his father, while all of the daughters bore the family name as their own. "Julia" was included in the name of every daughter of the Julii, for example. Younger sons often adopted a name or a modified version of a name from their mother's family— Vespasian, himself a second son, had been named for his mother's family, the Vespasii. This is why adding modifiers like "the Younger" and "the Elder" is necessary when referring to Romans. In this case, Titus Flavius Clemens's maternal uncle was the consul Arrecinus Clemens, whose family had been associated with the Praetorian Guard since at least the reign of Caligula. He was a "Clement" who could have known Paul in Rome. And, coincidentally, he, too, was sentenced to death by the purging Domitian. (9)

* * * * * * * *

By the time of the early Christian scholar Eusebius in the 4th Century, Christians themselves would have been at a loss to explain how it was that a great-nephew of a Roman emperor could also be a 1st Century pope. It is so baffling that we can understand why they might have created separate traditions for two separate histori- cal figures in order to avoid confronting the paradox. The niece of Titus and Domitian was also moved further away from the throne, becoming the "niece" only of *Clemens*, her husband, even as she is positively identified as a Christian.

However, since these steps appear to be purely artificial when weighed against all the other sources, we are left staring at the same extraordinary mystery that early Christians must have confronted.

To this day, the anchor is associated with St. Clement of Rome, who was almost certainly Titus Flavius Clemens, a victim of Domitian's apparent purge of those associated with Titus's semi-Jewish cult of "Christianity" that recognized the emperor as both a Jewish messiah and a literal "prince of peace."

We know Domitian quickly discontinued the dolphin-and-anchor motif used by his brother when he became emperor and began associating himself instead with traditional Roman gods on his coins and monuments. Twelve years younger than Titus, Domitian had remained a world apart from his heroic brother and father and their triumphs in Judea.

We have mentioned the Catacombs of St. Domitilla, the old-est known Christian burial site with perhaps the oldest known archeological evidence of Christianity in the world. One of the original inscriptions that identified this archeological site suggests that it was not only the original burial place of the "St. Flavia Domitilla" who is mentioned by Eusebius, but also of the Flavian family. This was the inscription that identified it as the Flavian family's sepulcher:

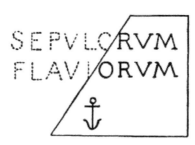

Inscription from the Catacombs of St. Domitilla with anchor

Known today as the Catacombs of St. Domitilla, it also contains the very first acknowledged Christian use of the anchor-and-fish symbol:

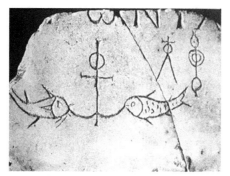

Anchor and fishes in the Catacombs of St. Domitilla

So the first Christian use of fish-anchor symbols is directly connected through Domitilla to her uncle, Emperor Titus, who used the symbol on his coins—and this tomb also happens to be the oldest archeological evidence for Christianity in the world. Here is Titus's own symbolism at his own niece's gravesite in the Flavians' own sepulcher in Christianity's first catacombs.

This extraordinary archeological evidence sheds more light on why the late 1st Century "pope," Clement of Rome, who was Domitilla's husband and also a Flavian, is associated with an anchor. An anchor is carved beneath the inscription on the Flavian family sepulcher, a unique imperial symbol used by Flavian emperors on their coinage and adopted as the symbol of a 1st Century pope who bore their name and was martyred at the same time their royal cousin was executed. We can only conclude St. Clement of Rome *was* that cousin.

* * * * * * * *

With no way to explain these coincidences, Christian tradition has simply split these historical figures into completely different people. However, considering what we now know, let us examine the letter that Christians attribute to St. Clement, which many scholars hold to be a letter or parts of letters written at the end of the 1st Century, precisely when both "Clemens" and "St. Clement" flourished. As we shall see, it reads exactly like something that could have been penned by an imperial Christian.

The subject of Clement's letter is his concern for discord and strife that has apparently arisen among Christians in the city of Corinth in Greece. Praising their former virtue, "Clement" reminds them that they had "walked in the commandments of God, being obedient to those who had the rule over you, and giving all fitting honor to the presbyters among you." (10)

Notice that Clement is keen to emphasize the doctrine of obeying political authorities, a theme we find so often in the New Testament. Notice, too, that he admires their former obedience to Church authorities, as well—the "presbyters"—even at this very early stage of the Church.

Clement then warns them of what seem to be earthly punishments for those who might instigate strife:

> For we shall incur no slight injury, but rather great
> danger, if we rashly yield ourselves to the inclinations
> of men who aim at exciting strife and tumults, so as to
> draw us away from what is good.

And he quotes scripture as follows: "Preserve innocence, and look on *equity*: for there shall be a remnant to the *peaceful* man." (Emphasis added.) (11)

While Clement emphasizes humility and virtuous conduct, like

Paul, he clearly believes that salvation is a matter of faith rather than deeds. (12) Well aware of the conflict between the Apostles that Paul reported in Galatians, Clement's exhortation for peace sounds decidedly Pauline. Here's an excerpt:

> Take up the epistle of the blessed Apostle Paul. What did he write to you at the time when the Gospel *first began to be preached?* Truly, under the inspiration of the Spirit, he wrote to you concerning himself, and Cephas, and Apollos, because even then parties had been formed among you. (Emphasis added.) (13)

Quite curiously, Clement's letter assumes Paul's mission as the point when the Gospel "first began to be preached"—decades after the supposed death of Jesus.

While Clement makes extensive use of the Hebrew Bible and certainly believes in the one God who created everything, he also cites the following distinctly pagan example for the resurrection:

> Let us consider that wonderful sign [of the resurrection] which takes place in Eastern lands, that is, in Arabia and the countries round about. There is a certain bird which is called a phoenix. This is the only one of its kind, and lives five hundred years. And when the time of its dissolution draws near that it must die, it builds itself a nest of frankincense, and myrrh, and spices, into which, when the time is fulfilled, it enters and dies. But as the flesh nourished by the juices of the dead bird, brings forth feathers. Then, when it has acquired strength, it takes up that nest in which are the bones of its parent, and bearing these it passes from the land of Arabia into Egypt, to the city called Heliopolis. And, in open day, flying in the sight of all men, it places them on the altar of the sun, and having done this, hastens back to its former abode. The priests then inspect the registers of the dates, and find that it has returned exactly as the five hundredth year was completed. (14)

The phoenix is a mythological beast from the lore of Egypt and "Arabia," as Clement makes clear, and not from Hebrew scripture. And, while mentioning this pagan creature, Clement also cites examples of virtue that are not only Jewish but also *pagan*:

> To bring forward some examples from among the heathen: Many kings and princes, in times of pestilence, when they had been instructed by an oracle, have given themselves up to death, in order that by their own blood they might deliver their fellow-citizens [from destruction]. (15)

As might be expected from a Pope, however, Clement stresses obedience to Church authorities. And here, rather amazingly, he compares the properly functioning Church to the Roman army:

> Let us then, men and brethren, with all energy act the part of soldiers, in accordance with His holy commandments. Let us consider those who serve under our generals, with what order, obedience, and submissiveness they perform the things which are commanded them. All are not prefects, nor commanders of a thousand, nor of a hundred, nor of fifty, nor the like, but each one in his own rank performs the things commanded by the king and the generals. The great cannot subsist without the small, nor the small without the great. (16)

Clement certainly seems to freely wield the authority of the Church at this very early stage, as if backed by the authority of the state:

> Ye, therefore, who laid the foundation of this sedition, submit yourselves to the presbyters, and receive correction so as to repent, bending the knees of your hearts. Learn to be subject, laying aside the proud and arrogant self-confidence of your tongue. For it is better for you that you should occupy a humble but honorable place in the flock of Christ, than that, being

highly exalted, you should be cast out from the *hope*
of His people. [Empasis added.] (17)

Clement even seems to foreshadow the ironic method of his
own martyrdom, in much the same way that Jesus does, and his
letter may itself be a source for the tradition concerning his death:

Yea, it were better for him that a millstone should be
hung about [his neck], and he should be sunk in the
depths of the sea. (18)

* * * * * * * *

During its infancy, we should expect a new religion to be flush with
the excitement of a new doctrine, its unique message, and the
inspirational qualities and deeds of its founder(s). We should expect
"organizational issues" to develop only after the new faith has accumulated a large enough number of followers to require attention.

Should there even be a formal Church? If so, how should it be
organized? Are bishops to be obeyed on matters of doctrine? Or
presbyters? These are questions for an already burgeoning religion on its way to wider acceptance. For this reason, among others, most scholars have rejected the self-identified authorship of
the New Testament epistles of both Titus and Timothy. Though
these letters claim to have been written by Paul, most researchers
believe these documents were composed towards the end of the
1st Century or the start of the 2nd Century precisely because they
discuss such "organizational" issues. For many it just doesn't make
sense to imagine the need for an elaborate hierarchy or for mech-
anisms to enforce doctrinal purity among the small underground
group of Christians that must have existed before the end of the 1st
Century.

However, since the earliest Christian writers, perhaps even
those writing in the first half of the 2nd Century, appear to cite
these letters, we know that they could not have been composed
much later.

This presents a puzzle. Part of the reason these critical scholars have questioned the dating and authorship of these works is

linguistic, and quite technical. But a large part of it is based on their content.

For example, at 1 Timothy 3:1-13, the moral qualifications for such Church officers as "bishops" or "overseers" and "deacons" are laid out. Paul's own lifetime (which is believed to have ended in the 60s) seems to be far too early for such top-down organizational developments to be happening for a presumably "grass-roots" movement. (If our hypothesis is right and it is an *imperial Roman* program, however, this presents no problem, and these sophisticated administerial arrangements make perfect sense even at the outset of Christian history.)

The authorship of the first letter attributed to Peter in the New Testament is also considered fraudulent by most scholars, and one of the most important reasons is that the letter is addressed to "Peter's" fellow "elders." How could the Church be so officially constituted so *early*?

Even more noteworthy, in the Book of Titus 1:5-7, the attributed author, Paul, orders the appointment of elders *in every town* and again discusses their moral qualifications. "The reason I left you in Crete was that you might put in order what was left unfinished and appoint elders in every town, as I directed you."

Many biblical scholars don't believe it is possible that Christians were so numerous as to maintain (much less require) leaders in every town on the *island of Crete* during Paul's lifetime.

Even if these surviving letters were composed as late as the 2nd Century, however, these passages are striking in their implications. The so-called Apostolic Fathers of the 2nd Century not only made use of these letters themselves, they also exhibit precisely the same very early concern for organizational questions that the first Church fathers were apparently considering.

Writing in the first decades of the 2nd Century, for example, St. Ignatius of Antioch commands his flocks:

> Let nothing be done without the bishop.
>
> See that you follow the bishop, even as Jesus Christ does the Father, and presbytery as you would the apostles; and reverence the deacons as being the institution of God. Let no man do anything connected

with the Church without the bishop. Let that be deemed a proper Eucharist, which is [administered] either by the bishop, or by one to whom he entrusted it. Wherever the bishop shall appear, there let the multitude [of the people] also be; even as, wherever Jesus Christ is, there is the Catholic Church. It is not lawful without the bishop either to baptize or to celebrate a love-feast; but whatsoever he shall approve of, that is also pleasing to God, so that everything that is done may be secure and valid." (19)

If there seems to have been a "top-down" organization to Christianity as early as the end of the 1st Century or the start of the 2nd Century, the Book of Acts preserves an even earlier tradition that a group called the "church elders" existed in Ephesus in Asia Minor when Paul visited there. (20) Of course, these may have been *Jewish*-Christian leaders that Paul was referring to, like those associated with James.

As we have already seen in his letter to the Galatians, Paul was opposing an existing "church" authoritatively led and organized by "Jewish Christians" such as James—against whom Paul appeared to be establishing an alternate leadership—even at this primitive stage.

It is also hard not to see an acute concern for Church hierarchy even in the Gospels themselves in passages like this famous prediction by Jesus:

And I tell you that you are Peter [literally "rock"], and on this rock I will build my church, and the gates of Hades will not overcome it. I will give you the keys of the kingdom of heaven; whatever you bind on earth will be bound in heaven, and whatever you loose on earth will be loosed in heaven. (21)

At their inception the Gospels seem to exhibit a well-developed organizational attention to hierarchical authority, and these early letters, some of them quite possibly from the late 1st Century, suggest an orderly, well-funded and authoritarian organization focused on establishing itself simultaneously across wide-ranging parts of the Roman Empire. (And notice how the leadership role of James, the martyred "Brother of Christ" and Paul's greatest adversary, has completely disappeared in the Gospels.)

Had the Roman authorities been aware of these large-scale activities, they would certainly have been alarmed and prosecuted such efforts as seditious, especially in the immediate wake of the Jewish War—just as they prosecuted rebel and Jewish-Christian leaders—unless these activities were authorized by the Roman government in the first place. Such sponsorship would explain the Church's rapid, well-funded, highly organized and empire-wide launch (as well as explaining Christianity's mild treatment at the hands of most of the emperors who followed the Flavians, such as Trajan.)

The existence of Christians in the imperial family gives us reason to re-examine the relationships Flavian emperors (especially Titus) had with the many traditionally identified "Jews" populating their inner circle of friends and associates. (22)

Let us turn our focus now to this extraordinary group of historical figures.

* * * * * * * *

As we have seen in Part I, the ancient historians Tacitus and Suetonius, pagan Romans of the 2nd Century, sometimes called rebellious 1st Century messianic Jews "Christians" or followers of "Chrestus." Paul himself refers to a very similar group of Jews as "apostles" of Christ. These historically troublesome Jews, like Paul's adversaries, fundamentally differ from the followers of the New Testament who are today identified as Christians.

Any "Christians" causing trouble in Rome or elsewhere at those early dates must have advocated the strictly observant form of messianic Judaism that sparked their rebellion against Rome and their conflict with Paul in the New Testament.

These militants were still awaiting the arrival of their messiah, albeit in the form of a warrior who would deliver them from foreign bondage. And of course they expected a thoroughly human messiah, as predicted in ancient Hebrew scripture—and certainly not a sacrificial divine human who modeled obedience to Rome. Their "Christianity," therefore, despite its other similarities, included none of these things now considered essential to "Christianity" as we know it today.

Among pagan observers at the time, like Tacitus, merely professing a belief in the imminent arrival of the prophesied Jewish messiah may have been sufficient to earn the name "Christian"—and even somehow associated with Jesus. Even in the New Testament, the strict Torah practitioners who follow James and Peter and defy Paul are considered "apostles of Christ," although exactly what that meant to *them* is unclear.

It seems only later, after the near annihilation of the Jewish rebels by the Romans, that the name "Christian" would become exclusively associated with the peace-loving adherents of the New Testament. Indeed, by the middle of the 2nd Century the Romans had ruthlessly exterminated or driven out of the Empire all of the militant variety of messianic Jews.

The only forms of Judaism to survive the two Jewish wars against Rome and their aftermath within the Empire were the rabbinic Jews, who de-emphasized the idea of "messiah" for the sake of their own survival, and the cheek-turning, peace-loving Pauline believers of the "New Testament," who inherited the title of Christians from that point forward. Any Zealot groups that survived at all after the bloody wars with Rome were driven underground or outside the eastern fringes of the Empire. Some known as "Ebionites" and others, forever scornful of their fellow Jews, carried forward many traits in common with a religion that subsequently emerged in the same geographic region centuries later—Islam.

Given the events unfolding today, it is perhaps more important than ever to realize that it was the Roman wars with Jewish fanatics that begat what we know as Christianity and shaped the relatively apolitical form of modern Judaism that enabled it to survive. Indeed, all three monotheisms today echo this same ancient and largely forgotten conflict that cracked the foundations of the Western World.

* * * * * * * *

Many friends of the Emperor Titus who are commonly identified as "Jews" are actually better understood as *Christians*—at least as the term was defined at that time.

For example, Titus's Jewish friends must have publicly acknowledged that he and his father were Jewish messiahs, which made them all *messianic* Jews.

Also, Titus's Jewish friends undoubtedly were not rebellious against Rome. Hebrews such as Josephus, Epaphroditus, Agrippa, Bernice or any of the other Jewish confidants of Titus could hardly follow their radical brothers while remaining friends with the emperor.

Finally, although they were from Jewish families, they must have been renegades of a sort, simply by attaching themselves to Titus, the man who would be reviled forever in the Talmud and by their fellow Israelites for reducing God's Temple to a Wailing Wall.

Titus's loyal Jewish friends were therefore of a non-observant kind and yet still messianic—the rather paradoxical combination of ingredients that comprises a Pauline Christian. Titus's Jewish friends in particular would have found it most convenient to embrace the Gospels themselves since they so readily accommodate their own non-Kosher but still nominally Jewish lifestyles. Moreover, the prophecies of Jesus in the Gospels readily lend themselves to establishing Titus as the Jewish Messiah.

Emperor Titus, the Vatican

And, as it happens, Titus's Jewish associates were some of the most powerful and influential people in the Roman Empire.

Among the emperor's personal friends was King Herod Agrippa II (properly, *Marcus Julius Agrippa*), the son of the famous Herod Agrippa I, who had himself been raised at the Julio-Claudian court and was a childhood friend of the Emperor Claudius.

This younger Agrippa inherited his crown from the "client" kings of Judea loyal to Rome. These kings were descended from Herod the Great, a Roman-installed monarch on what was then the Empire's eastern frontier and who had famously expanded and remodeled the Temple that Titus would destroy. Marcus Antonius (Mark Anthony), the famous Roman triumvir who married Cleopatra, had appointed Herod the Great as ruler of the Jews even though Herod hailed from an Idumaean family who had only recently converted to Judaism.

Courting both sides of Roman politics, Herod had deftly kept and augmented his position after Augustus became the first Emperor of Rome. Although Herod had married into royal and priestly Jewish families, he and his heirs were Roman appointees and, as such, became objects of hatred for nationalist Israelites.

Such was the background of Herod's great-grandson Herod Agrippa II, one of Titus's personal friends.

Marcus Julius Agrippa (Herod Agrippa II)

Titus's elite acquaintances also included Agrippa's sisters. In fact, Agrippa's sister Bernice was his mistress for a time, though she was ten years his senior. Bernice even became Titus's fiancée before conservative Senatorial opinion against a "new Cleopatra" in Rome prevented the politically ambitious Titus from following through with that marriage, according to our surviving sources. (23)

Both Bernice and her brother, Agrippa, were actually present with Titus as his legions sacked Jerusalem and razed the Temple that had been lovingly embellished by their great-grandfather.

Julia Bernice, 18th Century bust

Bernice's sister, Drusilla, was the wife of a well-connected (and Gentile) Roman governor of Judea named Felix.

We will hear more about Felix, Agrippa and Titus's one-time fiancée, Bernice, later. *All of them appear in the New Testament.*

The third sister of Titus's friend Agrippa, Mariamne, married first her Herodian cousin, Archelaus, and later one Demetrius, who was a wealthy Jewish "Alabarch" (a kind of tax collector) in the bustling Egyptian port of Alexandria.

Herod the Great and his son Antipas, and the whole Herodian dynasty, are criticized liberally in the New Testament. Titus was friendly with some of the Herods. So—is this evidence against a Flavian provenance for the New Testament?

Herod the Great killed not only strangers but members of his own family, as well, including three of his own sons. And one of those sons was the father of Agrippa I and the grandfather Titus's friends, Herod Agrippa II and Bernice.

Herod the Great by Theophile Lybaert (1883)

The Jewish historian working for the Flavians, Flavius Josephus, exhibits the same mixed relationship toward the early Herodian kings that appears in the New Testament. Josephus condemns the cruelty of Herod the Great as well as the unjust execution of John the Baptist by Herod Antipas. And yet he, too, simultaneously shares a close personal friendship with Titus's friend, Herod Agrippa II, who, as we shall see in the New Testament, was also friendly toward St. Paul.

As for the Flavian emperors, they were likewise critical of previous *Roman* rulers, such as Nero. What is remarkable is not the way both Josephus and the Bible depict Herod, but how early Christian literature seems to be sympathetic to *any* later Herodian, as well, in the same unique pattern that matches Titus's personal biases.

Another important Jewish figure in Titus's inner circle was a man named Tiberius Julius Alexander. For a time he was the Roman-appointed governor of Judea and later the Governor of Egypt. He was also a general who gave his early support to the Flavians' ambitions in both Judea and Rome. He, too, was present with Titus, as his second-in-command, at the Siege of Jerusalem and the sacking of the Temple.

Tiberius Alexander was the brother of Marcus Alexander, who was a husband of the aforementioned Princess Bernice before his unfortunate death. Their father, Julius Alexander, once an Alabarch himself in Alexandria, is described by Josephus as "an old friend" of the Emperor Claudius and a "steward" of the emperor's mother, Antonia. (24)

This relationship may suggest that connections between the Flavians and this family of Alexanders existed long before the Jewish

War, since Vespasian's own long-time mistress was Antonia's sec-retary. Antonia was a daughter of the triumvir Marcus Antonius, a niece of Augustus, and the mother of the Emperor Claudius. It was Claudius who had appointed Vespasian and his brother to their commands in the conquest of Britain during the early 40s, resulting in military successes that advanced the Flavians to the front ranks of Roman politics. (25)

Antonia

The Flavian family may have had connections to other high-ranking Jews in the East, as well, according to Vespasian biogra-pher Barbara Levick. (26) These relationships with important east-ern Jews who were collaborating with official Rome could actually help explain why Nero appointed Vespasian the task of quelling the Jewish revolt in 66 CE.

Vespasian

The elder Alabarch, Alexander, who was the Emperor Claudius's friend, was also the brother of the Jewish philosopher Philo of Alexandria. This means that his sons, including Titus's second-in-command at Jerusalem, were nephews of this famous sage.

Philo

This makes Philo's ideology well worth noting. We have seen that imperial politics sometimes inspired religious syncretism, like the god Serapis. But in the case of Philo we see an example of that kind of syncretism naturally occurring among the Jewish people as they assimilated into Hellenistic and Roman culture, with or without official influence. Alexandria, the diverse, cosmopolitan, and highly cultured city at the Nile's delta—and the home of Serapis—was just where one might expect a syncretism like Philo's to independently arise.

Like both Josephus and the Gospels, Philo's ideas blended aspects of his native Judaism with pagan ideas, specifically with the ideas of Plato and the Stoics. Some earlier Jewish works, especially *The Wisdom of Sirach*, had already shown signs of Platonic influence, but it was in the work of Philo that this marriage was fully consummated.

Philo transformed the Jewish God Yaweh into the neo-Platonic Absolute of the Hellenistic philosophers. For Philo, Yahweh became a World-soul, or Form of the Good, or the One, as this Platonic idea has been variously named. In truth, Jewish monotheism already fit more comfortably with this expanding Greek ideology than polytheism ever could and therefore held increasing attraction to pagans. Philo was the first to attempt a complete integration of these two systems of belief.

Philo also employed an *allegorical* approach to interpreting Hebrew scriptures, one that did not necessarily deny the literal meaning while seeking a deeper, more universal understanding of the text. He developed no less than an integration of Jewish and

Stoic thought, taking its concept of *Logos* to be the agency of the one God's creation. This is, coincidentally, the basic ideological blend underlying much of the New Testament. (27) It is these very ideas that directly foreshadow the opening lines of the Gospel of John as they are traditionally translated:

> In the beginning was the Word [*logos*], and the Word was with God, and the Word was God. He was with God in the beginning. Through him all things were made; without him nothing was made that has been made. In him was life, and that life was the light of all mankind. The light shines in the darkness, and the darkness has not overcome it. (28)

While Philo did not live to see the Flavian dynasty come to power, he probably had a considerable intellectual influence on his nephews, Marcus and Tiberius Alexander. In any case, Philo's joint Judaic-Hellenic ideology is well known. His nephews connect Philo to Titus's inner circle.

The Herodian princesses who were friends of Titus were quite notorious for their sexual conduct. While Bernice's reputation, for example, suffered from her affair with Titus, more damaging were accusations of incest with her brother.

Clearly, Titus also associated with "Alabarchs," who literally helped the Romans collect taxes.

Both sexual licentiousness and tax collecting were objectionable activities among the pious and revolutionary Jews of this period. Even so, the notorious Herodians and the family of Alabarchs from Alexandria were nominally "Jews" themselves. The Flavians, who had been proclaimed Jewish messiahs, were also a family of tax collectors. Both Titus's grandfather and great-grandfather were tax-collectors. (29)

So the Herodian royals and wealthy Alexandrian Jews connected with Titus are rather strikingly similar to the unconventional company Jesus keeps in the Gospels; i.e., prostitutes and tax collectors, characters reviled by contemporary Hebrews. (30) At Matthew 21:31 Jesus himself informs the chief priests and the elders of the Jews, "Truly I tell you, the tax collectors and the prostitutes are entering the kingdom of God ahead of you." So, we have another curious parallel between the Emperor Titus and the Jesus of the Gospels.

"The Triumph of Titus" by Sir Lawrence Alma-Tadema

The most notable of all the Jewish associates of Titus, of course, is the famous historian Titus Flavius Josephus.

A self-described scion of royal and priestly Jewish lines, Josephus was a reluctant rebel general who was originally named Joseph Ben Mathias ("son of Matthew"). He infamously switched to the Roman side following his defeat at General Vespasian's hands. Thereafter, he enjoyed official favor and fortune as a writer and historian at the Flavian court, according to his own account.

Josephus tells us he was with Vespasian at Alexandria, although he does not report the celebrated healing miracles that the Roman general performed there. He, too, was present with Titus at the prophetic Siege of Jerusalem along with the others we have mentioned.

Josephus boasts that, after the war, he was awarded a comfortable property near Rome while writing his encyclopedic tome of Hebraic history with Flavian support and approval.

The Siege and Destruction of Jerusalem by the Romans Under the Command of Titus, A.D. 70, by David Roberts (1850)

We shall return to this central and yet elusive figure, of whom there is much more to be said, later.

* * * * * * * *

How should we characterize all of these "Jews" who were intimately connected to the Flavians?

Mingling with the highest elites in Rome, they certainly did not have any of the qualms concerning pagan "pollution" that was condemned by the Dead Sea Scrolls sectarians. They would have welcomed the message of any critic of Jewish purity regulations, like the Jesus Christ of the Gospels, with enthusiasm.

At least in their youth, the Herodians that Rome appointed to rule the Jewish territories, along with their immediate family members, attempted to live a somewhat Kosher lifestyle even when they were "in Rome." We are told, for example, that Drusilla, the sister of Bernice and Agrippa II, was first married to the King of Emessa only on condition that he be circumcised—an obviously painful concession for an adult man. Likewise, her sister Bernice's marriage to King Polemon of Cilicia commenced on condition that the groom convert to Judaism and be circumcised, as well. (31) This kind of report suggests that the family was trying, initially, to be observant Hebrews, at least for public consumption.

Whatever the cost to the groom, Drusilla's first marriage didn't take, however. Upon his arrival in the east, Felix, the newly appointed governor of Judea, immediately fell for the beautiful Drusilla, and Drusilla's marriage was soon dissolved as Governor Felix married her. Unlike her first husband, the Greek Felix did not forfeit his foreskin, it seems, since Josephus reports Drusilla's marriage tellingly "transgress[ed] the laws of her forefathers." (32)

Tragically, Drusilla would die in the eruption of Mt. Vesuvius in 79 CE, along with her son by Felix, as would Titus's friend, the polymath Pliny the Elder.

Felix's brother, it should be noted, was a man named Pallas, an important secretary to the Emperor Claudius and a supporter of the Emperor Nero's mother, Agrippina (the woman who had hired the philosopher Seneca to tutor her son, the future emperor), while Felix's own first wife had been a granddaughter of the Roman general

Marcus Antonius and the famous Egyptian queen Cleopatra. (The level of political power and influence Felix enjoyed had undoubtedly given him additional leverage during his marriage negotiations.)

Drusilla's sister Bernice, who would later be engaged to Titus, had only a short-lived marriage to King Polemon despite his own encounter with the surgeon's knife. It seems their union had been shaky from the start. Josephus, in fact, records that Bernice only married him to dispel rumors that she was engaged in an incestuous relationship with her brother, Agrippa II. As for Polemon, he had been persuaded by Bernice's fabulous wealth to acquiesce to the short and painful marriage.

When Bernice left this husband, as Josephus reports it, she was still widely suspected of "impure intentions." (33) She and her unmarried brother, with whom she was still suspected of incest, visited Rome together after Vespasian was named emperor.

Regardless of their scandalous behavior, these late Herodian royals were not entirely false Jews. After all, as the children of Herod Agrippa I, they could all claim descent from his grandmother, who descended from the authentically Jewish Hasmonean dynasty of kings and high priests. Before the violent rebellion that erupted in Judea during the reign of Nero, however, these Herodian princesses seem to have abandoned the strictures of Jewish tradition, at least with respect to circumcision and marrying men outside of their faith. Indeed, the private conduct of the Herodian royals no doubt provoked the rebels in Judea and helped foment the outbreak of war in 66 CE. In the eyes of Jewish purists, the Herods may as well have been foreigners, polluted by consorting with the Roman elites and authorities who occupied Jewish land.

Some "collaborating" Jews dropped even the pretense of Jewish practice. Tiberius Alexander, Titus's second-in-command at the Jerusalem siege, for example, "did not continue in the religion of his country" according to Josephus. (34) And, as Dead Sea Scrolls translator Robert Eisenman observes, Josephus's description of Tiberius is "the equivalent of the pot calling the kettle black." (35)

Flavius Josephus himself resembles Paul in his opposition to forced circumcision. Though it was the practice of the Jewish rebels to require circumcision of any new allies and converts, Josephus boasts in his autobiography that he would not permit the forced circumcision of new rebel allies under his jurisdiction, arguing that "[e]veryone ought to worship God according to his own inclinations, and not to be constrained by force..." (36) This mirrors the language in Galatians where Paul considers and rejects the requirement that converts should be "compelled to be circumcised." (37)

Circumcision would have been a considerable obstacle for Jewish assimilation with the Empire, as well as for any Gentiles considering anything more than dabbling in Judaism. From the stories told about these Herodians, we can see that it was, indeed, a problem, and that Paul's position on the subject would have been extremely appreciated.

In addition to dispensing with circumcision, we can be reasonably sure that these "Jews" around Titus also ignored orthodox reservations about "eat[ing] with Gentiles" and sharing their non-Kosher food. Paul scornfully ascribed such stodgy rules to the James community (38), whose reservations seem identical to those of the so-called "Qumran sectarians" of the Dead Sea Scrolls and to those causing conflict with Rome. Indeed, Josephus informs us that the Essene sect, usually identified today as being the Qumran sectarians who wrote the Dead Sea Scrolls, were so devout that they could not even be tortured into eating forbidden foods. (39)

Obviously, then, the privileged and powerful Hebrews who were cooperating with the Romans had to reject the xenophobic politics of purist Zealots as well as the nationalist terrorists who called themselves the "Sicarii." As agents of Rome they were compelled to do so, since they were all, *ipso facto*, representatives of the *Pax Romana*.

We know from the reports of Tacitus, Suetonius, and Josephus that Vespasian and Titus proclaimed themselves to be the Jewish messiahs of prophecy. We must assume that, like Josephus, the other "Jews" in Titus's circle must have also publicly acknowledged this imperial claim.

Judea Capta

The agreement of the Flavians' Jewish friends on this point of propaganda would have been *especially* important. There is no doubt that certain "public relations" demands would have applied specifically to them in the aftermath of the Jewish War. These Jewish associates of the Flavians, simply for professing loyalty to Rome, would have had to agree that Vespasian and Titus, both father and son, had fulfilled the messianic prophecy of their faith. This imperial obligation alone, therefore, qualifies them as "messianic Jews," and more: they were pro-Roman and pro-peace messianic Jews.

In all of these ways, these Jewish figures who populated the Flavian court were more closely akin to "Christians" of Paul's school than to the "Jews" they are all assumed to have been.

Just as the rebellious messianic Jews of the 1st Century were conflated with "Christians," so, too, have these likely Flavian *Christians* been conflated with religious "Jews."

From all of this, we can surmise that the well-connected Jewish figures surrounding Titus would have been most receptive to Paul's message. Paul preached that it was possible to be both a good believer in the Jewish God, even a messianic one, and yet be "free" from the culturally-alienating constraints of Mosaic practice, such as circumcision, Kosher diet, and avoiding close association with Gentiles. Since among them were tax collectors and women of notorious repute by conventional Hebrew standards, the fact that Jesus is shown approving of such company would also have been appreciated by them.

As tax collectors and personal associates of Caesar, it goes without saying that they would have agreed with the "render unto Caesar" rhetoric, as well. Many of the key issues that concerned Paul, like circumcision, were the same concerns of these followers of the Jewish messiah, Titus, at his imperial court.

All of this seems highly likely from inference alone. Taken at face value, however, the New Testament confirms it—as we shall now see.

* * * * * * * *

A number of these friends and associates of the Emperor Titus actually appear in the New Testament—and are depicted in a surprisingly favorable light.

Wherever they appear they are shown offering friendly assistance to St. Paul himself. They even express sympathy for Paul and an avid interest in his radical Jewish gospel.

For the best detailed account of the activities of Paul, at least as described in the New Testament, the reader is once more directed to the work of Thijs Voskuilen and Rose Mary Sheldon, in their book, *Operation Messiah*. (40) However, any reader of the New Testament can readily see official Roman assistance repeatedly being provided to Paul's mission.

Acts of the Apostles, or as it is sometimes called, the Book of Acts, purports to be the second part of the Gospel of Luke. It is the only part of the New Testament to describe the activities of the Apostles after the Resurrection.

In Acts we are told that after the Jewish Sanhedrin accused Paul of crimes against Jewish Law and what is described as an attempted "desecration" of the Temple, Paul was taken to the Roman governor Felix—the husband of Drusilla and brother-in-law to Titus's future fiancée, Bernice. (41)

Paul and the attorney for the Sanhedrin both present their cases to Felix, who we are informed was well acquainted with "the Way" (as Christianity is often called in Acts). Although Paul was allegedly under arrest, Felix orders the centurion in charge "to give him some freedom and permit his friends to take care of his needs." (42) So, Paul's arrest seems to be an "arrest" in name only.

According to Acts:

> Several days later Felix came *with his wife Drusilla, who was Jewish.* He sent for Paul and *listened to him as he spoke about faith in Christ Jesus.* As Paul talked about righteousness, self-control and the judgment to come, *Felix was afraid* and said, "That's enough for now. You may leave. When I find it convenient, I will send for you." At the same time he was hoping that Paul would offer him a bribe, so *he sent for him frequently and talked with him.*
>
> When two years had passed, Felix was succeeded by Porcius Festus, but because Felix wanted to grant a favor to the Jews, he left Paul in prison. (Emphasis added.) (43)

It seems to have been standard practice to bribe officials to obtain one's release from custody, and Felix, it is implied, wants to release Paul. Apparently, though, no bribe had yet materialized.

But why should Paul be in any hurry here? A Jewish mob is waiting to tear him to pieces outside and, while in custody, he seems to be enjoying an extraordinary degree of "freedom" even as his friends are allowed to attend to his needs. He also seems to have had an interested and captive audience in the exalted Roman Governor Felix, who pays him regular visits while in his "captivity." Moreover, Felix is actually said to have become *afraid* when Paul spoke about the Final Judgment. Does this Roman governor actually believe in Paul's gospel?

Felix seems to respect Paul to an inordinate degree since political issues make releasing him or granting "the Jews" their trial of him inconvenient for a very long time.

For two years, in fact, Paul seems to be a rather important "prisoner." And his enemies do not like the situation. When the new Governor Festus (a Gentile with no known "Jewish" connections) is installed in the province, we are told that after only three days:

> Festus went up from Caesarea to Jerusalem, where the chief priests and the Jewish leaders appeared before him and presented the charges against Paul. They requested Festus, as a favor to them, to have Paul transferred to Jerusalem, for they were preparing *an ambush to kill him along the way.* (Emphasis added.) (44)

Festus opts instead to give them a hearing of their case back in the Roman port city of Caesarea. There, once more, both sides make their arguments, but rather than render a decision on whether to transfer the case to Jerusalem, Festus somewhat unbelievably asks Paul's own opinion about having his case transferred to Jerusalem. According to Acts, Festus does this in order to "do the Jews a favor." (45)

In reply, Paul famously appeals his case to Caesar himself (in Rome). After conferring with his own council, Governor Festus answers: "You have appealed to Caesar. To Caesar you will go!" (46)

The next characters to enter the New Testament are none other than Titus's friends Herod Agrippa II and his future fiancée, Bernice:

> A few days later King Agrippa and Bernice arrived at Caesarea to pay their respects to Festus. Since they were spending many days there, Festus discussed Paul's case with the king. He said: "There is a man here whom Felix left as a prisoner. When I went to Jerusalem, the chief priests and the elders of the Jews brought charges against him and asked that he be condemned.
>
> I told them that it is not the Roman custom to hand over anyone before they have faced their accusers and have had an opportunity to defend themselves against the charges. When they came here with me, I did not delay the case, but convened the court the next day and ordered the man to be brought in. When his accusers got up to speak, they did not charge him with any of the crimes I had expected. Instead, they had some points of dispute with him about their own religion and about a dead man named Jesus who Paul claimed was alive. I was at a loss how to investigate such matters; so I asked if he would be willing to go to Jerusalem and stand trial there on these charges. But when Paul made his appeal to be held over for the Emperor's decision, I ordered him held until I could send him to Caesar."
>
> Then Agrippa said to Festus, "I would like to hear this man myself."
>
> He replied, "Tomorrow you will hear him."
>
> The next day Agrippa and Bernice came with great pomp and entered the audience room with the high-ranking military officers and the prominent men of the city. At the command of Festus, Paul was brought in. Festus said: "King Agrippa, and all who are present with us, you see this man! *The whole Jewish community* has petitioned me about him in Jerusalem and here in Caesarea, shouting that he ought not to

live any longer. *I found he had done nothing deserving of death*, but because he made his appeal to the Emperor I decided to send him to Rome. *But I have nothing definite to write to His Majesty about him.* Therefore I have brought him before all of you, and especially before you, King Agrippa, so that as a result of this investigation I may have something to write. For I think it is unreasonable to send a prisoner on to Rome without specifying the charges against him." (Emphasis added.) (47)

Notice the respect that the author of Acts has for the Roman legal system—far greater respect than he shows for the Jewish counterpart, the Sanhedrin. Also observe that Festus had expected the Christian to be charged with real crimes, such as sedition or making rebellion, rather than the sectarian disagreements of religious doctrine Jewish authorities had with Paul. The now obvious political implications of Paul's message are simply glossed over in the text of Acts. Finally, once more we have a Roman governor who, just like Pilate before him, can find nothing worth punishing in a "New Testament" Christian accused by Jewish authorities.

In Acts, we continue as Paul begins his defense by saying:

King Agrippa, I consider myself fortunate to stand before you today as I make my defense against all the accusations of the Jews, and *especially so because you are well acquainted with all the Jewish customs and controversies.* Therefore, I beg you to listen to me patiently. (Emphasis added.) (48)

Titus's friend Agrippa listens patiently to Paul as he recounts his personal travails in some detail, and also the many plots of "Jews" who have been attacking him. When Paul explains his vision of Christ and his project to convert the Gentiles, "Festus interrupt[s] Paul's defense. 'You are out of your mind, Paul!' he shout[s], '*Your great learning* is driving you insane.'" (Emphasis added.) (49)

Notice that even the skeptical Governor Festus with no known Jewish connections, acknowledges Paul's "great learning."

"I am not insane, most excellent Festus," Paul replied. "What I am saying is true and reasonable. *The king [Agrippa] is familiar with these things, and I can speak freely to him.* I am convinced that none of this has escaped his notice, because it was not done in a corner. King Agrippa, *do you believe the prophets? I know you do.*"

Then Agrippa said to Paul, "Do you think that in such a short time you can persuade me to be a Christian?"

Paul replied, "Short time or long—I pray to God that not only you but all who are listening to me today may become what I am, except for these chains."

The king rose, and with him the governor and Bernice and those sitting with them. After they left the room, they began saying to one another, "This man is not doing anything that deserves death or imprisonment."

Agrippa said to Festus, "This man could have been set free if he had not appealed to Caesar." (Emphasis added.) (50)

Again, echoing Pilate and Festus, both of Titus's friends are likewise convinced of the Christian leader's innocence. The mutual admiration exhibited between Paul and Agrippa II is clear in any translation. Later generations would grapple with the following declaration with considerable difficulty because of what appears to be Agrippa's impossible Christian sympathies: *"Do you think that in such a short time you can persuade me to be a Christian?"*

The Greek original of this pregnant quote ascribed to Agrippa has given birth to a contentious litter of translations:

1. "In a little thou persuadest me to become a Christian." (Douay-Rheims, American)
2. "Almost thou persuadest me to be a Christian." (King James)
3. "You almost persuade me to become a Christian." (New King James)

4. "In a short time you think to make me a Christian!" (Revised Standard Version)
5. "Are you so quickly persuading me to become a Christian?" or, alternately, the footnote suggests, "Quickly you will persuade me to play the Christian." (New Revised Standard Version)
6. "Do you think that in such a short time you can persuade me to be a Christian?" (New International Version)

The first three versions straightforwardly report Agrippa II saying that Paul had almost made him Christian. The next begin to transform the "almost" into "in so short a time" but make it sound as if just Paul thinks he is making headway with King Agrippa. The last two remove that implication but transform what had been an assertion into a question, while the footnote to the NRSV translation makes a bizarre implication that Paul is rapidly making the king "*play the Christian.*" One need not know the original Greek to find this linguistic evolution both fascinating and enlightening.

Paul asserts that King Agrippa believes in "the prophets" and here the king does not contradict him. This means that King Agrippa II believes in the coming of the Messiah.

As we will see, Paul is not the only apostle to enjoy such agreeable relations with officials of the Roman Empire in the New Testament.

* * * * * * * *

The Book of Acts may not be reliable history to many scholars, but it is, for the most part, consistent in its theology. In it we find that Peter, like Paul, finds fellowship with Gentiles and, like Jesus before him, reserves his highest praise for a Roman centurion he meets in the course of his ministry. This entire extraordinary account from Acts is noteworthy:

> At Caesarea there was a man named *Cornelius, a centurion in what was known as the Italian Regiment.* He and all his family were devout and God-fearing; he

gave generously to those in need and prayed to God regularly. One day at about three in the afternoon he had a vision. He distinctly saw an angel of God, who came to him and said, "Cornelius!"

Cornelius stared at him in fear. "What is it, Lord?" he asked. The angel answered, "Your prayers and gifts to the poor have come up as a memorial offering before God. Now send men to Joppa to bring back a man named Simon who is called Peter. He is staying with Simon the tanner, whose house is by the sea."

When the angel who spoke to him had gone, Cornelius called two of his servants and a devout soldier who was one of his attendants. He told them everything that had happened and sent them to Joppa.

About noon the following day as they were on their journey and approaching the city, Peter went up on the roof to pray. He became hungry and wanted something to eat, and while the meal was being prepared, *he fell into a trance*. He saw heaven opened and something like a large sheet being let down to earth by its four corners. It contained all kinds of four-footed animals, as well as reptiles and birds. Then a voice told him, "Get up, Peter. *Kill and eat.*"

"Surely not, Lord!" Peter replied. "I have never eaten anything impure or unclean."

The voice spoke to him a second time, "Do not call anything impure that God has made clean."

This happened *three times*, and immediately the sheet was taken back to heaven.

While Peter was wondering about the meaning of the vision, the men sent by Cornelius found out where Simon's house was and stopped at the gate. They called out, asking if Simon who was known as Peter was staying there.

While Peter was still thinking about the vision, the Spirit said to him, "Simon, *three men* are looking for you. So get up and go downstairs. Do not hesitate to go with them, for I have sent them."

Peter went down and said to the men, "I'm the one you're looking for. Why have you come?"

The men replied, "We have come from Cornelius the centurion. He is a righteous and God-fearing man, who is respected by all the Jewish people. A holy angel told him to ask you to come to his house so that he could hear what you have to say." Then Peter invited the men into the house to be his guests.

The next day Peter started out with them, and some of the believers from Joppa went along. The following day he arrived in Caesarea. Cornelius was expecting them and had called together his relatives and close friends. As Peter entered the house, Cornelius met him and fell at his feet in reverence. But Peter made him get up. "Stand up," he said, "I am only a man myself."

While talking with him, Peter went inside and found a large gathering of people. He said to them: "You are well aware that it is against our law for a Jew to associate with or visit a Gentile. But *God has shown me that I should not call anyone impure or unclean. So when I was sent for, I came without raising any objection.* May I ask why you sent for me?"

Cornelius answered: "*Three days* ago I was in my house praying at this hour, at *three in the afternoon.* Suddenly a man in shining clothes stood before me and said, 'Cornelius, God has heard your prayer and remembered your gifts to the poor. Send to Joppa for Simon who is called Peter. He is a guest in the home of Simon the tanner, who lives by the sea.' So I sent for you immediately, and it was good of you to come. Now we are all here in the presence of God to listen to everything the Lord has commanded you to tell us."

Then Peter began to speak: "I now realize how true it is that God does not show favoritism but accepts from every nation the one who fears him and does what is right. You know the message God sent to the people of Israel, announcing the good news of peace through

Jesus Christ, who is Lord of all. You know what has happened throughout the province of Judea, beginning in Galilee after the baptism that John preached—how God anointed Jesus of Nazareth with the Holy Spirit and power, and how he went around doing good and healing all who were under the power of the devil, because God was with him.

"We are witnesses of everything he did in the country of the Jews and in Jerusalem. They killed him by hanging him on a cross, but God raised him from the dead on the third day and caused him to be seen. *He was not seen by all the people, but by witnesses whom God had already chosen—by us who ate and drank with him after he rose from the dead.* He commanded us to preach to the people and to testify that he is the one whom God appointed as judge of the living and the dead. All the prophets testify about him that everyone who believes in him receives forgiveness of sins through his name."

While Peter was still speaking these words, the Holy Spirit came on all who heard the message. The circumcised believers who had come with Peter were astonished that the gift of the Holy Spirit had been poured out even on Gentiles. For they heard them speaking in tongues and praising God.

Then Peter said, "Surely *no one can stand in the way of their being baptized with water. They have received the Holy Spirit just as we have.*" So he ordered that they be baptized in the name of Jesus Christ. Then they asked Peter to stay with them for a few days. (Emphasis added.) (51)

The first thing to note in this passage is that, in the Gospels, Jesus clearly abolished the laws that Peter is still unaccountably obeying during Paul's time. The whole new doctrine Jesus delivered in the Gospels does not seem to have made any impression on Peter, at all. He seems to have forgotten that Christ said much the same thing about pure and impure foods as the voice he heard in his mystical trance. Peter has also seemingly forgotten that Jesus had said that many would come to "feast with Abraham," that the Gospel should be spread to the whole world, and that Jesus himself had praised a centurion. In fact, Peter states, point -blank: "You are well aware that it is against our law for a Jew to associate with or visit a Gentile" as if Jesus hadn't associated with unclean persons himself, and as if Christ had been a Jewish nationalist or a stickler about ritual purity. Peter clearly never read the Gospels—and he certainly never lived them.

As we have previously observed, it is far more likely that such a Pauline position on Gentiles and the Mosaic Law was not attributed to Jesus until later, when the Gospels were written, *after* the Jewish War. Only this can explain Paul's emotional confrontation with Jewish Christians over these very issues in his letter to the Galatians.

Acts describes Peter's centurion as a "God fearer," or Jewish convert, implying that he was not circumcised, nor were the others in his house, it seems. We are told that the "circumcised believers who had come *with Peter* were astonished that the gift of the Holy Spirit had been poured out *even on Gentiles.*" (Emphasis added.) (52)

Recall that in Galatians' account, Paul confronts Peter for hypocrisy after eating with Gentiles and then later returning to the more orthodox "Jewish-Christian" fold. (53) This account may be no more reliable, but Peter allegedly also wavers after his personal epiphany from God that instructed him to eat with Gentiles.

Notice, too, that in Peter's vision, he resists eating impure food *three* times—despite God's direct command—just as he had infamously denied knowing Christ three times on the night of Jesus's arrest and trial, according to all four Gospels. Recall that Jesus had predicted that Peter would do so—"before the cock crowed"—at the Last Supper. The number *three* rattles around this story so many times that it becomes clear: Peter's resistance to non-Kosher foods is being associated with his betrayal of Jesus. And the issue of Kosher diet is precisely the subject of the heated argument between Paul and Peter (in Aramaic, "Cephas," meaning "rock") that we read about in Galatians.

While there is nothing unusual about a Christian having a mystical vision or experience in the Bible, the Book of Acts' account of Peter's vision is among the least credible reports in the New Testament. If he actually had such a visionary experience, it is hard to imagine Peter returning to his former Kosher ways only to be "confronted to his face" by Paul, as recounted in Paul's letter. Notwithstanding Paul's hypocrisy as one who boasted of chameleon-like adaptability himself, if Peter vacillated so readily after such a direct revelation, he was certainly no "rock."

We are asked to believe that Peter backslid into Jewish ways *twice*—the second time after receiving his own personal revelation of Christ's true message—in addition to ignoring what would be reported in the Gospels as Jesus's own teachings on the matter of pure and impure foods. (54) This only further suggests that the Pauline doctrine had not yet been attributed to Jesus when this confrontation took place, and that only after Paul's vision had two very different camps of "Christians" emerged. Until then, however, it appears that "Christians" were counted among the messianic rebels of the period, and may have been their ideological leaders.

* * * * * * * *

If the mutual admiration between Paul and King Agrippa II and other Roman officials is remarkable, the consistent enmity of the Jews to Paul's message makes a symmetrical bookend. As friendly, respectful, and open-minded as Roman officials and their allies are invariably shown to be with Paul and his friends, the Jews are equally depicted as violently opposed to Paul's message at every turn.

When Paul is threatened or seized by the Jews he is placed in protective custody by Romans and brought before the highest authorities. And those Roman authorities uniformly give him special freedoms, display respect for his message, and render favorable decisions about his fate.

Only days after his famous conversion on the road to Damascus, Paul, still called "Saul" at this point, faced "a conspiracy among the Jews to kill him." (55) Indeed, "[d]ay and night they kept close watch on the city gates in order to kill him." (56) Even "Hellenic Jews" tried to kill him, and we are told that following his departure a period of peace broke out in the region. (57)

Given the anti-Torah message Paul was preaching, it is easy to understand why many Jews reviled him, and Acts reports that "[w]hen the Jews saw the crowds [Paul drew], they were filled with jealousy. They began to contradict what Paul was saying and heaped abuse on him." (58) Despite Paul's strong rebuke, "the Jewish leaders... stirred up persecution against Paul and Barnabas..." (59) The two escaped to Iconium, and then to Lystra, where "some Jews from Antioch and Iconium" incited the crowd to have Paul stoned and left for dead. (60)

It should be kept in mind that even Jews who wanted peace with Rome had reason, at least initially, to be skeptical of any messianic missionary. Normally, these were the trouble makers. And when messianic hardliners soon learned of Paul's anti-Torah message, it seems, nearly every variety of Jew became his opponent.

Paul had become a paradox: a messianic Jew who argued for peace with Rome and a moderation of the strict religious practices that were behind the conflict.

After its account of the Council of Jerusalem (the same meeting Paul records in his letter to the Galatians), Acts tells us that Paul returned to Antioch in Syria, and from there traveled through the provinces of Cilicia, Phrygia, and Galatia (in modern-day Turkey) to the Greek city of Philippi. According to Acts, Philippi was the very first city in Europe where Paul preached his message. (61) Paul did, however, find some initial resistance at Philippi and was arrested by the magistrates there, the charges being these:

> They brought them before the magistrates and said, "These men are Jews, and are throwing our city into an uproar by advocating customs unlawful for us Romans to accept or practice." (62)

From what we know about Paul's message of "freedom in Christ," we know that the author of Acts intends this accusation to be seen as slander.

Incited by this accusation, however, the crowd beats Paul and his companion, and they are both arrested.

We are then told that a miraculous earthquake not only opens the doors of the jail where they are held but loosens all of the prisoners' chains, as well. (63) Paul's jailer is on the verge of committing suicide as a result when Paul stops him. After some preaching at the jailer's house, all there are converted to Christianity by Paul. (64)

The question, of course, is not whether these reports are historically accurate or represent later invention, but rather: why does Christianity consistently preserve only a tradition of Roman sympathy and even Roman assistance when trouble is encountered during its founding evangelical acts?

Even Paul's Roman jailer, we are shown, is more righteous than the many Jews who are persecuting Paul. The earthquake, for example, had been for the benefit of the jailer and his family (not Paul) since the city magistrate later ordered Paul released the next morning anyway; the jailer meanwhile was "saved" and converted to the Way. (65)

Paul's quick release was not enough for him, however. His remarkable boldness in the face of Roman authorities is almost as remarkable as their obsequious response:

> But Paul said to the officers: "They beat us publicly without a trial, even though we are *Roman citizens*, and threw us into prison. And now do they want to get rid of us quietly? No! Let them come themselves and escort us out."
>
> The officers reported this to the magistrates, and when they heard that Paul and Silas were *Roman citizens, they were alarmed*. They came to *appease them* and escorted them from the prison, requesting them to leave the city. After Paul and Silas came out of the prison, they went to Lydia's house, where they met with the brothers and sisters and encouraged them. Then they left. (Emphasis added.) (66)

It is useful here to consider the location of this event. Philippi had been the site of the famous Battle of Philippi, in which the forces of Marcus Antonius and Octavian (Mark Anthony and Augustus) defeated the forces of the assassins of Julius Caesar in 42 BCE. The victors settled veteran legionaries in this city and refounded it as *Colonia Victrix Philippensium*, only to be renamed again later as *Colonia Augusta Iulia Philippensis* around 27 BCE after Octavian officially received the title "Augustus" from the Senate. The Book of

Acts actually describes Philippi as a "colony" and the most important city in the area. This, again, provides valuable context for our theory. According to one historian:

> The population of *Colonia Augusta Iulia Philippensis,* which included Romans, Greeks, and Thracians, guaranteed that pluralism and syncretism would mark the religious life of the colony. The Augustan character of the colony, and the control of Philippi by the Roman elite, however, *assured the imperial cult of a position of prominence at the very center of the settlement's religious and social life.* (Emphasis added.) (67)

So it should not be so surprising that it was to his Philippian converts years later that Paul would write from Rome, thanking them for the gifts they had sent through his "brother, co-worker and fellow soldier," Epaphroditus. Paul also commends his other co-worker, who is named Clement, and closes that letter with warm greetings from those "in Caesar's household." (68)

We will return to this astonishing postscript later. For now, we must note that key associates of Paul are named Titus, Clement, Epaphroditus and Joseph (who takes the name "Barnabas").

As Paul travels to Thessalonia, Athens, and Corinth, making new converts along the way, he continues to irritate, above all, the Jews. (69) One exception in the New Testament is when Paul makes converts of two Jews who had been expelled from Rome under Claudius for those disturbances caused by "Chrestus" that were reported by the historian Suetonius. Possibly, these two had been messianic Jews of the rebellious kind. (70)

This particular act of Paul may reveal an underlying imperial purpose for his mission that would explain why it enjoyed so much official support by Nero's government: the pacification of militant messianic Hebrews by converting them to something more palatable to the Romans and more easily assimilated into their Hellenized culture. Both the narrative in Acts and the content of Paul's message suggest that he was acting as a Roman operative in a "psyops" program that anticipated the later Flavian project by trying to convert messianic Jews into good Roman citizens.

A measure of the success of Paul's program, in the long run, at least, is the subsequent triumph of Christianity itself.

Paul had, after all, offered a way for Jewish messianic theology to co-exist with Roman society, thereby permitting its survival. In Part I, we read from a Pauline (if not Paul's own) letter to the Christians in Ephesus how "the dividing wall of hostility" had been "broken down" with Christ's sacrifice "by abolishing" aspects of the Mosaic Law. We have also read Paul's commands for obedience to the state as *God's own agent on earth* in one of his earliest epistles. The alternative way Paul offered, however, became viable only after the total victory of the Flavian generals in Judea. And, since it was designed as a religious justification for Roman rulers, Christianity would become the perfect validation for a thousand years of kings to follow, a "divine right" surviving long past the empire that created it for this purpose.

In Corinth, once more, Paul reports that the Jews attacked him. And once more the Roman governor steps in to protect him:

> While Gallio was proconsul of Achaia, the Jews of Corinth made a united attack on Paul and brought him to the place of judgment. "This man," they [the Jews] charged, "is persuading the people to worship God in ways contrary to the law."
>
> Just as Paul was about to speak, Gallio said to them, "If you Jews were making a complaint about some misdemeanor or serious crime, it would be reasonable for me to listen to you. *But since it involves questions about words and names and your own law*—settle the matter yourselves. I will not be a judge of such things." So he drove them off. (Emphasis added.) (71)

Acts reports that the crowd then turned against a Jewish leader who had led the assault on Paul and beat him in front of the Roman governor, who shows no concern whatsoever for the fate of the Jew—and none of the same solicitude he had previously shown Paul. (72) Once more, we have a Roman governor who believes an accused Christian leader to be innocent, and, once more, we see what can only be official sanction of Paul's mission by Roman authorities. And this time, the governor is a high-ranking "proconsul," and none other than Lucius Junius Gallio Annaeanus, the older brother of the Stoic philosopher Seneca, whose ideas bear such a striking resemblance to those found in the New Testament. Yes—even the philosopher Seneca's brother makes a favorable appearance in the Bible.

Parallels to the ideas of Seneca are only to be expected in Paul's own ideological counter-insurgency—that is, if it took shape early in the reign of Nero or late in that of the Emperor Claudius.

At Ephesus, again, we are told that a "city clerk"—one with the apparent authority to "dismiss the crowd"—intervened to quell rioters at an anti-Christian demonstration. (73) This time, however, the rioters comprise both pagans and Hebrews, but the official Roman response is once again favorable to Paul.

Time and again in the New Testament we are told how Paul's continuing missionary efforts are dogged by "Jews" who "plotted against him." (74) Paul's followers warn him not to visit Jerusalem, according to Acts, and one can certainly see why. But fear of Romans was not one of their reasons.

Apparently, their warnings to Paul were well-grounded. The Christian community in Jerusalem, that is, the Jewish-Christian community of Torah purists, seems to share the same worries of Paul's followers. After hearing news of Paul's many conversions in the area of Greece, they tell him:

> "...You see, brother, how many thousands of Jews have believed, and all of them are zealous for the law. They have been informed that you teach all the Jews who live among the Gentiles to turn away from Moses, *telling them not to circumcise their children or live according to our customs.* What shall we do? They will certainly hear that you have come, so do what we tell you. There are four men with us who have made a vow. Take these men, join in their purification rites and pay their expenses, so that they can have their heads shaved. *Then everyone will know there is no truth in these reports about you, but that you*

yourself are living in obedience to the law. As for the Gentile believers, we have written to them our decision that they should abstain from food sacrificed to idols, from blood, from the meat of strangled animals and from sexual immorality." (Emphasis added.) (75)

Notice that Paul's accusers are not just any Jews—they are *Jewish-Christians*, those who "have believed," according to the description of the Jerusalem Apostles. Far from Christ's message as reported in the Gospels, it is they who are "zealous for the law." It is they who are a violent threat to Paul. Remarkably, Paul does not defend his doctrine against circumcision in Jerusalem. If Acts is to be believed, he didn't have to—the established Apostles accept his message without the slightest complaint at this point. This flies in the face of the argument suggested in Paul's heated letter to the Galatians.

Instead, Paul complies with their strange dietary demands that, along with "sexual immorality," are mentioned. Nowhere else are Christians subject to such rules in the New Testament. So, it is likely that the "Gentile" converts were then subjected to more than dietary restrictions, at the edge of a knife.

The account in Acts is clearly papering over the intense conflict between Paul and the Jewish-Christians. Silently and almost completely, James and his opposition to Paul have vanished from the story, something both incredible and most convenient to later Pauline Christians, although James is clearly the leader of the Christian movement in Paul's letter to the Galatians. Still, according to Acts, before the seven days were up, "some Jews from the province of Asia" see Paul at the Temple, seize him and begin to beat him. So even Acts must confess to violent tensions during this period of time.

Once more, the Romans intervene on Paul's behalf:

While they were trying to kill him, news reached the commander of the Roman troops that the whole city of Jerusalem was in an uproar. He at once took some officers and soldiers and ran down to the crowd. *When the rioters saw the commander and his soldiers, they stopped beating Paul.* (Emphasis added.) (76)

The Romans had Paul "bound with two chains" but the officer in charge—incredibly, if this was really an "arrest"—allowed Paul to address the crowd. (77)

The very idea that anyone arrested by the Romans would be allowed to make a public speech is simply not credible. That someone arrested for inciting unrest among the general population such that the whole city was "in an uproar" would be granted permission by Roman authorities to address the angry crowd is inexplicable. If it is true, we must assume the Roman government endorsed Paul's mission.

As in the case of Jesus, the Jewish crowd at Jerusalem demands that the Romans get rid of Paul, and it is only in compliance with their demands that the Roman commander orders Paul to be flogged and interrogated. Paul then raises the legal issue of his Roman citizenship, brazenly "one-upping" the Roman officer in charge by observing that he was born a Roman citizen while the officer had to purchase his own Roman citizenship at some expense.

The commander then, we are told, is "alarmed" at this news and releases Paul *before* he is flogged, in spite of the ugly crowd demanding his punishment. (78) It is almost as if the benefits of Roman citizenship are being advertised in the narrative of Paul's journeys in Acts.

Once more, as in Jesus's story, it is the Jewish Sanhedrin, not the Romans, that proves to be the Christians' worst foe. While Paul argues with them, "[t]he dispute became so violent that the commander was afraid Paul would be torn to pieces by them. He ordered the troops to go down and take him away from them by force and bring him into the barracks." (79)

Paul is arrested. (Early 1900s Bible illustration)

Again, his "arrest" by the Romans can only be seen as a kind of protective custody to save him from his zealous Jewish rivals. And, again, official Roman sanction seems to be behind the intervention.

Hearing of a plot that "some Jews" had hatched to assassinate Paul, the Roman commander "called two of his centurions and ordered them, 'Get ready a detachment of two hundred soldiers, seventy horsemen and two hundred spearmen to go to Caesarea at nine tonight. Provide horses for Paul so that he may be taken safely to Governor Felix.'" (80) If this is not pure fiction, which is possible, Paul was a prisoner of enormous importance to the Romans, and his wider "Christian" movement can hardly have been the small underground group most scholars assume Christianity to have been at this early stage of its history. Not only was Paul provided with an entire *cohort* of Roman security forces, the commander informs Felix that "there was no charge against him that deserved death or imprisonment." (81)

Just as with Jesus, and with all of Paul's previous experiences, the Roman official finds no wrongdoing despite the hostile Jews' accusations.

These, then, are the circumstances under which Paul was first brought before Governor Felix. And, according to Acts, under Felix (the husband of Titus's future mistress, Bernice), Paul would spend two years in what must be described as protective custody. Felix's replacement, Festus, would finally send Paul away from Judea, where calls for his head were mounting, to Rome for trial before Caesar himself in compliance with Paul's own demand.

On his way to trial in Rome, Paul's extraordinary luck with Roman authorities continues. This time the centurion in charge of him, one Julius from the "Augustan" or "Imperial" regiment, no less, "in kindness to Paul, allowed him to go to his friends so they might provide for his needs." (82)

Once more, then, Paul's "arrest" seems more like a formality. Once more, Roman moderation, toleration—even kindness and respect—are dutifully accorded him.

* * * * * * * *

Christian tradition holds that Paul, like Peter, suffered martyrdom in Rome at the hands of the Romans during Nero's reign. However, these deaths are not described anywhere in the New Testament.

The Gospels, Acts, and even Paul's letters, show Romans in only one invariably positive light. From Jesus's centurion to Paul's own jailer, they are always portrayed as the good guys who are uniformly unwilling to name a Christian guilty of any crime or worthy of any punishment. Only when Jews and Jewish authorities are explicitly blamed, we can be sure, will any martyrdom be recorded in the New Testament, such as that of St. Stephen and, of course, of Jesus. This strict rule would no doubt have applied to the martyrdom of Paul and Peter, too, if it were possible.

So, while it is difficult to argue from a lack of evidence, this failure to discuss the deaths of Paul or Peter in any canonical text may be the best evidence that they were in fact executed by the Romans. After all, such a cruelty would contradict the portrayal of Romans that is thematically consistent everywhere else in the New Testament. The omission of their deaths looks just like the odd void of information we might inherit if the theory we are developing is true.

As a leader of the militant Jewish-Christians, Peter's execution at Rome is rather easy to understand. And, by bringing his contentious mission to Rome itself, Paul may have helped fuel the Fire of Rome, which, as we noted in Part I, is likely to have been set by Paul's Jewish-Christian foes. After the Great Fire, Nero may understandably have decided that Paul had outlived any usefulness he had once promised. Indeed, the narrative of Paul's journey in Acts may be a clue to why Nero might have seen his execution as an expedient way to placate the dangerously aroused Jewish populace.

The outright villainy of "the Jews" as a whole as presented in the New Testament, and the sharply contrasting portraits of not just Romans but Roman *officials* in the stories of Jesus, Peter, and Paul, goes well beyond cosmetic touches to appease the Romans or to convince them that Christians were harmless to their empire. This constant chorus in the New Testament is too consistent to be coincidental.

The positive Roman portraits and good relations Christians enjoyed with Romans in Acts and the Gospels are a deliberate demonstration of the ethics of Jesus and the theology of Paul. They are not incidental but fundamental to the New Testament's theme. They are not exceptions, they are the rule.

* * * * * * * *

An oddity largely overlooked in the New Testament is how often we are reminded of Paul's high-ranking connections, friends and associates.

For example, according to the Book of Acts, one of the early Christians associated with Paul's mission at Antioch was a man named "Manaen," who was "brought up with Herod the Tetrarch." (83) In his letter to the Romans, Paul asks his friends to "Greet those who belong to the household of Aristobulus. Greet Herodion, my fellow Jew." (84) Paul, here, appears to be name-dropping *royal* Herodians! (85)

According to Acts 19:31, "some of the officials of the province [of Asia Minor]" were "friends of Paul," and sent him warnings about the resistance he would face there.

In addition, we are told that among Paul's early converts was Sergius Paulus, probably of consular rank and the *Roman governor of Cyprus.* (86)

All of Paul's powerful connections strongly suggest that the "greetings" he sends from those "in Caesar's household" in his letter to the Philippian community should be taken at face value. (87) Which brings us, at last, to one of Paul's most important allies: Epaphroditus.

This most extraordinary figure has been remarkably unsung in history, though he is not only likely to have been a revered associate of St. Paul but also a powerful administrator for Roman emperors including Nero, Vespasian, Titus, and Domitian. Having had a hand in four imperial administrations, Epaphroditus no doubt had considerable influence over the great events of his time.

Paul wrote to his friends in Philippi:

> I am *amply supplied*, now that *I have received from Epaphroditus the gifts you sent.* They are a fragrant offering, an acceptable sacrifice, pleasing to God. And my God will meet all your needs according to the riches of his glory in Christ Jesus.
>
> To our God and Father be glory for ever and ever. Amen.

> Greet all God's people in Christ Jesus. The broth-
> ers and sisters who are with me send greetings. All
> God's people here *send you greetings, especially*
> *those who belong to Caesar's household.* (Emphasis
> added.) (88)

Previously, in the same letter to the Philippians:

> I think it is necessary to send back to you *Epaphroditus,*
> *my brother, co-worker and fellow soldier, who is also*
> *your messenger,* whom you *sent to take care of my*
> *needs.* For he longs for all of you and is distressed
> because you heard he was ill. Indeed he was ill, and
> almost died. But God had mercy on him, and not on
> him only but also on me, to spare me sorrow upon
> sorrow. Therefore I am all the more eager to send
> him, so that when you see him again you may be glad
> and I may have less anxiety. So then, welcome him
> in the Lord with great joy, and *honor people like him,*
> because he almost died for the work of Christ. He
> *risked his life* to make up for the help you yourselves
> could not give me. (Emphasis added.) (89)

Given the extraordinary credit he is paid in Philippians,
Epaphroditus is curiously never mentioned in Acts. If he was a native
of Philippi, as some have supposed, he makes no appearance in
Christian literature until after Festus delivers Paul to Rome and only
in this letter to the Philippians where Epaphroditus is shown personally attending to Paul's needs.

Another of Paul's important companions (one named "Titus") is
also not mentioned in Acts, even though he played such an important role in the circumcision controversy between Paul and James
described in Paul's letter to the Galatians, in which Titus is uniquely
spared from that initiation. At the very least, the narrative in Acts is
deficient for neglecting to follow these two previously instrumental
New Testament figures, just as it largely ignores the leadership role
played by James the Just.

Icon of Epaphroditus

Leaving that aside, let us consider what Paul says about Epaphroditus, a man who was probably a loyal friend of both the emperors Vespasian and Titus. Paul tells us that "Epaphroditus" helped deliver material support and messages from Paul's friends in Philippi, enough for Paul to say that he was now "amply supplied." Epaphroditus had apparently been ill and this may have brought him close to death, much to his Philippian friends' distress, but he has also "risked his life" in order to help Paul in a way that the Philippians could not.

For all of their "ample" material support, the Philippians could not do the risky thing that Epaphroditus did for Paul, suggesting that Epaphroditus was in a position to assist Paul in some unique way in the city of Rome. This alone suggests that Epaphroditus may have had some special sort of influence that others did not.

It was to Caesar himself that Paul had appealed his case. Apart from material support, what Paul needed in Rome were friends in high places. Epaphroditus, if he had such influence there, apparently used it for Paul at this time—successfully, it seems, but at some personal risk. Paul urges the Philippian Christians to honor men like Epaphroditus.

Any doubt about Paul's relative freedom under Roman captivity is dispelled by Paul himself in the same letter, in which he reassures his Philippian friends:

> Now I want you to know, brothers and sisters, that what has happened to me has actually served to advance the gospel. As a result, *it has become clear throughout the whole palace guard and to everyone*

else that I am in chains for Christ. And *because of my chains, most of the brothers and sisters have become confident in the Lord and dare all the more to proclaim the gospel without fear.* (Emphasis added.) (90)

Given the nature of Paul's imprisonment, it is easy to see why other Christians would have lost any fear of "proclaiming the gospel"; at least, *Paul's* gospel. Paul's friends are allowed to attend to his needs, Paul is free to correspond, and, even more remarkably, Paul is free to communicate with the whole of the Praetorian Guard about his situation. He has somehow gained the sympathy of the entire *imperial bodyguard* in Rome!

It is clearly implied that the Philippians to whom Paul is writing have some special relationship with Epaphroditus. They also seem to have a connection to those "in Caesar's household," since Paul winds up his letter with greetings from the imperial palace.

Remember, we have previously seen that Philippi, as a colony comprising many retired legionaries, was a community with a special relationship to the imperial cult.

Whom else could Paul have meant when, writing from Rome, he makes such a casual, unexplained reference to "Caesar's household"—other than Caesar himself? The progress he has made in persuading Caesar's Praetorian Guard to Christianity only reinforces the authenticity of this imperial reference.

But how is this possible? That St. Paul should have connections to the highest levels of the administration of the Roman emperor is baffling under any traditional assumptions about Christian history. And it might simply be speculative—if other sources did not actually verify that a real person named "Epaphroditus" did in fact live in Rome at this time.

This Epaphroditus did enjoy just the sort of influence over Emperor Nero that Paul could use. He was so close to the emperor, in fact, that he would personally "help" Nero commit "suicide."

When Jesus states that his Second Coming will occur within a lifetime, when Josephus calls his imperial master the true Jewish messiah, and when Paul refers casually to Caesar and the Praetorian Guard, we must first consider these astonishing claims at face value if we are to understand what is actually happening.

Modern Christianity dismisses or deflects the import of these statements, and yet, without evidence to contradict them, we must start
by testing the literal meaning, since—in contrast to so much else
in the New Testament—they are factually specific, non-miraculous
assertions found in contemporary personal correspondences of St.
Paul and some of the oldest Christian literature.

The wider context of Paul's high-ranking connections, along
with the friendly way Roman officials uniformly treat him, all support
taking him literally when he name-drops Epaphroditus, "Caesar's
household," and the Praetorian Guard in the same letter to his com-
patriots in Philippi.

Epaphroditus was certainly of "Caesar's household." As the
Roman historian Suetonius recounts, he was Nero's powerful
"Secretary of Letters." While he may have already been working for
the emperor previously, Epaphroditus might have won his exalted
position by exposing to Nero the famous "Piso Conspiracy," as
Tacitus reports. (91) This was the same conspiracy prosecution that
led to Seneca's demise. What connections Epaphroditus may have
had to Seneca and his circle, perhaps allowing him to become an
effective informer against them, is unknown.

Nero

Suetonius informs us that Epaphroditus had a heavy hand in
history, indeed. According to Suetonius (92), Epaphroditus helped
Nero stab himself in the throat following the outbreak of the Vindex
Revolt in Gaul. The ancient historian Cassius Dio echoes this, (93)
telling us that Epaphroditus accompanied Nero in his final flight from
rebels and that it was he who delivered the fatal blow to Nero's neck

during Nero's prolonged and reluctant suicide.

The historian Cassius tells us this about the end of Epaphroditus's own life, many years later:

> As a consequence of his cruelty the emperor [Domitian] was suspicious of all mankind, and from now on ceased to repose hopes of safety in either the freedmen or yet the prefects, whom he usually caused to be brought to trial during their very term of office. He had first banished and now slew Epaphroditus, Nero's freedman, accusing him of having failed to defend Nero; for he wished by the vengeance that he took on Nero's behalf to terrify his own freedmen long in advance, so that they should venture no similar deed. (94)

This opens the possibility that Epaphroditus himself may have somehow been involved with the anti-Nero conspirators, although we cannot be completely certain.

Suetonius plainly reports that Domitian executed Epaphroditus because he had helped Nero kill himself. (95) This is interesting because the official Flavian position on Nero was quite negative as the Flavians sought to reassure Rome that they were a new breed of emperor following Nero's calamitous reign—and also because Domitian's own enemies accused him of being a "new Nero," in contrast to his father Vespasian and his much-beloved brother, Titus.

The Flavian emperors who employed Epaphroditus in the same position of "Secretary of Letters" that he had enjoyed under Nero had long known about his role in Nero's death without it ever being a concern until the latter years of Domitian's reign. Even if Suetonius correctly reported Domitian's stated motive, therefore, the charge was a remarkable change in the Flavians' previous policy.

Suetonius tells us about Epaphroditus's execution immediately after describing the execution of Titus Flavius Clemens. The two events seem to be connected, chronologically at least, and they suggest that Domitian's real motive may have been the purging of the "Jewish" elements within the Flavian court that he had inherited from his father and brother.

Emperor Titus Flavius Domitianus (Domitian)

This man named Epaphroditus is thus connected to Christians in yet another way. As we have already seen, the "Clemens" who was executed at about the same time with Epaphroditus was the 1st Century pope, St. Clement of Rome, the cousin of Titus and Domitian.

St. Clement of Rome, St. Peter's Basilica, the Vatican

And Epaphroditus had yet another imperial and "Jewish" connection to the Flavians. In a sort of dedication at the start of his monumental work, *Antiquities of the Jews*, the Jewish historian Titus Flavius Josephus praises "Epaphroditus" as his beloved patron who encouraged him to undertake the task of recording the heritage of the Hebrew people.

Josephus describes this "Epaphroditus" as a lover of all kinds of learning with a special love for history, and someone who participated in the "great affairs" of their time. Josephus notes that Epaphroditus experienced different "turns of fortune" as a result of his participation in these great affairs. (96)

Josephus also dedicates his own autobiography to Epaphroditus. (97) And Josephus addresses to Epaphroditus his later work, *Against Apion*, in which the historian defends the Jewish religion from the slander of the Greek writer Apion. Josephus ends that work with yet another dedication to "Epaphroditus." (98)

That the Epaphroditus referred to by Paul, Suetonius and Josephus is the same person is a controversial proposition—but there is no credible reason to doubt it and every reason to believe it.

According to Suetonius, the same Epaphroditus must have served emperors from Nero to Domitian. The charge of participating in killing an emperor that he reports as the reason for Epaphroditus's execution would make utterly no sense if Nero and Domitian had not been served by the same "Epaphroditus."

Since we know that both Josephus and the Epaphroditus mentioned by Suetonius worked for the Flavian emperors, it is highly probable that Josephus's Epaphroditus is the same man. In the unlikely event that there had been two men named "Epaphroditus" connected to the same Flavian court, we would expect our sources to distinguish them for us. Furthermore, Josephus mentions that his Epaphroditus had participated in the *great events of his time*. This can only be the same man who exposed an important conspiracy to Nero and who "helped" that emperor commit suicide, precipitating a tumultuous civil war that was finally pacified by the Flavians.

From Nero to Domitian, this is the one Epaphroditus prominent in public affairs who is remembered in history—the only one mentioned, for example, by the historians Suetonius and Dio to have existed during this period—a prominent Secretary of Letters who served four emperors.

That Paul's Epaphroditus is the same man Suetonius mentions is suggested by the fact that he was in a unique position to offer Paul assistance in Rome, help of a type that the Philippians apparently could not provide, and help that somehow risked Epaphroditus's own life. Such help, which arrived after Paul appealed his case to Nero Caesar himself, might uniquely come from the emperor's own Secretary of Letters. Such an imperial position also explains the otherwise inexplicable references in the same letter to members of "Caesar's household," and Paul's access to the emperor's own Praetorian Guard.

That *Josephus*'s Epaphroditus is the same man Paul refers to is suggested by the avid interest in Jewish history Josephus ascribes to him. Paul's lengthy historical exegeses are not as voluminous as Josephus's histories, but they are strikingly similar in their pride in Jewish history and their simultaneously pro-Roman outlook. Paul's focus is theology as revealed in history; Josephus's focus is history proper. But, in their "moderate" Jewish positions and their interest in Jewish religion and heritage, the work of both Paul and Josephus would have the same appeal to the same man for the same reasons.

Moreover, the life and influence of the Epaphroditus mentioned by Suetonius spans the entire gap between Paul and Josephus, and, indeed, between Nero and the last of the Flavians before he was executed by Domitian.

To be sure, "Epaphroditus" was not an uncommon name in the classical world. We know of multiple individuals named Epaphroditus. Augustus had a servant of this name. We have a famous inscription from the reign of Trajan in the early 2nd Century with the name "Epaphroditus." We also know of a grammarian from Alexandria named "Mettius Epaphroditus."

Predictably, scholars once thought that the Epaphroditus mentioned by Paul could *not* be the same one that is mentioned by Josephus. Their reason is that in both *Against Apion* and his autobiography, Josephus addresses Epaphroditus as a person still living, while in his autobiography Josephus also mentions the death of the Herodian king, Agrippa II. Since the 9th Century Byzantine writer Photius of Constantinople places the death of Agrippa II in the "third year of Trajan," or 100 CE, for a long time scholars believed Josephus's later works could not have been composed until around 100 CE. From this they reasoned that the "Epaphroditus" Josephus mentions could not be the same Epaphroditus executed by the Emperor Domitian in the year 95 CE as reported by Suetonius.

However, today most scholars regard Photius as inaccurate and recognize that Herod Agrippa II probably died *before* 93 CE. (99) This means that the works of Josephus may well have been composed before 95 CE. If this is correct, then the Epaphroditus of Nero and Domitian would have been alive when Josephus dedicated his works to him.

Considering the interest that Epaphroditus devoted to the work of both Paul and Josephus, it is likely that he was Jewish himself, at least by birth. This would also shed light on why his execution is associated with that of Flavius Clemens, who was executed, according to Cassius Dio, for "adopting Jewish ways."

Epaphroditus would not have been the only person at Nero's court interested in things Jewish. From suggestions by Josephus, it may be possible to infer that Nero's second wife, Poppea, was a "God fearer," the term given to "soft" converts to Judaism who did not follow strict Jewish practice. (100) Josephus himself reports that Poppea was sympathetic and helpful to him during his own mission to Rome in his youth before he would become the Flavian historian. (Poppea was later kicked to death by Nero while she was pregnant, according to one ancient report.)

Poppea Sabina

The main objection by scholars to this three-way identification of Paul, Josephus and the historians' Epaphroditus has always been the mere incredulity that Christian connections could reach so high at this foundational stage of the Church. And yet, as we have so often seen now, when all of the evidence is simply taken at face value, the position most supported is that all of these Epaphrodituses are the same person, who, by himself, joins the roots of Christianity to imperial Rome and the Flavian dynasty itself.

Scattered throughout the New Testament are many references to prominent political figures from the Roman Empire of the 1st

Century, and many of these mentions do not involve any controversial identification. Princess Bernice, for example, the mistress of an emperor who claimed to be the Jewish Messiah, and her brother, the last prince from a house of Jewish kings, are both recalled positively in the New Testament, as are all Roman governors, state officials, and even Paul's jailer. One of the consistent thematic concerns of both the Gospels and the Acts of the Apostles is depicting the relationship of the first Christians to the Roman state *positively*.

It is now time to focus on the most famous Jewish figure in the inner circle of Emperor Titus: the seminal historian, Titus Flavius Josephus.

II. Josephus and the New Testament

As we have previously noted, the historian commonly known as Josephus was a self-described priest from an ancient line of Jewish priests. He also boasted of royal connections as a descendant of the Hasmonean family that had achieved both the crown and the high priesthood. (1)

After starting out as a conflicted and reluctant rebel general in Galilee whose doubts constantly irritated his countrymen, Josephus tells us that he switched over to the Roman side after the city he was defending, Jotapata, fell to the Romans. Thereafter, Josephus informs us, he enjoyed official favor as a writer and historian at the Flavian court who would not only earn his freedom but also Roman citizenship, as well as valuable estates.

Josephus tells us that he was with Vespasian at Alexandria, where the new emperor performed his healing miracles that exactly mirror Jesus Christ's. Perhaps the reason we don't have Josephus's own account of these miracles is that they happened at the pagan temple of Serapis. Josephus does attest to having been present with Titus during the Siege of Jerusalem, along with all of Titus's other New Testament friends. Of that momentous event he provides us with a vividly detailed account. (2)

Titus Flavius Josephus

During Vespasian's reign Josephus produced a history of the Jewish revolt, with official Roman approval, entitled *Wars of the*

Jews. About 20 years later, he finished his comprehensive history of the Hebrews from the Creation to the eve of the Jewish War entitled *Antiquities of the Jews*, which he dedicated to Epaphroditus. This monumental work was a more detailed, parallel account of the legendary history found in the Old Testament itself, supplemented by subsequent history.

In addition, Josephus wrote *Against Apion*, his defense of Jewish history and culture against the attacks of one "Apion" and other anti-Semitic writers (whose works no longer exist), which he also dedicated to Epaphroditus, and, finally, he penned his own autobiography.

Today, there is near consensus among scholars that the Gospels (and the Book of Acts), or the material comprising them, were largely composed between the time of the Jewish War and the end of the 1st Century (although some place the completion of the more theologically sophisticated Gospel of John in the early 2nd Century). These texts underwent further editing and redaction, but this dating for the basic material has become widely accepted. This means that most of the New Testament was written during the same time that Josephus wrote his books, while the Flavians were in power.

The Gospels were composed in Greek, rather than Aramaic or Hebrew, as were the works of Josephus, who was learned in all three.

In his theology and political outlook, Josephus is remarkably Christian to a degree that is not generally acknowledged. Although nominally "Jewish," the works of Josephus were preserved only by Christians. Understandably, he was regarded as a traitor by his fellow Israelites. His military and political betrayal of the rebellion is only the first basis for Josephus's popularity among Christians and his infamy among his own people.

As Josephus describes it, his change of heart was not a sudden matter. He had long predicted that the Romans would inevitably win any conflict with the Hebrews. He claims that from the start he had repeatedly urged peace among the rebels. (3) In response, he tells us, his countrymen denounced him and literally flung excrement at him.

So, like Jesus, Josephus advocated an unpopular peace to the Jews. Josephus also believed in "loving thine enemy." He reminds us in his autobiography that Jewish law prohibited the Hebrews from despoiling "even of their enemies," (4) and, in *Apion*, he asserts that to *treat one's enemies well* is God's own command. (5). Josephus criticizes Herod the Great for not showing "mercy" on those whom he "hated" (6), and he tells us that the virtue that the crazed Zealot rebels entirely lacked was "mercy" (*clementia*). (7)

Apparently, like both Paul and the author of the epistle of Peter, Josephus even believed that the Roman authorities were *appointed by God.* (8) He tells the rebels themselves at one point that they are fighting against not only the Romans, but against God himself. (9) If hearing this doctrine expressed by Paul is somewhat more surprising than reading it in the works of the Flavian apologist Flavius Josephus, the two men, nevertheless, share exactly the same political doctrine—one that endorses the legitimacy of Roman rule with the Jewish God's own favor during an age of religious war.

Like Paul, Josephus also opposes forced circumcision. (10) In his recounting of the story of Abraham, Josephus actually "omits the connection between circumcision and the covenant of God with Abraham," as one scholar has observed, even though this is the whole point of the story for any faithful Jew. (11)

If Vespasian, an uncircumcised Roman general who did not observe a Kosher diet and did not submit to Mosaic Law, could still be the true Messiah of Jewish prophecy, as Josephus himself proclaimed him to be (12), then how crucial was a Kosher lifestyle to being a "good Jew"? Josephus's political motivations are obvious—yet they match the agenda of Paul and Jesus exactly.

Josephus advocates the same religious compromises that caused an uproar in Jerusalem when Paul advocated them and helped fuel the Jewish War. He shares, in other words, the same moderating objectives of his triumphant Roman masters. And he shares them at the same time when scholars agree the Gospels themselves were being written—even as he was writing his recapitulation of the Old Testament, so many passages of which are echoed in the Gospels.

We must note here that after the Temple in Jerusalem was destroyed and the holy scriptures inside were plundered by the Romans, Titus gave all the Jewish holy books found there to Josephus. (13) (The Dead Sea Scrolls, of course, eluded capture by the Romans, as they had been secreted away in caves and would not be discovered until the 20th Century.)

Plunder from the Jewish Temple, detail from the
Arch of Titus, c. 81 CE

Perhaps most remarkably, Josephus also paradoxically combines his belief in the Messiah, the nationalistic and militaristic lightning rod from Jewish history that had incited rebellion, with a *peacemaker*—just as Paul and Jesus do. Josephus's master, Vespasian, advertised himself throughout the Empire as a peacemaker and the father of a new *Pax Romana* (Roman Peace). His son Titus was literally a "prince of peace." Vespasian erected a temple of peace in the city of Rome, even as he erected the Colosseum.

Not only are all of these peace advocates (Paul, Vespasian, Titus and Josephus) strangely adopting the idea of the Jewish messiah as their own, they are all turning it upside-down, transforming the Jewish concept of a national redeemer into a Roman advocate of transnational harmony.

First Paul, and then the Gospels, provide the cultural and theological argument needed to transform the Jewish Messiah into a Hellenized, Platonic and Stoic "Christ" figure who submits to established Roman authority. Josephus's works provide authority for this same mission in a number of surprising ways in addition to his liberal take on circumcision.

Most interesting, however, is that Paul and Josephus arrived at precisely the same politically paradoxical conception of the "messiah."

* * * * * * * *

The Gospels depict Jesus associating with persons who are "unclean" according to contemporary Jewish prejudices, including prostitutes and tax collectors. Jesus is shown allowing his disciples to work on the Sabbath, criticizing Kosher dietary laws, praising a Roman centurion for greater faith than any Jew, and so forth, seemingly checking off every issue that had created friction between the Jews and Rome.

It is easy to understand why Jews accused early Christians of conspiring to subvert Mosaic Law. Jesus directly answers that criticism by saying, paradoxically: "Do not think that I have come to abolish the Law or the Prophets; I have not come to abolish them but to fulfill them." (14) However, in order to "fulfill" Jewish law and prophecy, Jesus presents an entirely "new" testament that is rewritten within acceptable Roman specifications.

Josephus's claims to be a faithful Jew are no less incredible than that of Jesus in the Gospels. After all, Josephus became a turncoat who even helped the Romans interrogate Jewish captives under torture and later made public excuses for the Romans even after they had razed the Temple.

When Josephus was still fighting on the rebels' side, his own Jewish critics accused him of intending to betray not just the rebels but the *laws* of his country. (15) This is, of course, the same charge leveled against Jesus—and Paul.

Josephus recounts for us his prayer to God as he was making his fateful decision to go over to the Roman side:

> Since it pleaseth thee, who hast created the Jewish nation, to depress the same, and since all their good fortune is gone over to the Romans, and since thou hast made choice of this soul of mine to foretell what is to come to pass hereafter, I willingly give them my hands, and am content to live. *And I protest openly that I do not go over to the Romans as a deserter of the Jews, but as a minister from thee."* (Emphasis added.) (16)

Just like Jesus, therefore, Josephus regards himself as a faithful believer in the Jewish God even as he is branded a traitor to the law by fellow Jews.

Of course, Josephus himself also went on to associate with

"unclean" persons. He reserves some of his highest religious praise for Roman officials—just as Jesus praises a Roman centurion and Paul praises Titus's and Josephus's personal friend, Agrippa II. (Josephus tells us that he, too, was a friend of Agrippa.)

However, in addition to the shared ideological beliefs expressed by Jesus Christ and Flavius Josephus, there are also specific biographical parallels between them that warrant attention. In their royal heritage, early histories, and later acts, the coincidences between the lives of Jesus and Josephus are too plentiful to ignore. Obviously, both kept the same kind of unorthodox company and both faced the same criticism from orthodox Jews as a result—but there is much more that Jesus and Josephus strangely have in common.

* * * * * * * *

Between the Nativity and Jesus's baptism by John—the event that signals the commencement of Jesus's vocation as teacher and healer—we are told almost nothing about the early life of Jesus in the canonical Gospels.

The major exception is the story of the child Jesus at the Jerusalem Temple, which is relayed in some detail in the Gospel of Luke:

> Every year Jesus' parents went to Jerusalem for the Festival of the Passover. When he was twelve years old, they went up to the festival, according to the custom. After the festival was over, while his parents were returning home, the boy Jesus stayed behind in Jerusalem, but they were unaware of it. Thinking he was in their company, they traveled on for a day. Then they began looking for him among their relatives and friends. When they did not find him, they went back to Jerusalem to look for him. After three days they found him in the *Temple courts, sitting among the teachers*, listening to them and asking them questions. Everyone who heard him was amazed at his *understanding* and his answers. When his parents saw him, they were astonished. (Emphasis added.) (17)

Here is Flavius Josephus's story about himself from his auto-biography:

> Moreover, when I was a child, and about fourteen years of age, I was commended by all for the love I had to learning; on which account *the high priests and principal men of the city* came them frequently to me together, in order to know my opinion about the accurate *understanding* of the law... (Emphasis added.) (18)

In both cases, a child prodigy impresses religious authorities at the Jerusalem Temple with his religious learning. The only difference is their age: Jesus was twelve and Josephus was fourteen.

There is an additional coincidence in the exalted family status of Jesus and Josephus. Josephus came from a royal family, the Hasmoneans, while Jesus is alleged to have descended from the more exalted and ancient line of King David.

The slight difference in both cases is also telling. As with the stories of the elders at the Temple, Jesus's family is *one notch higher* than Josephus's. If his own Flavian masters were to be associated with the Jewish messiah—and therefore with the stories of their pre-incarnation in Christ—then Josephus may be making sure not to equate himself with the Flavian emperors or their status as messiahs by ranking himself just below Christ. After all, Josephus describes himself as merely his Roman masters' prophet (having prophesized Vespasian's ascension to the throne) and not a messiah.

Where Jesus associated with a "Baptist" who wandered in the "wilderness," Josephus, he tells us, lived for three years with a holy man named "Banus" in "the desert" who "bathed himself in cold water frequently" in order to preserve his chastity. (19) The Baptist famously wore clothing made of camel's hair while Josephus's "Banus" wore only what grew on trees. The Baptist ate "locusts and wild honey." Banus ate only food that "grew of its own accord." (20)

Details about the dress, vegetarian diets and bathing rituals of these two wilderness holy men known by Jesus and Josephus, respectively, are probably provided for the same end, namely to associate both Jesus and Josephus with the famous "Essene" movement of Jewish purists precisely in order to add authoritative messianic credibility to their unorthodox message. Both of these desert figures, John the Baptist and Banus, also share their dietary tradition with the leader of the Christian community in Paul's time, James the Just, who scholar Robert Eisenman has identified as the leader of the Qumran community called "The Righteous One" in the Dead Sea Scrolls. This is the same James who would come into such bitter conflict with Paul over what "Christianity," or messianic Judaism, actually meant decades after Christ had supposedly settled the question. (21)

Since the sectarians of the Dead Sea Scrolls also described themselves as dwelling in the "Wilderness," all of these Holy Men, the sectarians of the Dead Sea Scrolls, James the Just, John the Baptist, and Banus, have significant similarities. (22) All of them echo the messianic prophecy of Isaiah (23) about a "voice calling" for the Jewish people "to clear a path [or 'Way'] in the desert" for the Lord. In the Gospels, this reference to Isaiah is explicitly linked to the Baptist, as he famously identifies himself as "a voice of one calling in the wilderness, 'Make straight the way of the Lord...'" (24) In Isaiah's prophecy, however, that "voice crying in the wilderness" was originally a call to reject pollution, to restore cultural purity and reaffirm the Covenant with God in order to become worthy of the coming of the messiah.

Josephus's mentor "Banus" seems to associate Josephus with the sect known as the Essenes at an early stage of the historian's life. However, Josephus tells us that he ended up being a Pharisee. This evolution interestingly reflects the same ideological mix allegedly adopted by Paul. St. Paul claims to be a Pharisee (25) even though his celibate lifestyle is more akin to the behavior of the Essenes as described by Josephus in his book on the Jewish War. (26) Since both oppose forced circumcision, however, they must be paradoxically (for Pharisees) classified as critics of Mosaic Law, just as Jesus himself was with respect to issues like Kosher diet, strict Sabbath observance and Jewish purity regulations.

Josephus insists that Pharisees like himself are ideologically related to the Hellenistic philosophy that was popular among the

Romans, namely Stoicism, as it was "called by the Greeks." (27) Scholars have likewise observed that Josephus's work exhibits deeply Platonic and other Hellenistic influences, influences that often supersede his Jewish heritage. As one scholar of Josephus puts it, in "seeking to accommodate Greek and Jewish wisdom," Josephus "clearly depart[s] from the tradition in which he had been trained." (28)

This matches Paul's ideological leanings exactly: both are proud of their Jewish heritage though each has adopted Hellenistic style and ideas.

According to both Josephus and the Book of Acts, one of the defining features of the Pharisees was their belief in the Resurrection of the Dead (29), something they distinctly shared with both Essenes and Christians, but not the third sect of Jews, the Sadducees, who, according to Josephus's description in *Antiquities of the Jews*, did not believe in an afterlife.

Josephus expresses the same combination of pagan and Jewish elements, therefore, that we find in the original Christian literature, i.e. the same transcultural syncretism that characterizes the New Testament.

In his earlier work, *Wars of the Jews*, Josephus focuses largely on the Essene sect that is probably also represented by the figure of Banus. His sympathy for this group of purists, who were also probably the ideological leaders of the Jewish conflict with Rome, curiously shifts in his later works.

Like the wider Hellenistic world, according to Josephus, both Pharisees and Essenes believed in an immortal soul, an Afterlife, and a Judgment with rewards and punishments meted out as deserved, mirroring the Elysian Fields and Hades of pagan belief. In fact, in his earlier *Wars of the Jews*, Josephus himself compares the Essenes' views of an afterlife to the Greeks' and finds them to be substantially similar. In *Wars*, Josephus says that the Essenes followed restraint and reason like the Stoics.

However, in his later work, *Antiquities,* Josephus claims that it was the *Pharisees* who showed a Stoic restraint. (30)

In the earlier *Wars*, Josephus concedes that the Essenes were closest to the warlike rebels:

And as for death, if it will be for their glory, they esteem it better than living always; and indeed our war with the Romans gave abundant evidence what great souls they had in their trials, wherein, although they were tortured and distorted, burnt and torn to pieces, and went through all kinds of instruments of torment, that they might be forced either to blaspheme their legislator, or to eat what was forbidden them, yet could they not be made to do either of them, no, nor once to flatter their tormentors, or to shed a tear; but they smiled in their very pains, and laughed those to scorn who inflicted the torments upon them, and resigned up their souls with great alacrity, as expecting to receive them again. (Emphasis added.) (31)

Josephus depicts the Essenes' political zeal as rooted in their fervent adherence to the Torah and Kosher diet in particular. He therefore implicitly claims that his own bona fides reside in both the Pharisees *and* those who went into the "wilderness" such as the Essenes and the Dead Sea Scrolls sectarians. But something has definitely changed in Josephus between his early writing of *Wars* and his later writing of *Antiquities*—something ideological has happened. Josephus has begun to contradict himself about the identity and nature of the rebels with whom he associated in his youth.

Like Jesus and Paul, Josephus, too, ran afoul of the Jewish priesthood in Jerusalem who, he says, "contrived how [they] might catch [him] by treachery." (32) It seems the same elite priesthood of the Sanhedrin that convicted Jesus and condemned Paul also accused Josephus of betraying the Jewish people.

The striking similarities in the stories told about Jesus, Josephus, and the Apostle Paul are hard to miss. The most remarkable coincidence between Josephus and Paul, however, is a dramatic event that both of them experienced: a shipwreck on their way from Judea to Rome.

We shall now consider and compare the details of these accounts.

* * * * * * * *

St. Paul and Flavius Josephus tell extraordinarily coincidental stories. First, Josephus's:

> But when I was in the twenty-sixth year of my age, it happened that I took a voyage to Rome, and this on the occasion which I shall now describe. At the time when Felix was procurator of Judea there were certain priests of my acquaintance, and very excellent persons they were, whom on a small and trifling occasion he had *put into bonds*, and *sent to Rome to plead their cause before Caesar*. These I was desirous to procure deliverance for, and that especially because I was informed that they were not unmindful of piety towards God, even under their afflictions, but *supported themselves with figs and nuts*. Accordingly I came to Rome, though it were through a great number of hazards by sea; for as our *ship was drowned in the Adriatic Sea*, we that were in it, being *about six hundred* in number, *swam for our lives all the night*; when, upon the *first appearance of the day*, and upon our sight of a ship of Cyrene, I and some others, eighty in all, by God's providence, prevented the rest, and were taken up into the other ship. And when I had thus escaped, and was come to Diearchia, which the Italians call Puteoli... (Emphasis added.) (33)

Here, we see vegetarian Jewish sectarians of the John the Baptist and James the Just type, and like Josephus's own one-time rabbi, Banus. Josephus refers to these Essene-like prisoners as eaters of "figs and nuts."

Now let us consider Paul's account of his own shipwreck, in the same vicinity, from the Book of Acts:

> On the fourteenth night we were still being driven across the *Adriatic Sea* [It should be recalled that for the ancients, the "Adriatic Sea" extended well south of the Italian peninsula], when about midnight the sailors sensed they were approaching land. They took

soundings and found that the water was a hundred and twenty feet deep. A short time later they took soundings again and found it was ninety feet deep. Fearing that we would be dashed against the rocks, they dropped *four anchors* from the stern and prayed for daylight. In an attempt to escape from the ship, the sailors let the lifeboat down into the sea, pretending they were going to lower some anchors from the bow. Then Paul said to the centurion and the soldiers, "Unless these men stay with the ship, you cannot be saved." So the soldiers cut the ropes that held the lifeboat and let it drift away.

Just before dawn Paul urged them all to eat. "For the last fourteen days," he said, "you have been in constant suspense and have gone without food— you haven't eaten anything. Now I urge you to take some food. You need it to survive. Not one of you will lose a single hair from his head." After he said this, he took some bread and gave thanks to God in front of them all. Then he broke it and began to eat. They were all encouraged and ate some food themselves. Altogether there were *276 of us on board*. When they had eaten as much as they wanted, they lightened the ship by throwing the grain into the sea.

When *daylight came*, they did not recognize the land, but they saw a bay with a sandy beach, where they decided to run the ship aground if they could. Cutting loose the anchors, they left them in the sea and at the same time untied the ropes that held the rudders. Then they hoisted the foresail to the wind and made for the beach. But the ship struck a sandbar and ran aground. The bow stuck fast and would not move, and the stern was broken to pieces by the pounding of the surf.

The soldiers planned to kill the prisoners to prevent any of them from swimming away and escaping. But the centurion wanted to spare Paul's life and kept them from carrying out their plan. He ordered those who could swim to jump overboard first and get to land. The rest were to get there on planks or on other pieces of the ship. *In this way everyone reached land safely.* (Emphasis added.) (34)

In contrast to Paul, Josephus's wrecked ship carried about 600 people, more than twice the 276 on Paul's ship. Oddly, both accounts specify the number of passengers, a detail that establishes a difference between them.

In Josephus's case, the ship's passengers desperately swim to another ship that takes them to Pueoli, while, after Paul's shipwreck, they improbably swim all night and make it to the island of Malta.

In both stories, parties of Jewish prisoners are on their way to Rome to try their cases before Nero. Just as in Paul's story, Josephus's friends were "in bonds" for what can only be messianic beliefs that the Romans consider threatening.

Apparently, both ships full of suspected Jewish rebels took on water in the Adriatic Sea and sank, forcing their passengers to swim for their lives only to be miraculously saved on their way to judgment before Caesar in Rome.

In one of these shipwreck stories, the dietary habits of the prisoners are mentioned; in the other, Paul urges them to eat bread and almost performs a Christian Communion or Mass while feeding them.

Both shipwrecks happen at night and end at dawn. And in both, all the passengers are miraculously saved.

Could these events, like other dubiously duplicated people and events we have already seen, be one and the same?

The Book of Acts says that Paul was sent to Rome by the order of the Judean governor Festus, who governed between 60-62 CE. Josephus says that he was about 26 years old when he went to Rome, and this would place his voyage in the year 63 CE, which would take the event into the next governorship of Albinus.

However, Josephus mentions that the prisoners he was accompanying to Rome as their advocate had been arrested under the governorship of Felix, who governed from 52-60 CE, just as the Book of Acts says that Paul was first arrested by Felix and kept under guard until the time of Festus, who then ordered him sent to Rome. (35) While Festus ordered Paul sent to Rome, however, the voyage itself might well have not occurred until early in Albinus's governorship, around 63 CE—the same year of Josephus's voyage.

Most Christians today place Paul's arrival in Rome in the year 60 CE, but Christian tradition has repeatedly associated the martyrdoms of Peter and Paul with the Great Fire of Rome (a tradition famously included in the historical novel *Quo Vadis?* by Henryk Sienkiewicz). (36) If this tradition is correct, then Paul could not have died until 64 CE, a date consistent with his arrival the previous year—the same year that Josephus arrived in Rome via shipwreck.

None of this suggests that either shipwreck story is historical. A story about either man surviving a "shipwreck" on their "way to Rome" is somewhat fantastic and may be allegorical however common real shipwrecks might have been on the ancient Mediterranean Sea. What's interesting is that Josephus's account can be correlated so closely in both time and metaphor with Paul's story in Acts. (37)

About the same time as these shipwrecks, James the Just had been assassinated on the steps of the Temple, a treachery that had provoked a massive reaction among the Jewish population and may have caused delegations from both sides of the dispute to be sent to Rome for adjudication. Both Josephus, as a young priest representing Jewish prisoners, and Paul, James's most bitter Jewish rival, could well have been among them. James's shocking murder in Jerusalem occurred in 62 CE—precisely during the interval between the governorships of Festus and Albinus, according to Josephus. (We shall consider Paul's possible role in the death of James shortly.)

It is noteworthy that when Josephus was composing his possibly metaphorical and certainly miraculous tale of Jewish rebels swimming from a lost ship to salvation in Rome, Titus had just put into circulation millions of coins with his dolphin-and-anchor motif and adorned public works with images like this:

Herculaneum mosaic buried by Vesuvius during the reign of Titus

They are both tableaus of the lost, swimming like fish in a tempestuous sea, desperately seeking salvation. Both ships carry Jewish prisoners accused of being agitators disturbing the peace against Rome. In both stories, all of these lost souls miraculously survive their shipwreck on their way to Caesar. (Paul's shipwreck story even mentions no less than four *anchors* being laid down.)

Regardless of whether these shipwrecks were real, metaphorical or one and the same, it is important to note that there are some unrelated historical discrepancies between Josephus and the New Testament. For example, Acts claims that a rebel named "Theudas" caused a disturbance *before* Judas the Galilean would emerge as the founder of the Zealots. But Josephus tells us that Theudas's uprising occurred decades *after* Judas's group came together. (38) Also, the Gospel of Mark tells us that Herod Antipas married his sister-in-law, wife of his brother Philip, something that Josephus does not say. (39) Moreover, the Gospels seem to place the death of John the Baptist in a different year than Josephus does. And there is no slaughter of innocent babies at the time of Jesus's birth recorded by Josephus. And there are a few other interesting differences.

However, Christians have also observed that some of these are only apparent contradictions. If Josephus failed to mention one of the many marriages among the Herodian royals, this does not mean it didn't happen. And as many have observed, ourselves included, Josephus sometimes contradicts himself.

Some of the differences are harder to explain by those who believe in the literal truth of the Gospels. And yet this problem vanishes, too, if we recognize that the New Testament authors knew their work to be allegorical in import and did not need to be strictly factual. If they were never intended to be taken literally by those few who might also read the scholarly historical tomes of Josephus, then there is no "problem" to solve. Just as Jesus taught in parables, so the Gospel narratives may have been originally intended this way. Josephus's texts were written for the educated seeking greater education and, as such, his works needed to meet a higher standard of accuracy. The Gospels, on the other hand, were religious and liturgical texts.

What is remarkable, however, is the degree to which the historical detail in Josephus and the New Testament does correlate. The

Christian imagery evoked by the strangely coincidental shipwrecks of Paul and Josephus remains remarkably similar, no matter how questionable the historical truth of these events.

* * * * * * * *

There are still more parallels between the lives of Josephus and Jesus. Speaking about himself, as always in the third person, Josephus tells the following remarkable story about his escape and his switch to the Romans' side during the Jewish War:

> [Josephus] was assisted by a certain supernatural providence; for he withdrew himself from the enemy when he was in the midst of them, and leaped into a certain deep pit, whereto there adjoined a large den at one side of it, *which den could not be seen by those that were above ground*; and there he met with forty persons of eminency that had concealed themselves, and with provisions enough to satisfy them for not a few days. So in the day time he hid himself from the enemy, who had seized upon all places, and in the night time he got up out of the den and looked about for some way of escaping, and took exact notice of the watch; but as all places were guarded every where on his account, that there was no way of getting off unseen, he went down again into the den. *Thus he concealed himself two days; but on the third day, when they had taken a woman who had been with them, he was discovered.* Whereupon Vespasian sent immediately and zealously two tribunes, Paulinus and Gallicanus, and ordered them to give Josephus their right hands as a security for his life, and to exhort him to come up. (Emphasis added.) (40)

So, after spending three days in a cave while presumed dead, Josephus is revealed by a woman to be alive after all. Jesus spent three days in his tomb, as well, which was also a cave, before he was discovered by a woman, Mary Magdalene, according to all of the Gospel accounts. (41) (Curiously, Jesus's tomb was owned by a man named "Joseph," just as Jesus's human father is also named "Joseph.")

The "new life" that Josephus emerges from the cave to find is just a figurative transformation. But that new life as "Titus Flavius Josephus" would certainly be akin to a new life "in Christ," as a devotee of the Messiah who is, paradoxically, set free from Mosaic Law, just as Paul describes this option for all Jews who converted to Christianity.

Jesus and Josephus share a royal background. Both were child prodigies who dazzled scholars at the Temple in Jerusalem. Jesus associated with a wilderness holy man who was a vegetarian "bather," as did Josephus.

Like Jesus *and* Paul, Josephus earned the enmity of Temple authorities, including the high priest. And, also like Paul, Josephus experienced a shipwreck on the way to Rome around the same time only to be miraculously saved on his way to Caesar.

Josephus, like Paul, describes himself as a "Pharisee." Doctrinally, however, both are better identified with Essenes, though only with the same measure of irony. Indeed, Josephus seems to have shared profound ideological similarities with both Paul and Jesus, ranging from his objection to forced circumcision, acquiescence to Romans, permitting association with "unclean" individuals, praising Roman army officers, "loving enemies," and believing in a paradoxically peace-loving "messiah." The outstanding difference, of course, is that Josephus claimed Vespasian was that messiah. Paul himself probably did not live to see Vespasian's reign.

Meanwhile, Vespasian was erecting a magnificent Temple of Peace in Rome (now destroyed) as he was calling for a new *Pax Romana*.

Josephus's views are so similar to those of a Christian, in fact, that the famous 18th Century translator of Josephus's entire corpus, William Whiston, concluded that Josephus must have been a secret Christian.

Despite his own wealth (Josephus tells us about the property he received from the Romans as a reward for his services), and thus, the hypocrisy that this opinion might imply, Josephus advocates the same position on wealth that we find in the New Testament. About the Essenes, for example, Josephus writes:

> It also deserves our admiration, how much *they
> exceed all other men that addict themselves to vir-
> tue*, and this in righteousness; and indeed to such a
> degree, that as it hath never appeared among any
> other men, neither Greeks nor barbarians, no, not for
> a little time, so hath it endured a long while among
> them. *This is demonstrated by that institution of theirs,
> which will not suffer any thing to hinder them from hav-
> ing all things in common; so that a rich man enjoys no
> more of his own wealth than he who hath nothing at
> all.* (Emphasis added.) (42)

Josephus admires the idea of communal property as a pinnacle
of virtue. This perfectly echoes the conduct of the earliest Christians
that we read about in Acts:

> All the believers were one in heart and mind. *No one
> claimed that any of their possessions was their own,
> but they shared everything they had...* And God's
> grace was so powerfully at work in them all that there
> were no needy persons among them. For from time
> to time those who owned land or houses sold them,
> brought the money from the sales and put it at the
> apostles' feet, and it was distributed to anyone who
> had need. (Emphasis added.) (43)

At Luke 3:11, we read that John the Baptist also advocated a
similar conception of communal property: "Anyone who has two
shirts should share with the one who has none, and anyone who
has food should do the same."
Christ also charges his disciples:

> Freely you have received; freely give. Do not get any
> gold or silver or copper to take with you in your belts—
> no bag for the journey or extra shirt or sandals or a
> staff, for the worker is worth his keep. (44)

The "blessing" of poverty is, of course, one of the repeated and central themes of the New Testament, from Jesus advising a "rich young man" to give all that he owns to the poor to the famous adage attributed to St. Paul, "the love of money is the root of all evil." (Although a better translation may be, "all kinds of evils.") (45) Paul instructs givers to give graciously and without complaint.

As Josephus tells us, the Essenes, too, believed in the virtue of poverty. According to the Dead Sea Scrolls, purist Jewish sectarians of the period actually called themselves "the Poor." As we have seen, the letter of James in the New Testament also contains a rebel-like threat against "the rich." (46)

Like the concept of the "messiah" itself, this love of poverty was rooted in the rebel movement, which surely must have appealed most to the poor and those oppressed by the Romans. It is therefore an idea that can only be hypocritically adopted by a wealthy Roman collaborator like Josephus who was working for a Roman emperor—even one who was known for his humble origins, ostentatious modesty and extravagant charity.

* * * * * * * *

There are many other fascinating religious parallels between the Gospels and Josephus. Like Christ, for example, Josephus also gives special veneration to the Jewish prophet Daniel (47), whose messianic prophecy has profound echoes in Jesus Christ's own prophecy of the Temple's destruction, the prophecy we have considered in such detail. According to Daniel:

> In my vision at night I looked, and there before me was one like a Son of Man, *coming with the clouds of heaven.* He approached the Ancient of Days and was led into his presence. He was given authority, glory and sovereign power; all nations and peoples of every language worshipped him. His dominion is an everlasting dominion that will not pass away, and his kingdom is one that will never be destroyed. (Emphasis added.) (48)

The term literally rendered as "son of man" in this passage simply means "human being" in Aramaic—but many translations of the Old Testament use the phrase "son of man," instead, since this is the title given to Jesus in the Gospels.

Jesus echoes Daniel's prophecy thus: "… you will see the Son of Man sitting at the right hand of the Mighty One and *coming on the clouds of heaven.*" (Emphasis added.) (49)

In perfect fulfillment of this prophecy, Tacitus tells us that before Titus destroyed the Temple in Jerusalem:

> Prodigies had occurred, which this nation, prone to superstition, but hating all religious rites, did not deem it lawful to expiate by offering and sacrifice. *There had been seen hosts joining battle in the skies, the fiery gleam of arms, the Temple illuminated by a sudden radiance from the clouds.* (Emphasis added.) (50)

Josephus may be Tacitus's source for this report since Josephus himself tells us this:

> …on the one and twentieth day of the month Artemisius, a certain prodigious and incredible phenomenon appeared: I suppose the account of it would seem to be a fable, were it not related by those that saw it, and were not the events that followed it of so considerable a nature as to deserve such signals; for, before sunsetting, *chariots and troops of soldiers in their armor were seen running about among the clouds, and surrounding of cities.* (Emphasis added.) (51)

Christians who still await such a vision to appear above the skies of Jerusalem should be aware that such a vision has already been reported, right down to that very specific detail.

* * * * * * * *

According to standard Christian assumptions, the Second Coming of Christ has not yet happened. If that is true, of course, Jesus

Christ made a mistake in the timing of his prophecy. He clearly and unequivocally predicted that the generation hearing him speak would not "pass away" before the events transpired. Jesus is quoted twice in the Gospel of Mark at Mark 9:1 and Mark 13:30 predicting the imminent arrival of the Kingdom of Heaven and the Coming of the Son of Man in Power within the current "generation," and this is repeated in the Gospels of Luke and Matthew at Luke 21:32, and Matthew 24:34.

If this was a mistake, Jesus must be counted as the first of many Christian prophets to come who would incorrectly predict the timing of the Apocalypse. Such an embarrassing error, if it is one, could not be a later Christian interpolation, for obvious reasons. This makes these well-attested passages all the more credibly authentic to the Gospels and fixes the date of their writing even more credibly no later than the 1st Century.

Scholars wrestling with these problems have come to believe that Jesus's earliest followers were convinced he was returning quite soon. They were so convinced that they confidently put the idea into the mouth of Jesus himself. There can be little doubt that the author of this passage intended his readers to believe the Second Coming was to be a 1st Century event. As a prophecy, that would have been a terribly bold assertion for such followers to make since the prediction also associated the Messiah's return with the destruction of Jerusalem and the defeat of Jewish hopes.

On the other hand, Jesus may have been right—but only if the thesis we have been exploring is right—i.e. only if Titus's entry into Jerusalem to level the Temple after spectral armies churned in the clouds *was* his glorious Second Coming. Again, the Gospels were written after Titus had accomplished these deeds.

If we accept at face value Jesus's own apocalyptic prophecy, and accept that his plainly stated prediction means precisely what it says, then Jesus himself perfectly justifies Josephus's own belief in a Flavian messiah. So convenient is this prophecy for Titus's claim to be the returning messiah that it was quite probably written after the events transpired as prophetic "proof" supporting the Flavians' messianic propaganda.

Titus Destroys the Temple in Jerusalem
by Nicolas Poussin (1638-1639)

Short of Josephus actually attesting his own belief in the Jesus Christ of the Gospels, Josephus's beliefs already match all of Christianity's main tenets. However, there may even be evidence that Flavius Josephus himself was aware of—and actually personally endorsed—Jesus Christ himself.

It's time to look at the most controversial evidence in support of this theory.

* * * * * * * *

Even though Josephus's own mentions of Christ, if they are credible, would predate by about two full decades the earliest surviving mention of Jesus by anyone outside Christian literature itself (which is widely conceded to be historically unreliable), the existence of such extraordinary evidence linking the Flavians so directly to Christianity probably shouldn't be as surprising as it is to most scholars, given what we have now seen.

The hypothesis of a Roman pedigree for the New Testament that we have been presenting has already been thoroughly demonstrated by all of the evidence without contradiction by simply taking that evidence at face value. It should be almost predictable, therefore, that the literature of the Flavian dynasty must, somewhere, actually sanction Christianity itself if this theory is correct.

All of the evidence suggests that the Gospels were written during the time of the Flavians as a kind of proof text for their messianic ascension to the throne after their victory over the messianic Jewish rebels. They seem tailored for the imperial cult of the

Emperor Titus Flavius Caesar Vespasianus Augustus, the son of God (his deified father) who was born on December 30 and who personally fulfilled the prophecies of Jesus at the time predicted to presage his return.

Bust of Titus, Herculaneum

Christian tradition holds that Jesus was 33 years old when he made his "triumphant" entry into Jerusalem and predicted the destruction of the Temple before he was crucified.

Born just a few years after the Crucifixion, Titus was 33 years old when he made his triumphant entry into Jerusalem and destroyed the Jewish Temple, *40 years later.*

Their humble origins, their claims to being the Jewish messiah (but with pagan elements added), their anti-Jewish status as man-gods, their advocacy of peace, Titus's fame as a healer of sickness, Vespasian's identical healing miracles, Titus's loving compassion, his fulfillment of Jesus's prophesied return within a generation coinciding with the Temple's destruction, and so much more, all reflect Jesus Christ as clearly as the symbol on Titus's coins.

The Gospels' story of Jesus unmistakably blames his death on the Jews and exonerates the Romans—to such an extent that Christians concluded the destruction of the Temple and Jerusalem must have been God's punishment for their treatment of Jesus. Both early Church writers Origen and Eusebius quite explicitly argued this, centuries later. The Gospel of Mark (thought to be composed around 71 CE by many scholars) could already reflect this causal relationship since in it Jesus warns Jerusalem of the destruction to come only days before his crucifixion. Jesus predicts false messiahs, war, and a catastrophic end to the rebellion against Roman rule.

Jesus even asks God to forgive the very Roman soldiers nailing him to the Cross, excusing them because they "know not what they do." (52) The Romans don't know any better, since they think they are executing a rebel who claimed to be "King of the Jews." It is only on these mistaken grounds that they proceed to "mock" and "kill him," and they are therefore forgiven by Christ himself.

Even the scene in the Gospels depicting Roman soldiers casting lots for Jesus's robe during the Crucifixion is, in fact, a veiled attack on the Jewish rebels, who, according to Josephus's own contemptuous account, at one time awarded high priesthoods by what Josephus views as a corrupt process of casting lots. Jesus's robe is a clear allusion to priestly vestments. (53) According to the Gospel of John, the garment was of one single piece—just as Josephus describes the garments of the high priests. (54) This famous scene is therefore a criticism not of Romans but of the corruption of the Jewish rebels' own process of selecting their religious leaders.

Jesus's forgiveness of his Roman executioners does not extend to his Jewish accusers in the Sanhedrin, however. Nor does he ask forgiveness for Judas, the disciple who had betrayed him. Nor does he ask it for the Jewish crowd that three times demanded his execution. In these cases, the excuse Jesus gives for the Roman soldiers driving nails into his flesh is denied the Jews—for they do know better.

Jesus had already condemned the Temple establishment for converting God's house into "a den of thieves." (55) In doing so he had provided justification for Titus's destruction of the Temple 40 years later, which Josephus, who was there, would describe in such strikingly similar visual details, including the ominous specter of armies in the clouds.

General Titus tears the curtain of the
Temple and enters the Holy of Holies

Upon witnessing the Crucifixion, we are told that it is a Roman "centurion" who "praised God" and said, "Surely this was a righteous man," according to Luke's Gospel. (56)

The Gospels are unfailingly consistent with a pro-Roman/anti-Jewish agenda, with the political and religious views of Josephus—and with the theory of their Roman provenance we have been presenting.

A Roman and, indeed, an imperial origin for the New Testament integrates and harmonizes all of the earliest evidence we have inherited about Christianity, including the pagan sources Tacitus, Suetonius, and Pliny the Younger, the archeological evidence, the historical evidence, the contemporary iconography, the works of Josephus, the New Testament, and even the Talmud. Such an interpretation stands independently simply on the agreement of all of these sources without any direct evidence that Titus Flavius Josephus, an employee of the Flavian emperors, personally endorsed Christianity or actually referred to Jesus Christ by name.

But there is evidence that he did. And it is time that we take a look at that evidence.

III. The Flavian Testimony for Christ

If the Gospels sprang from 1st Century Flavian propaganda, then we should, some might argue, expect to find actual textual evidence of a Flavian Christianity, in addition to the coins, iconography, art, architecture, history, politics, and the historical and personal relationships of the Flavians that we have already presented.

If the Flavians were bolstering their titles as Jewish messiahs by way of the Gospels, why shouldn't we expect Flavius Josephus, their own "Jewish" historian, to have directly participated in such an important effort?

Titus Flavius Josephus

On the other hand, could a man in Josephus's profession risk alienating his wider audience by admitting to such a belief or make any positive mention of Christianity to a 1st Century audience without compromising his credibility as an historian? The absence of such evidence might not be conclusive, therefore, one way or the other.

However, as remarkable as it may sound, Flavius Josephus says precisely what our theory predicts. And what he said about Jesus Christ has been a textual battlefield for theologians and scholars for centuries.

Flavius Josephus, the Flavians' own court historian, not only mentions Jesus Christ, but he does it before anyone else outside of Christian literature by decades. His description of Jesus Christ is, on its face, so extraordinary that it is often dismissed outright.

We have seen the same incredulity before: how could anyone so highly placed in Roman government, especially so early, have expressed such open sympathy for Christianity? And, once again, this is the same foundation for much of the doubt concerning the passage we are about to examine.

We must set aside mere incredulity now and try to see Josephus's reference to Jesus for what it means—as well as what it does not. As it has been passed down to us, *Antiquities of the Jews*, Josephus's exhaustive account of Jewish history, contains this amazing passage:

> At this time there was Jesus, a wise man, *if indeed one ought to call him a man*. For he was one who performed *wonderful works*, and a teacher of people who received the truth with pleasure. He stirred up both many Jews and many Greeks. *He was the Christ*. And when Pilate condemned him to the cross, since he was accused by the leading men among us, those who had loved him from the first did not desist, for he appeared to them on the third day, having life again, *as the prophets of God had foretold* these and countless other marvelous things about him. And until now the tribe of Christians, so named from him, is not extinct. (Emphasis added.) (1)

This passage is known as the *Testimonium Flavianum,* that is, the "Flavian Testimony for Christ."

If verified, this passage would be the very first mention of Jesus Christ by any historian or any other Roman source, predating even Pliny the Younger by two decades. In fact, if it was truly written by Josephus, it would predate all *archeological* evidence of Christianity currently accepted by historians (which does not include the new evidence we have presented in this book).

Yet, on a number of grounds, Josephus's testimony is just too good to be true for most scholars to accept.

The very fact that this passage paints Josephus as a Christian has been considered justification enough for most scholars to reject it. The generally accepted explanation for it appearing in a work by Josephus is that Christians must have added material to the text that was not original to his work. Maybe the entire passage was simply added at a later date.

This process of adding to an existing text is called "interpolation." Interpolation has been detected in the texts of certain other ancient writers whose works were manipulated by later editors. We have more than one example of this kind of deliberate Christian forgery, such as the aforementioned "correspondence" between St. Paul and the philosopher Seneca. Their work may have shared similar ideas, it is true, but the letters themselves look in every other respect to have been written much later and they have been uniformly rejected by Christian scholars for this reason.

Scholars have located the precise time that the suspected interpolation in Josephus's text must have taken place. But the problem with wholly dismissing Josephus's highly positive mention of Jesus is complicated by his positive references to other characters from the New Testament, such as John the Baptist and James, to whom Josephus elsewhere refers as "the Brother of Christ" in yet a *second* reference to Jesus by Josephus.

Here, then, is what Josephus says about John the Baptist:

> Now some of the Jews thought that the destruction of Herod's army came from God, and that very justly, as a punishment of what he did against John, that was called the Baptist: for Herod slew him, who was a good man, and commanded the Jews to exercise virtue, both as to righteousness towards one another, and piety towards God, and so to come to baptism; for that the washing [with water] would be acceptable to him, if they made use of it, not in order to the putting away [or the remission] of some sins [only], but for the purification of the body; supposing still that the soul was thoroughly purified beforehand by righteousness. Now when [many] others came in crowds about

him, for they were very greatly moved [or pleased] by hearing his words, Herod, who feared lest the great influence John had over the people might put it into his power and inclination to raise a rebellion, (for they seemed ready to do any thing he should advise,) thought it best, by putting him to death, to prevent any mischief he might cause, and not bring himself into difficulties, by sparing a man who might make him repent of it when it would be too late. Accordingly he was sent a prisoner, out of Herod's suspicious temper, to Macherus, the castle I before mentioned, and was there put to death. Now the Jews had an opinion that the destruction of this army was sent as a punishment upon Herod, and a mark of God's displeasure to him. (Emphasis added.) (2)

This is extraordinary. As we have seen, Josephus elsewhere claimed that God Himself was on the Roman's side. And yet we find him expressing sympathy for John the Baptist—just the sort of "innovator" who stirred up trouble, like the Zealots, for whom Josephus normally expresses contempt.

King Herod Antipas views the head of
John the Baptist by Henri Leopold Levy (1872)

King Herod Antipas is said to have feared just such trouble might be instigated by the Baptist. Yet, far from criticizing him, Josephus only reports that the people believe John's execution deserves divine punishment. Given his declarations that the Jewish rebellion was doomed from the start, Josephus shows an unusual sympathy for a messianic prophet who is suspected of inciting rebellion. He is an employee of the Flavians, and yet he is expressing the same kind of sympathy Christ exhibits for this Biblical figure.

Josephus also positively reports that John preached a version of the so-called "Love Commandments," which were advocated by Jesus and regarded in earlier Jewish thought as the apex or summary of the law. (3) Josephus shares with the Baptist, and with Jesus, the belief that loving God and loving one's neighbor comprise the essence of morality.

And John the Baptist is not the only New Testament figure that Josephus admires. He also mentions James the Just, referring to him as the "brother" of Jesus in an equally positive way. Once more, we find him defending a messianic ideologue rather than the "authority" figures opposing him:

> ...Ananus...took the high priesthood, was a bold man in his temper, and very insolent; he was also of the sect of the Sadducees, who are *very rigid in judging offenders*, above all the rest of the Jews, as we have already observed; when, therefore, Ananus was of this disposition, he thought he had now a proper opportunity. Festus was now dead, and Albinus was but upon the road; *so he assembled the Sanhedrim of judges*, and brought before them *the brother of Jesus, who was called Christ, whose name was James, and some others;* and when he had formed an accusation against them as *breakers of the law*, he delivered them to be stoned: but as for those who seemed *the most equitable of the citizens, and such as were the most uneasy at the breach of the laws, they disliked what was done*; they also sent to the king, desiring him to send to Ananus that he should act so no more, for that what he had already done was not to be justified; nay, some of them went also to meet Albinus as he was on his journey from Alexandria, and informed him that it was not lawful for Ananus to assemble a Sanhedrim without his consent—whereupon Albinus complied with what they said, and wrote in anger to Ananus, and threatened that he would bring him to punishment for what he had done; on which king

Agrippa took the high priesthood from him, when he had ruled but three months, and made Jesus, the son of Damneus, high priest." (Emphasis added.) (4)

"Innovators" to whom Josephus is typically hostile are here once again depicted approvingly. True, there is no Roman governor requiring exoneration and the Roman governor's imminent arrival soon spells trouble for the high priest who killed James. Still, Josephus here is representing a messianic idealist as an innocent victim.

To properly analyze these controversial passages requires us to explore a few technical arguments in order to understand the scholarly debate that has raged over what might be the very first historical evidence of Jesus outside the New Testament itself.

* * * * * * * *

One common Christian objection to the *Testimonium Flavianum* is that a true Christian would have faced persecution and death rather than admit that any man other than Jesus was the Messiah. Since Josephus claimed Vespasian was the Messiah, he could not be a Christian, according to this argument.

Our theory answers this objection, of course: for Josephus, the victory of his Flavian masters *was* the Glorious Coming of the Messiah, and its timing miraculously fulfilled Christ's own words. Indeed, by the conventional understanding, whether he was a pious Jew or a Christian, Josephus would face the same "problem" worshipping an emperor. In either case, he seems to have found an elegant solution: by identifying the emperor *as* the Messiah, he could retain his Jewish faith *and* honor the emperor above all other men, simultaneously.

He could worship the emperor as divine—but only if he shared the distinctly un-Jewish Christian idea that the Messiah could also be divine, like a pagan man-god or a Roman emperor, living in the flesh on earth, like Caesar, or like Christ.

Some scholars argue that Josephus proclaimed Vespasian the Messiah in order to justify his betrayal of the Jewish cause—and to justify the treachery of many other Jews who had assisted Rome in the war. (5) This is certainly true, but it does not preclude Jewish messianic claims actually being part of the new imperial cult that Josephus would probably have been enlisted to help develop for the Flavians after the war.

Could a pious Christian have ever served a Roman emperor? What if the Roman emperor was the second coming of Jesus Christ?

Roman emperors themselves would become pious Christians in time, of course, and pious Christians would become Roman emperors.

Another argument against the passage's authenticity: If Josephus actually was Christian, how could he advertise it like this without fear of prosecution by his Roman patrons? How could he write anything like the *Testimonium Flavianum* under the watchful eye of the emperor while on his payroll? Again, we can readily see the answer to this objection, too.

Perhaps the most common objection of all to the authenticity of the *Testimonium*, however, insists that Josephus is simply too highly connected with Roman authorities to credibly have any sort of sympathy with Christianity during this nascent stage in Church history. And again, a Flavian provenance for the Gospels and a Roman hand behind most of the rest of the New Testament answers this objection, easily and with no conflict or contradiction.

If the Gospels were part of the Flavian imperial cult's propaganda effort to establish their claims as authentic Jewish messiahs after the conquest of Judea, and their mission was to reform Judaism into something manageable by the Roman state, then of course this controversial passage would have enjoyed official sanction. It would follow that Josephus's attributed works were themselves important and foundational elements of this imperial project.

According to the theory of Christian origins now emerging from all of the facts, we should actually expect only a Flavian apologist to make any reference to Jesus Christ at so early a date—especially any positive one. So the fact that no other contemporary historians mention Jesus at all is quite predictable and perfectly explained.

However, we must still wonder: even if we are right and Josephus had no fear of prosecution himself for praising Christ, could he risk alienating his wider pagan and Hellenized Jewish audience by expressing partisan sympathy for Jesus Christ in a work of history?

If Christianity is conventionally seen as a splinter group of messianic Jewish rebels spreading their gospel in the face of Roman opposition, then any positive mention of Jesus or those associated with him by a highly placed Roman operative like Josephus in the 1st Century must be absurd on its face. Even if the original Josephus passage was more tepid in its assertions, that such an uncritical reference to Jesus Christ could exist at all in Josephus's work, without any other supporting evidence or political qualifications, implies at least a Flavian sanction of Christianity.

Therefore, we must be extremely careful as we consider what, if anything, might have been added to the *Testimonium Flavianum* and what, if anything, was original to Flavius Josephus's text.

* * * * * * * *

First, we must recognize that there is very good reason to believe that this crucial passage was originally far less grand in its claims about Jesus Christ.

We know this because the early 4th Century Christian historian Eusebius quotes the *Testimonium* just as we have it in our texts today, but his 3rd Century predecessor, Origen, the first Christian writer to make substantial use of Josephus, repeatedly states in his work that Josephus did *not* accept Jesus *as the Christ.*

So something must have happened in between these two sources.

Despite the historian Josephus's heavy influence on theologians, no Church Father cited the famous *Testimonium* prior to Eusebius, author of the earliest history of the Christian Church, in the 4th Century. Josephus's influence on Christian writers down through the centuries is profound. While his influence grew over time, his impact came relatively early and was widespread. According to scholar Louis Feldman, at least eleven Church Fathers prior to or contemporary with the early Christian historian Eusebius cited Josephus. (6) As Feldman also observes, the widely respected translator, St. Jerome, cited Josephus no less than 90 times, calling him a second Livy. (7) Yet, before Eusebius, all of them failed to mention the *Testimonium.*

And it is interesting that even Josephus does not mention Jesus in *Wars of the Jews*, his earlier work. However, in the part of his later work, *Antiquities of the Jews,* that overlaps his earlier work, he does. Why?

Most Christian writers in Eusebius's own time do not mention this passage, either, and Jerome, who does, modifies it to read only: Jesus "was believed" to be the Messiah.

So, it is easy to see how all of this scholarly controversy might weigh heavily in favor of dismissing the *Testimonium* as an outright forgery.

Yet, the reluctance of Church Fathers to mention this passage may reflect Jerome's motive for modifying it: they might have shared the same doubt that has lead so many recent scholars to disbelieve that Josephus, whether as Jew or Roman, could mention Jesus at all, let alone so positively, given his proximity to Roman emperors. Their reluctance to cite Josephus's passage may simply be another example of the same baseless incredulity that has deflected so much evidence of Christianity's Roman provenance.

When the Gospels are considered as Flavian propaganda, it becomes easy to see why other historians contemporary to Josephus never mentioned Jesus Christ. Indeed, that would explain why *none* of them did. And the absence of a similar reference in Josephus's earlier work also becomes explainable, as this aspect of Flavian propaganda had probably not yet been fleshed out when Josephus had written his earlier chronicle of the war.

Most importantly, it is also highly probable that if the original passage had been a more neutral mention of Jesus, as we shall see was probably the case, Christians would have overlooked what they disdained as a "Jewish source" for being insufficiently enthusiastic about Christ. The Church father Origen leveled that very criticism at Josephus, as we shall see. Contemporary scholars, however, are far more focused on finding corroboration for the historically dubious Gospels than early Christians, who believed the Gospels were all the textual "evidence" they needed.

And yet, over time, this confidence would have yielded to an increasing need for the historical attestation of Jesus that Josephus uniquely provides for the Church. After all, no one else substantiates the existence of Christ so early outside the New Testament itself.

The deep impact of Flavius Josephus's work on Christians, whether they made use of his *Testimonium* or not, demonstrates how fundamentally sympathetic his work is to Christianity in general. Many less sympathetic texts from other authors of this period, such as Justus of Tiberius, did not survive in Christian libraries at all and are lost to history.

Why would Origen in the 3rd Century be the very first Christian writer to make substantial use of Josephus? He may simply have studied Josephus because of his field of interest, which seemed to encompass themes "closely related with the Bible [Old Testament] and the Jews," and possibly also because of Origen's own "background and interests" in history, as one scholar suggests. (8) So why does Origen's work present a serious problem for the authenticity of Josephus's testimonial to Christ?

Origen

The most important Christian philosopher before St. Augustine, Origen was a prolific writer and a well-read scholar in the 3rd Century who appreciated the work of Hellenized Hebrews like Philo and Josephus. He also appreciated how much the work of Josephus could contribute to a deeper understanding of Christianity.

The 2nd Century pagan writer Celsus, the critic of Christianity who first reported the story that Jesus was the illegitimate child of a Roman soldier, is known only through Origen's critique of his work. For obvious reasons, Celsus's own writings were not preserved by Christians and don't exist today. (We can never know how much we will never know because of such censorship.) But in his critique of Celsus, *Contra Celsus*, Origen makes use of Josephus to rebut Celsus's charges, writing:

> I would like to say to Celsus, who represents the Jew as accepting somehow John as a Baptist, who baptized Jesus, that the existence of John the Baptist, baptizing for the remission of sins, is related by one who lived no great length of time after John and Jesus. For in the 18th book of his *Antiquities of the Jews*, Josephus bears witness to John as having been a Baptist, and as promising purification to those who underwent the rite. Now this writer, *although not believing in Jesus as the Christ, in seeking after the cause of the fall of Jerusalem and the destruction of the Temple, whereas he ought to have said that the conspiracy against Jesus was the cause of these calamities befalling the people, since they put to death Christ, who was a prophet, says nevertheless—being, although against his will, not far from the truth*—that these disasters happened to the Jews *as a punishment for the death of James the Just, who was a brother of Jesus (called Christ)*—the Jews having put him to death, although he was a man most distinguished for his justice. Paul, a genuine disciple of Jesus, says that he regarded this James as a brother of the Lord, *not so much on account of their relationship by blood, or of their being brought up together, as because of his virtue and doctrine.* If, then, *he says that it was on account of James that the desolation of Jerusalem was made to overtake the Jews, how should it not be more in accordance with reason to say that it happened on account (of the death) of Jesus Christ*, of whose divinity so many Churches are witnesses, composed of those who have been convened from a flood of sins, and who have joined themselves to the Creator, and who refer all their actions to His good pleasure. (Emphasis added.) (9)

Origen accepts Josephus's self-identification as a "Jew." Any assistance he provides Christians, therefore, according to Origen, is against his will, and even more compelling. The fact that Origen finds Josephus so compelling an authority is itself significant. Yet, writing in the 3rd Century, Origen is explicit on this point: Josephus did *not* accept "Jesus as the Christ," in direct contradiction of the Josephus text that we have inherited today.

Eusebius, who wrote in the early 4th Century, quotes the full *Testimonium*, with all the bells and whistles that we have today, however.

So, we know that the passage was tweaked sometime between Origen and Eusebius, around the turn of the 4th Century.

Other things that bothered Origen about Josephus are very interesting. He decries Josephus's claim that the Temple was destroyed "on account" of James's death rather than because of Jesus's death. Origen seems to be correcting Josephus on something that does not exist in any Josephus text that we possess today. So something *else* was changed.

Origen elsewhere writes:

> [The Jewish War] began in the reign of Nero, and lasted till the government of Vespasian, whose son Titus destroyed Jerusalem, on account, as Josephus says, of James the Just, the brother of Jesus who was called Christ, but in reality, as the truth makes clear, on account of Jesus Christ the Son of God. (Emphasis added.) (10)

Here he is relating that Josephus *justified the deeds of the Emperor Titus* by way of the Jews' murder of *James*. This reference in Josephus does not survive at all now. But such a motive would make sense coming from Josephus, the Flavian apologist. To show that internal strife among the Jews was responsible for the events that led to the destruction of their Temple certainly distracts from the Roman role in that deed, even if it falls short of a full "justification" for it, while the murder of a good man, such as James, might meet the case. In yet another work, Origen says:

And James is he whom Paul says in the Epistle to the Galatians that he saw, "But other of the Apostles saw I none, save James the Lord's brother." And to so great a reputation among the people for righteous-ness did this James rise, that Flavius Josephus, who wrote the *Antiquities of the Jews* in twenty books, *when wishing to exhibit the cause why the people suffered so great misfortunes that even the Temple was razed to the ground*, said, that these things hap-pened to them *in accordance with the wrath of God in consequence of the things which they had dared to do against James the brother of Jesus who is called Christ*. And the wonderful thing is, that, *though he did not accept Jesus as Christ, he yet gave testi-mony that the righteousness of James was so great*; and *he says that the people thought that they had suffered these things because of James*. And Jude, who wrote a letter of few lines, it is true, but filled with the healthful words of heavenly grace, said in the preface, "Jude, the servant of Jesus Christ and the brother of James." (Emphasis added.) (11)

Well. Origen is not only reporting (for the third time) that Josephus said the Temple's destruction was God's punishment for the murder of James, an assertion no longer found in Josephus's work, but here he adds that Josephus claimed the people understood this divine punishment was for the murder of James. So this was a widespread belief at the time. This seems to further elaborate what Origen was objecting to in the previous passage.

If Origen is correctly reporting this Josephus passage, this, too, makes sense. As Josephus's passage about John the Baptist shows, divine punishments for the murder of a good man were to be expected by both contemporary Jews and, apparently, by Josephus himself.

Origen once more makes clear that the original passage in Josephus as he read it, however, could not have said, "Jesus was the Christ," as it appears in the text passed down to us.

Many scholars have tried to "fix" the text of Josephus so that it agrees with Origen's description of it. This is a useful exercise. If we omit what must have been missing from Origen's copy of Josephus, we get something like this:

> At this time there was Jesus, [a wise man. For he was one who performed wonderful works, and a teacher of people who received the truth with pleasure. He stirred up both many Jews and many Greeks.] And when Pilate condemned him to the cross, since he was accused by the leading men among us, those who had loved him from the first did not desist. And until now the tribe of Christians, so named from him, is not extinct.

Any of the bracketed material may have also been omitted, but its omission is not strictly necessary to approximate the text that Origen described.

So, from Origen we can tell that the reference to Jesus was significantly augmented at a later date. We can also see that a passage Origen found objectionable suggesting that James's death, instead of Jesus's, precipitated God's punishment of the Hebrews appears to have been completely excised from the text. Origen refers to this missing material on no less than three separate occasions. Both later "adjustments" of Josephus's text seem to "fix" the problems Origen complained about.

If we eliminate the *Testimonium* altogether, we are left to puzzle over Josephus's admiration for James, whom he calls "the brother of Jesus." This *second* reference to Jesus by Josephus suggests that Josephus's original account of Jesus, though doubtlessly tampered with by Christians, must have at least been present in the original text and that it was positive even if it was not overtly proclaiming the exclusive truth of Christianity. This alone would be unexplainable in any context other than the theory we are considering.

Josephus's passages about James and John the Baptist, in contrast to the *Testimonium* itself, have almost never been challenged by scholars as later interpolations. As a result, Christians still frequently cite Josephus as an important historical source to this day. So, let us look at Flavius Josephus's *second* mention of Christ.

This one is contained in his description of the death of James, whom he calls: "the brother of Jesus, who was called the Christ." Not surprisingly, this reference to Christ by Josephus has recently been challenged, too. And, because the scholar who challenges it provides us with an illustrative example of recent historical reasoning in this field, analyzing it will prove instructive.

Scholar Richard Carrier has made the unusual claim that there was no mention of Christ at all in the original James passage from Josephus's work. He suggests that the part that reads James's brother Jesus "was called Christ" is *also* an interpolation. This leaves us, he claims, with no authentic mention of Jesus Christ in any of the works of Flavius Josephus. (12)

What is Carrier's argument?

Immediately after Josephus describes the murder of James he relates that a "Jesus, son of Damneus" was named high priest to replace Ananus, who was removed for killing James. Carrier suggests that the "James" whose murder Josephus had just recounted is the brother of this Jesus (the new high priest) and not the "Jesus who was called the Christ." According to Carrier, this last phrase, "who was called the Christ," was interpolated later by Christians just like the *Testimonium*. After all, Carrier explains, replacing the high priest Ananus, who killed James, with James's brother may have been part of King Agrippa's remedy for the crime.

A lot of suppositions are being made with no evidence whatsoever here. How does Carrier propose such a change in the text could have happened?

Carrier offers that a Christian reader of Josephus may have missed the connection between the appointment of the High Priest Jesus and the previously mentioned "James, the brother of Jesus" and mistook "James, the brother of Jesus" for James, who is called "the brother of our Lord" by Paul in Galatians. Carrier imagines that such a Christian might have written in the *margin* of his copy of Josephus "who was called the Christ" next to "brother of Jesus," and his mistake was memorialized for all eternity after a second mistake was made when subsequent transcribers copied the margin note into the text. All ancient texts were copied by hand, and there are other known instances where marginalia was introduced into ancient texts in this fashion, but there is no evidence any of this happened in this particular case.

Why any Christian would eccentrically note "who was called the Christ" instead of simply "who was the Christ" remains unexplained in Carrier's theory.

There is no reason to think that "Jesus, son of Damneus" was even of the same political party as the "James" who was murdered, let alone that he was his brother. And, if James did not belong to a party hostile to the Temple establishment, why would the high priest have had him killed in the first place? And if so, why would the King replace the High Priest responsible for his execution with someone hostile to the Temple establishment?

Aside from this obvious political *non sequitur,* Josephus adds to Carrier's difficulties by next telling us that the new high priest "Jesus" who replaced Ananus was bribed right along with the new Roman governor, Albinus, and that inter-priestly relations did not improve, as one might have expected if an ally of the murdered James had been appointed in response to his murder. (13)

In fact, the new high priest seems to have intensified the unrest, for Josephus tells us that the Temple establishment still took the "tithes" traditionally reserved for the lesser or poorer priests during this time, and that this, in turn, set off a new reaction from the rebel Sicarii—who responded by kidnapping the son of Ananus and demanding the release of ten rebel prisoners in exchange for his life. (14)

It is obvious that the rebels would not have reacted like this if the murdered James was not one of them. And if the new high priest had been the brother of such a rebel martyr, this would surely have been mentioned. And if James was *not* a rebel ideologue then the motive for killing him is left entirely unexplained by Josephus.

If, on the other hand, as pre-interpolation Origen reports, Josephus claimed James's death precipitated God's wrath and the Jewish defeat, then the rest of Josephus's narrative makes perfect sense. That murder, not Jesus's four decades earlier, set off an immediate uprising that led to the war and ultimately the Temple's destruction by Titus. This was the actual history of events suppressed by Christian scholarship in subsequent centuries.

The lesser priests' violent reaction to further abuse by the high priests would also remain inexplicable if it was not already stoked by the crime Josephus just related—the murder of James. This seems to confirm that Josephus made the argument Origen attributes to him, which Carrier suggests he never made.

Carrier also oddly complains that Origen would have commented on it if Josephus had mentioned Jesus Christ elsewhere. But Origen did comment—on Josephus's lack of belief in Jesus "as Christ," which clearly implies that Josephus did mention him. Had Josephus not mentioned Jesus at all, Origen would not have complained that Josephus had merely denied his status as "Christ."

Had the James passage been the only place Origen read about Jesus in Josephus's text, it could not have served as the basis for his complaint, either, for there Jesus is at least called Jesus "the Christ" in a phrase similar to one used in the Gospel of Matthew. Carrier concedes that Origen must have seen this passage and this phrase (at least as an interpolation) or Origen could not have thought that the "brother of Christ" was mentioned in Josephus's text, at all.

The reference to the "brother of Christ" suggests there must have been another mention of Jesus elsewhere, one in which Josephus passively observes that his followers thought him to be Christ without attesting to his own belief, as he does in the corrected version of the *Testimonium*.

Carrier also posits that Josephus would never have used any phrase like that found in Matthew, for example the phrase, "the one called the Christ." However, because it is a bland enough phrase that any non-Christian might have comfortably used, the real incongruity is its use in *Matthew*, not its use in Josephus. Why didn't the evangelist Matthew simply say "the Christ" in his Gospel—just as the interpolation of Josephus does? Why did Matthew say "the one called the Christ"? This is a case of Matthew strangely using a phrase that a cautious historian like Josephus might understandably employ. This tentative qualification is more out of place in the Gospels than it is in Josephus—indeed, this might have been the original wording of the Testimonium, the same hesitation that had irritated Origen. (As always, it is important to remember that Josephus was writing his history at the same time that the Gospel of Matthew was being written.)

Because no surviving Josephus text links the Jewish defeat to James's murder, Carrier argues that Origen must also have been mistaken about his own source for this idea. This only adds improbability on top of improbability. Where does Carrier think Origen got this idea if not from Josephus? Carrier's answer is that Origen's actual source must have been the 2nd Century Christian Hegesippus.

Carrier proposes that Origen misattributed to Josephus an argument made by the later Christian writer Hegesippus that claims that it was James's murder, not Jesus's, that precipitated the war. Thus, in addition to his marginalia mistake and transcription-error hypothesis, Carrier adds that Origen misattributed his sources, as well. Only if all these contorted improbabilities are true can Carrier's argument make any sense.

However, if Hegesippus or any other Christian was Origen's real source, then we are only more perplexed. Hegesippus may have been a converted Jew, but he was certainly a Christian. Origen's surprise comes from the fact that Josephus, someone he regards as a Jew, should have alleged that the Jews were punished in the war because of James's death—the martyrdom of a *Christian* leader, according to the Bible—at the hands of Jewish authorities. Origen is surprised by how *pro-Christian* the supposedly Jewish (and Roman) Josephus is, in addition to being disgruntled that Josephus did not go all the way and name the death of Christ himself as the cause of the Jewish defeat.

On the other hand, Origen would have no reason to be surprised at Hegesippus or any other Christian for showing sympathy for Christianity. In that case, the only surprise Origin might have expressed was that a *Christian* writer like Hegesippus failed to connect the punishment of the Jewish nation to the death of Jesus Christ rather than surprise that a Jew could show any sympathy for a martyred Christian like James. Why *would* Hegesippus, a Christian, ever claim such a thing?

Even if a Christian like Hegesippus did argue that the Jews lost the war because God was punishing them for killing James, as Carrier speculates, this doesn't mean that Josephus did not also make the same argument. If anything, Josephus would have been Hegesippus's likely source for such an idea. In any event, we don't have the passage of Hegesippus that Carrier suggests may have existed. And our only source for Hegesippus's text, Eusebius, attributes the argument that James's death caused the war to Josephus—just as Origen does.

This is the kind of roundabout Christian scholars often construct to circle around the Flavian and Roman relationships that seem too close to Christianity's origins. However, the fact remains: Origen plainly states that Josephus attributed the cause of the Jewish War to the murder of the Christian James. The normally careful scholar does so in no fewer than three works. And if Origen is to be believed when he suggests Josephus's text did *not* say "Jesus was the Christ," then he should be believed when he tells us what Josephus *did* say about James and Jesus.

Before Origen made use of the work of Josephus in the 3rd Century, and he was the first Christian writer to make extensive use of Josephus, there would have been no motive for Christians to embellish Josephus's work. Any failure to name Jesus "the Christ" by the "Jew" Josephus could have been explained away even as they made use of his historical works for other purposes.

However, by the time of Eusebius, when the full, glowing reference to Jesus Christ in Josephus was present, after Christianity enjoyed official sanction under the Roman Emperor Constantine, more than one copy of Josephus's histories surely existed, and these copies must have been housed in more than one pagan public library. Yet, Eusebius "quotes" the newly augmented Josephus text with no fear of being contradicted. This may well suggest that by this time Josephus's work had been *officially* "corrected," with the authoritative approval of the emperor himself.

We have another reason to believe that a passage about the impact of James's murder did exist in the original Josephus. In his passage about John the Baptist, Josephus tells us that the destruction of Herod Antipas's army was *punishment for killing the Baptist.* The argument is classic Josephus; it is just the kind of providential argument Origen reports Josephus making about James.

* * * * * * * *

So, from Origen's description of the text of Josephus, we know that Josephus's reference to Christ was tampered with. It is hardly a stretch to suppose that the offending passage about James's murder being the *casus belli* for the Jewish War (instead of the death of Jesus) disappeared around the same time the amplified *Testimonium* proclaiming Jesus to be the true Christ had appeared. As scholars have shown, in all probability both changes were made in direct response to Origen's complaints.

However, since Origen's criticisms of Josephus's text seem to have stimulated this Christian interpolation, what Origen reports about the original text should be regarded as highly credible.

As this book has proven, Carrier's additional assumption that Josephus, as a 1st Century historian employed by Roman emperors, could never mention Christ, is not a valid assumption. This is the faulty premise upon which the rest of his succession of suppositions relies. If Christianity was still just an underground group among Jews, as the conventional understanding assumes, why would Josephus, of all people, be mentioning Christ, or, indeed, be the very first person to mention Christ outside the New Testament? And how could the murder of James, by conventional understanding a Roman-accommodating, peace-loving *Christian,* incite war with Rome?

Of course, we have the answers: the *"Jewish*-Christian" movement James belonged to was an ideological wing of the rebels who were threatening Rome. James *wasn't* a pacifist. His sect was devoted to strict Torah observance, and for that reason was anti-Roman and in bitter conflict with Paul. It was these rebel "Christians" who could be most plausibly blamed for the Great Fire of Rome only two years after James's murder. And the Jewish War commenced only two years after that. The religious positions that brought James into conflict with Paul explain why the rebels regarded James so highly—and why they reacted so violently to his murder—and why there was anger directed at Paul—and why there was fury directed at Rome. *All is explained.*

When Origen refers to Josephus he almost never provides us the exact passage. As we have already observed, Origen may be the first Christian writer to make substantial use of Josephus simply because his "themes were closely related with the Bible [Old Testament] and the Jews" and because of his "background and interests" in history. (15) Other Christians would have ignored a Jewish writer who did not openly proclaim Jesus to be "the Christ." There is simply no reason to impute such extensive errors to Origen as

Carrier does, other than a prejudicial disposition to find the James passage fraudulent because it attests to Jesus's historical existence at too early a stage at too high a level of Roman government—assumptions we can now see are unfounded.

* * * * * * * *

We are not finished with the objections to the *Testimonium*. It is so controversial, its implications so profound, that it continues to be a field of pitched battles among scholars—and we can certainly see why.

Scholar G.J. Goldberg, for example, has observed a number of linguistic similarities between the *Testimonium Flavianum* and the Gospel of Luke's account of the Resurrection visions of travelers on the road to Emmaus. (16) This has suggested to him that a Christian versed in Luke must have been responsible for the Jesus Christ interpolation in Josephus's work. Yet this does not demonstrate that the *Testimonium* was a later interpolation at all, but merely that a dependency or shared provenance exists between these two sources. From this, for all we know, Josephus himself was the author of Luke or had read it himself. Or perhaps the author of Luke had read Josephus. Again, both works were being written during the same period.

For a long time scholars did not challenge the authenticity of Josephus's mention of James and John the Baptist, even while routinely challenging the *Testimonium* as a forgery or an error. Only recent skeptics, such as Carrier, have questioned the James passage, as well, since it, too, seems to require falsification—but only because it comes from the imperial pen of a Flavian historian at too early a stage to seem credible.

However, just as we wondered why Josephus was sympathetic to John the Baptist, we must also ask: if James was a rebel whose martyrdom (instead of Jesus's) really did ignite the Jewish War, then why was Josephus, a Roman collaborator, so positive about him unless Josephus was attempting to express sympathy for Christianity? If the theory that we are considering is correct, of course, and Josephus was in sympathy with a form of Christianity, the question virtually answers itself. Here we see Josephus doing precisely what Paul had done earlier by engaging with James: attempting to co-opt the messianic Jewish movement for pro-Roman ends.

The matter has become especially urgent as scholars have come to realize that Josephus's secondary mention of Christ through his "brother" may, by itself, confirm at least the partial authenticity of the deeply problematic *Testimonium*. The specific phrase used in Josephus's mention of James can be translated, "the brother of Jesus, *the aforementioned Christ*," and not just "Jesus, who *was called* Christ."

Even if this were just formula or linguistic filler, it would be out of character for Josephus to have mentioned someone with an unusual name or title like "Christ" without giving it an explanation elsewhere. Scholars have argued that the absence of such an explanation implies that there must have already been one somewhere in his work. (17) The very formula, "X, the brother of Y" seems to imply that Y has been previously mentioned, since Y is used to identify X.

As we have observed, why would Origen criticize Josephus for failing to identify Jesus as *the Christ* if he had not mentioned Jesus Christ at all? If Josephus had not mentioned Jesus, that would have been Origen's complaint instead, since Origen found Josephus so convenient to cite for many other historical purposes.

It would have been much easier to enhance an existing reference than to create an entirely new one. The interpolation itself may suggest that Josephus made at least some original mention of Jesus upon which later embellishments could be added.

Skeptics note that a Jewish historian contemporary to Josephus, Justus of Tiberias, whose work has not survived, did not mention Jesus at all even though his history covered the same period of time in which Jesus is alleged to have lived. (We know of his account only through a description of it by the Byzantine Christian, Photius, since the original work by Justus of Tiberias is lost to history.) (18)

But of course this cannot be regarded as evidence that Josephus's mentions of Christ are forgeries because a Flavian origin of Christianity easily explains this discrepancy. Only Flavian apologists would have had any reason to assert the existence of Jesus, much less mention him in a favorable light, at this time. Indeed, we should expect *only* a Jewish Flavian apologist such as Josephus to assert Jesus's existence so early if the Gospels were a creation of Flavian propaganda created to prophesy their status as Jewish messiahs.

In summary, the evidence suggests that Flavius Josephus is likely to have mentioned Jesus Christ. And his mention of him was probably just as positive as his references to John the Baptist and James the Just. The passage in which he praises Jesus and notes his death, however, was clearly tampered with by Christians around the time of Eusebius, dramatically augmenting his claims about Jesus while removing references to the murder of James as the incitement to the war.

As an historian, Josephus had to model himself after the great historians to whom a Roman or Hellenized audience was accustomed, such as Thucydides or Polybius. This required a nonsectarian detachment and objectivity. This kind of neutrality is exactly what is absent from Josephus's *Testimonium* of Jesus Christ as we have received it down through the centuries. For this reason alone, Josephus, whether or not he was Christian, would probably not have called Jesus "the Christ" even if he had been a sincere and devout Christian.

However, why should Josephus record Jesus *at all*, a person who supposedly died 60 years prior to his pen touching the page, an obscure founder of a minor sectarian offshoot of Judaism? And how could Josephus have ever referred to Jesus in any positive way while subject to his imperial masters' tacit approval unless Christianity enjoyed some form of imperial Flavian sanction, especially considering the war against messianic Judaism that had just been concluded? Only later Christians could view Josephus's history as inadequate for not openly declaring Jesus to be "the Christ."

Taken together, Josephus's positive mentions of any Christian protagonists is remarkable enough. Such references constitute an official sanctioning by Josephus, and at least implicitly by the Flavian dynasty itself, of the prominent Christian figures Jesus, James and John the Baptist. The only resistance to believing that the Flavians' historian could have mentioned Christ comes down to an instinctive aversion to its problematic imperial provenance at so early a date.

* * * * * * * *

If our theory is correct, then who could have written the Gospels?

For the answer to that, let us explore yet another remarkable set of literary connections between the life and works of Josephus and the New Testament.

We have already seen that stories and language from sacred Hebrew scriptures were liberally used by the authors of the Gospels to create accounts of Jesus's life, an aspect of the Gospels that has long been acknowledged and studied by New Testament scholars. The examples are numerous. Moses, in particular, seems to have served as an inspiration for the story of the "lawgiver" Jesus. The most obvious parallel to Moses is the slaughter of infant sons by a wicked king at the birth of both of these "deliverers." Also, both prophets deliver God's law from a "mount." We have also seen how the Old Testament Joseph parallels "Joseph" in the Gospel of Matthew. The former interpreted prophetic dreams in Egypt while the latter "father" of Jesus, named Joseph, had a prophetic dream that led him to Egypt.

We have also seen how Josephus's own life is reflected in the lives of both Jesus and Paul in the New Testament.

But there is another group of strikingly similar parallels in the New Testament between Josephus's life and the *Old Testament* that we should also consider.

Both Josephus and the New Testament usually rely on the Septuagint, which is the most famous Greek translation of Hebrew scripture, when referencing the Old Testament. However, both also sometimes cite material that is apparently from Hebrew or Aramaic editions. That mixture can be analyzed in both and compared.

In writing the *Antiquities*, Josephus mined the precious documents that the Romans had plundered from the Jerusalem Temple, given to him by Titus, as sources for his comprehensive recapitulation of Hebrew literature. Therefore, Josephus used precisely the same *mixture* of sources, Greek, Hebrew and Aramaic, that we know to have been incorporated into the life of Jesus in the Gospels.

Josephus and the New Testament not only use the same sources but employ the same *methodology* in using that mix of sources.

For example, according to the Book of Genesis, the Hebrew Joseph was sold as a slave by his envious brothers after he told them about his *prophetic dreams.* His dreams suggested that his brothers would one day "bow down" to him. (19) Resold in Egypt as a slave, according to Genesis, Joseph would become famous for interpreting other people's dreams. After interpreting Pharaoh's disturbing dreams with spectacular accuracy, Joseph was named governor of the land. This, in turn, helped Joseph save the lives of his family, the House of Israel. (20)

It appears that Flavius Josephus borrows this from the Biblical Joseph to describe himself in just the same way the Gospels borrow material from the same story to illustrate aspects of Jesus's life. Both "Josephs," the Biblical figure and the Flavian historian, were Hebrews who gained a foreign ruler's favor through miraculous predictions and the interpretation of prophetic dreams.

Josephus relates his prophetic dream to Vespasian

Like Joseph, Flavius Josephus claims to have had prophetic dreams and a talent for interpreting them. (21) He boasts about his ability "to give shrewd conjectures about the interpretations of such dreams as have been ambiguously given by God." (22) According to Josephus's own report:

> [Josephus] called to mind the dreams which he had dreamed in the night time, whereby God had signi-
> fied to him beforehand both the future calamities of

the Jews, and the events that concerned the Roman emperors. Now *Josephus was able to give shrewd conjectures about the interpretation of such dreams as have been ambiguously delivered by God.* Moreover, he was not unacquainted with the prophecies contained in the sacred books, as being a priest himself, and of the posterity of priests: and *just then was he in an ecstasy*; and setting before him the tremendous images of the dreams he had lately had, he put up a secret prayer to God, and said, "Since it pleaseth thee, who hast created the Jewish nation, to depress the same, and since all their good fortune is gone over to the Romans, and since thou hast made choice of this soul of mine to foretell what is to come to pass hereafter, I willingly give them my hands, and am content to live. And I protest openly that I do not go over to the Romans as a deserter of the Jews, *but as a minister from thee.*" (Emphasis added.) (23)

Of the Old Testament Joseph, according to Genesis, it was reported to Pharaoh that:

A young Hebrew was there with us, a servant of the captain of the guard. When we told him, he interpreted our dreams to us, giving an interpretation to each man according to his dream. (24)

The same methodology, therefore, that Josephus apparently used to write his own autobiography is used in the New Testament, as well, to construct the biography of Jesus. The story of "Joseph" in the Book of Matthew recalls that of Joseph in ancient Hebrew scripture in the same way that the life of Josephus does.

So, almost imponderably, we have at least some reason to doubt whether "Josephus" himself is even real. Is he too convenient for the Flavians or Christians to have actually existed? With such obvious sourcing in religious texts for *his* biography we must wonder whether he was a composited construction or whether we are merely looking at the same work and style of other authors who wrote both the

Gospels *and* the works of Josephus. The resources necessary to engage such a deliberate deception were all too readily available to a Roman imperial administration well-versed in the initiation of cults and the sophisticated propaganda of war.

Whatever the case, Josephus argues strenuously for the credibility of his dreams to underscore how seriously he believes his own proclamation that Vespasian is the Messiah. To be sure, Josephus may have been a fraud even if he existed, but he certainly lobbies his audience very hard to believe him. Simply *recalling* his own prophetic dreams, Josephus assures us, sent him into a religious "ecstasy" resembling the ecstatic visions related by St. Paul in the New Testament:

> I must go on boasting. Although there is nothing to be gained, I will go on to visions and revelations from the Lord. I know a man in Christ who fourteen years ago was caught up to the third heaven. Whether it was in the body or out of the body I do not know—God knows. And I know that this man—whether in the body or apart from the body I do not know, but God knows—was caught up to paradise and heard inexpressible things, things that no one is permitted to tell. (25)

Josephus describes exactly the same kind of experiences, therefore, as Paul. Despite being a Hellenistic and Stoic philosopher and an "objective" historian, Josephus is nonetheless, a *bona fide* mystic it seems. He accepts the miracles of Moses and by his own assertion believes in the messianic prophecies of the Jews, along with his own prophetic visions and dreams.

Josephus reports with all seriousness that a Jew exorcized demons in the presence of Vespasian, his sons, and himself. (26) Such exorcisms, of course, are analogous to many of Jesus's own "healing" miracles in the Gospels. And though he was a thoroughly Hellenized, Platonic and Stoic Jew, Josephus nevertheless believes in the Resurrection of the Dead and a Final Judgment, as well.

In the works of Josephus, we are surely at the confluence of the same ideological rivers that produced the Gospels. And, while it may never be possible to determine the authorship of the Gospels with certainty, in the circle of semi-observant "Jews" surrounding the Flavian court we have certainly found a number of leading candidates. They were at the same place at the same time and shared the same background, education, agenda, and even the same iconography with the earliest Christians. And they had the resources necessary to launch an empire-wide mission.

Professor Robert Eisenman has argued that this group around the Flavians, especially the figure of Epaphroditus, is likely to have produced the material comprising the Gospels. However, he does not think that Josephus himself could have written it, suspecting that his orientation was still too Jewish to have authored the sustained anti-Jewish drumbeat that is found throughout the Gospels. (27)

In response, we can only observe that Josephus had obviously abandoned any strict adherence to Mosaic Law. And more: he could actually take part in the Romans' torture of many of his own people—by his own account—and could watch thousands upon thousands of his countrymen crucified in the aftermath of the great war between the Romans and the Jews. And finally, we know that Josephus wrote pages and pages of justification for the Roman generals who were responsible for the mass carnage and enslavement of his own people.

Josephus's works reveal an author who possessed not only the education in history, philosophy, languages and Judaism that was necessary to have written the Gospels, but also the same outlook as the Gospel writers, politically and theologically. He used the same methodology to craft his autobiography that was used to construct Christ's biography. He even admired and was close friends with figures who appear in the New Testament itself, such as Agrippa II, Epaphroditus, Bernice, and possibly Paul if they shared a berth on that ill-fated sea voyage across the Mediterranean. Perhaps most importantly, he bore the same contempt for that generation of Jews that we find expressed in the Gospels.

And, of course, he worked for masters (as their loyal freedman, he took their name) who were friends of so many figures favorably depicted in the New Testament, some of whom stood with Titus during the Siege of Jerusalem as he fulfilled the prophecy of Jesus Christ.

* * * * * * * *

It is now time to reexamine the widespread unwillingness to accept at face value the evidence from so many fields suggesting Christianity's imperial Roman origins.

Conventional wisdom tells us that if Jesus says his glorious return will come within the lives of his contemporaries, at the moment when Jerusalem is sacked and its Temple is destroyed, we cannot take this at face value—even if it happened with exactly the same vivid portents of "armies in the clouds" predicted by Jesus himself.

If Josephus calls Vespasian the Jewish Messiah, this must be no more than shallow lip service—as it must also have been in the case of his contemporary, Rabbi Johanan ben Zakkai, when he, too, acknowledged Vespasian to be the true Jewish Messiah.

If St. Clement of Rome is, to every appearance, the cousin of the emperors Titus and Domitian, and if his wife St. Domitilla who originally occupied the first Christian catacombs is their niece and the granddaughter of the Emperor Vespasian, then we are told that Domitilla must be Clement's niece, not his wife, and St. Clement cannot be Titus Flavius Clemens but someone else altogether.

If we find friendly mentions of Epaphroditus and those in Caesar's household in Paul's own letters, then we are told he cannot be the "Epaphroditus" of "Caesar's household" known to Flavius Josephus and Suetonius, and Christian scholars warn us that there must be two or even three separate Epaphrodituses.

If Paul and Josephus are victims of shipwrecks at around the same time on their way to Rome with messianic Jewish prisoners, and all are miraculously saved, they must be two unrelated shipwrecks and such a miraculous salvation must have happened twice in virtually the same place and time.

If Josephus's life bears unique resemblances to the story of Christ in the New Testament, they must all be mere coincidences.

If Josephus thinks well of no fewer than three protagonists of the New Testament—including Jesus Christ himself—we are cautioned that this must involve at least two wholesale interpolations combined with two transcription errors.

If Vespasian performed the same miracles that Jesus performs in the Gospels, it must be yet another coincidence.

And, now that we know that the same unique symbols used by the Emperor Titus himself would be used by Christians to identify themselves for the first three centuries of their history, what new reasons will be offered to deny this physical evidence?

And yet the theory we have explored, the hypothesis that the Gospels originated as a form of Roman propaganda formulated to dampen the conflagration of Jewish resistance, reconciles all of the mysteries with no such tortured convolutions and explains all of the evidence whether it be chronological, ideological, historical, archeological, theological or political, whether it be in pagan, Jewish, or Christian literature, whether it be on Roman coinage or in the earliest Christian iconography. It solves everything by simply taking the evidence at face value.

The proponents of other theories must come up with a succession of elaborate explanations, a new one for each ancient text or image or discovery that presents a fresh problem for their assumptions in a perpetual game of cognitive dissonance, all to deny what the plain evidence is saying in perfect harmony.

IV. Engineering a Religion

From an historical perspective, the human sacrifice of Jesus Christ on the Cross could not have happened at a more convenient time for the Romans. Not only did Jesus predict Titus's destruction of the Jerusalem Temple but Jesus's own sacrifice ended forever the need for the Jewish practice of animal sacrifice, making redundant the annual plea of the high priest in the Holy of Holies on Yom Kippur for the atonement of the sins of the Jewish people. Jesus himself made the Temple he predicted would be destroyed *obsolete*, suggesting that he—indeed his bodily resurrection—would be a metaphorical lamb and a metaphorical Temple.

According to the Gospel of John:

> The Jews then responded to him, "What sign can you show us to prove your authority to do all this?"
>
> Jesus answered them, "Destroy this temple, and I will raise it again in three days."
>
> They replied, "It has taken forty-six years to build this temple, and you are going to raise it in three days?" But the temple he had spoken of was his body. After he was raised from the dead, his disciples recalled what he had said. Then they believed the scripture and the words that Jesus had spoken. (1)

Thus did Jesus indicate how his impending death and resurrection could *replace* the Temple. And this is perfectly consistent with Jesus's own condemnation of the Temple:

> On reaching Jerusalem, Jesus entered the Temple courts and began driving out those who were buying and selling there. He overturned the tables of the money changers and the benches of those selling doves, and would not allow anyone to carry merchandise through the Temple courts. And as he taught

them, he said, "Is it not written: 'My house will be called a house of prayer for all nations'? But you have made it 'a den of robbers.'" (2)

Having been corrupted, the Temple is therefore worthy of the destruction to follow at the hands of the Flavians. As a justification for razing the Temple, passages like these echo the goals that the Flavian apologist and historian Josephus promulgates as someone who both cherished the sacred building and sanctified its destruction at the hands of his imperial masters. Josephus even lays the blame for the Temple's destruction, at least in part, on the rebels themselves. Jesus's own words, "Destroy this Temple...," seem to suggest that his listeners will be the ones who will destroy it. In any case, Jesus's attack on the Jewish Temple prefigures, justifies and even *commences* the deeds of Titus.

Jesus lamented the Temple's impending destruction. According to Josephus, Titus himself sought to spare the "magnificent" structure. Yet notice how Jesus prophesies that the "construction" of his metaphorical temple, the Church, cannot begin until after the Temple is destroyed. Thus Titus's deed is a necessary part of God's plan. Jesus condemns the Temple as corrupt, predicts its destruction, his own sacrificial act removes all need for its existence as a place of further sacrifice, and Titus destroys it as predicted. In this way, instead of serving a purpose millennia after they were written, the Gospels served a very real political purpose in their time.

To be sure, Jesus is not alone in his condemnation; the Dead Sea Scrolls "sectarians" very much agreed that the Temple had become thoroughly polluted. But they entirely disagree with Jesus about why. The pollution of foreigners was not a concern for Jesus. Just the opposite.

The Scrolls community would be appalled that Jesus claimed the Temple was designed "for all nations" equally. That was a Roman, imperial goal. In this respect, the Jesus of the Gospels is again adopting the transnational agenda of the Jews' conquerors. Jesus's own physical attack on the Temple only begins the same physical attack the Roman general Titus would finish 40 years later.

Even the 40-year separation between these events is rife with Biblical significance and not just a random historical coincidence. It matches the same 40-year period that the children of Israel were compelled to wander in the wilderness for rebelling against Moses as they doubted that the Promised Land could ever be conquered. (3) For 40 days and 40 nights rains poured down on Noah when God collectively punished humanity for its sins. (4) In the Bible, *40* is the period of redemption.

If Noah experienced relief from the rains after enduring a period of 40, what relief was Jesus now promising? If the Children of Israel arrived at the Land of Milk and Honey after enduring their period of 40, what reconciliation with God would Jesus bring? If Moses brought down the stone tablets after 40 days of fasting on Mount Sinai, what good news was Jesus delivering?

If the answer was only the destruction of Jerusalem and its Temple, this would only have amounted to more punishment. Where was the Jewish deliverance this time? It came in the form of Christ's Glorious Second Coming 40 years later, in the persons of Vespasian and Titus, who would fulfill the traditional interval of redemption. This time, however, the Jewish people's deliverance was to *Rome*. And Christianity would assure that this message was delivered, loud and clear.

* * * * * * * *

In his letter to Trajan, Pliny the Younger refers to the decline of Christianity's popularity from its peak some 20 years earlier, during the Flavians' rule. This correlates with everything we have seen.

After Titus's death, the youngest of the Flavian emperors, Domitian, who was not associated with the Jewish War and who did not enjoy the status of Jewish Messiah with his father and brother, quickly discontinued his brother's dolphin-and-anchor motif on his own coinage. He also restored the recently burned-down Pantheon and rededicated it to the traditional gods of Rome. Domitian's own coins feature a different slate of deities from his brother and father, favoring Minerva and Jupiter.

Toward the end of his 15-year reign, Domitian purged Epaphroditus and Titus Flavius Clemens (the "pope" St. Clement of Rome) among "many" others, while banishing Clemens' wife (St. Domitilla).

It is only after Domitian's assassination that we see the first Christian images in the Catacombs of Domitilla herself, images that reflect iconography stamped on the coins of Titus and illustrated in the Herculaneum mosaic at the imperial baths buried during his reign.

Even after Domitian's death, it is quite possible that the descendants of the Flavian family held out hope that another of their kin might someday restore their imperial fortunes and reestablish their dynasty. Such hopefuls most likely would have been the descendants of Clemens and Domitilla who were adopted by Domitian to be his heirs. Such Flavians would have had an active interest in keeping their family's imperial cult alive. We can only speculate how many generations such hope persisted with the Flavians.

The imperial cult of Julius Caesar lasted for centuries after his death. After the deaths of Vespasian and Titus, there is no doubt their official cult continued for decades. For the period immediately following the death of Vespasian, we have evidence of a thriving cult of his divinity. More "Flamens" or priests of Vespasian have been identified than for any other emperor except Augustus. While we know that Trajan disfavored the worship of Vespasian—for some reason it did not share the same "pristine glamour" as the cults of the Divine Julius and Augustus for him, according to one historian— there were named priests of Titus as late as the 3rd Century. (5)

Maintaining such a family cult with too great a zeal could easily have been regarded as a threat by future emperors, however. And, after the Flavian dynasty was defunct, the Gospels' Jesus would have had no propaganda value for subsequent emperors or dynasties—with the possible exception of Hadrian, who also prosecuted a war against messianic Jewish rebels a few decades later. Without such a motivation, imperial sanction of Christianity by future emperors would have ended. The Flavian Christians would no longer benefit from advertising imperial connections. At that point, indeed, such connections could have become risky.

Hadrian, who would prosecute the second Jewish War that finally expelled the Jews from Judea, made use of Flavian propaganda by issuing a limited edition of coins bearing the dolphin-and-anchor symbol. By then, of course, it was recognized as a symbol of Christianity. Indeed, Eusebius seems to imply that Hadrian deliberately sent Christians to populate Jerusalem after he had expelled the Jews.

The letters of Paul, which are older than the Flavian dynasty and date to Nero's administration, and the Flavian-era Gospels themselves, would, over time, become more easily separated from Flavian politics, enabling them to develop a life of their own. Since the Christian project had likely begun under Nero with Paul's mission, Christianity could credibly be detached from the Flavians altogether after enough time had passed.

At the outbreak of the Second Jewish Revolt, Hadrian may have had reason to reestablish clandestine Roman support for Pauline Christianity. Though the Flavians were by then irrelevant, both the letters of Paul and the Gospels would have been too useful to set aside as Hadrian fought his own war with Jewish rebels.

By the start of the 2nd Century, Christianity had become almost entirely detached from its purported roots in Judaism, as well, as many Christians drifted from the doctrine expressed in the Gospels. Twentieth Century discoveries at Nag Hamadi and elsewhere in Egypt have dramatically revealed that during the 2nd and 3rd Centuries of the Common Era an anarchic variety of Christian doctrines sprang up. No longer anchored to any centralized authority, a wide range of disparate gospels and other Christian literature variously identified as Gnostic, "Pseudo-Clementine," or Arian emerged in this post-Flavian period, containing ideas that would seem startlingly strange and alien to contemporary Christians. (6)

Some of the doctrines from this period imply that Jesus was not a physical human being at all but only a spiritual entity. Some argue that he was a divine being but that this same divine element could be found in each of us. Some suggest that he was a divine man but a separate entity not to be equated with the God who created the universe.

Much of this literature never cites the Old Testament, at all. Other Christian writers, like Bishop Marcion of Sinope (whose lost work can only be inferred through rebuttals by Christian writers like Tertullian), simply did away with the Hebrew Bible altogether, using as canon only Paul's letters and the work of the evangelist Luke.

All of this demonstrates the radical break from Judaism that "Pauline" Christianity actually represented. And all of it is consistent with the hypothesis of Christianity's Roman origins.

In so short a time after being detached from the anchor of the Flavians, Christians were completely erasing whatever Judaic influences remained. The Jesus Christ presented in the Gospels proved so perfect a syncretism of ancient pagan religion and philosophical thought that it was easy to separate from the proximate historical and political purpose of its creation. Once decapitated from the imperial agenda, the religion quickly mutated into a plethora of pagan-influenced "Christianities."

The cults of deified Roman emperors continued long after their deaths. Deceased emperors were permanently enrolled in the pantheon of recognized state gods as their state-sanctioned rites continued to be performed. It was Vespasian who completed the Temple of the Divine Claudius, for example, an emperor from the previous dynasty. The worship of the Flavians, as well, continued throughout the 2nd Century, and there is evidence of *Sodales Titiales Flaviales*, that is, an official priesthood of the God Titus, up to the time of the Emperor Septimius Severus in the early 3rd Century. In time, however, the Temple of the God Vespasian became known as the Temple of Janus. (7)

The cults of the emperors Vespasian and Titus certainly contained many pagan elements and, therefore, could never have been exclusively associated with the God Jesus. As we have seen, however, these pagan elements would deeply influence Christian worship, belief and symbolism. Even the original structure of the Christian Church resembles a top-down empire-wide Roman administration instead of a humble, underground and organic grassroots movement. It is that organizational structure that may have helped it survive and might account for the surprisingly meticulous (if sometimes contradictory) tracking of its "Apostolic Succession" along with a special reverence for the original 1st Century documents that came in time to be regarded as canonical.

At some point, even the worship of an emperor comes to an end. In the case of the Flavians, however, this did not stop the worship of their Romanized Christ. The pre-Flavian Pauline tradition and literature under Nero enabled Christianity to maintain a separate identity from the Flavians that outlived its imperial patrons, while the later Emperor Hadrian had every reason to both continue using Christianity as propaganda while detaching it from its Flavian connections.

The hidden agenda of the Gospels—to demonstrate Flavian messianic claims to the freshly conquered Judea—would remain hidden, and thus could be easily forgotten. Eventually, any obsolete connection between Christianity and the Flavians could be discarded, including Titus's dolphin-and-anchor symbolism, leaving Jesus Christ eternally in error about the prophecy of his Second Coming.

* * * * * * * *

We have seen that religious manipulation and fraud were flagrantly practiced by governments during this period of ancient history, as illustrated by the creation of the god Serapis.

Miraculous healings were staged by the Emperor Vespasian at the temple of Serapis, and a Jewish captive foresaw a general's ascension to the imperial throne. Both obvious fabrications were key elements of Flavian propaganda.

The wide range of Greek, Egyptian, and Jewish portents, miracles, and prophecies the Flavian dynasty advertised on their way to the throne indicate the unprecedented level of religious manipulation they employed to validate their legitimacy as Roman rulers. No Roman leader before or after would claim to have performed actual miracles as did Vespasian—much less healing miracles identical to Christ's in the Gospels, which are known to have been written during the Flavian's rule.

Blatant politically-motivated fraud like Ptolemy's fabrication of the god Serapis set a bold precedent that the Romans readily adopted as a tool of statecraft. That the Romans applied to such state projects the same efficiency and organization that they applied to all public works and civil engineering projects is entirely predictable.

If the conventional assumption that the Roman government was hostile to Christianity is true, we must expect some of that hostility to be expressed somewhere in the New Testament. And yet not a single Roman governor finds fault with a Christian in the Gospels to justify this reputation for "persecution." Should we not see even one Roman official treating Paul unfairly or even one of Paul's guards abusing him? Why, instead, is *every* appearance of Roman centurions or government officials described so favorably—in the Bible?

Conversely, shouldn't Josephus, who worked for the Flavians, show at least some Roman disapproval when he mentions Jesus, James or John the Baptist? He *works* for the Flavians. Scholars attempting to grapple with the *Testimonium* of Josephus exhibit a blind spot to this fact. Even if his text was augmented and enhanced, Josephus seems to have been unreservedly sympathetic to other figures in the New Testament. Blotting out one reference does not explain away the others.

We have seen various translators of the New Testament grappling with how Agrippa II could sympathize with Paul's message. Knowing that Agrippa II was a friend of Josephus and Titus, they have tortured and tweaked his words over and over instead of seeking to explain their implications.

Again, the eternal "problem" for beleaguered scholars is the same: high-ranking Romans simply could not sympathize with Christianity, or *vice versa*, at such an incipient stage.

Christianity urges complete obedience to authority, paying taxes, going the extra mile for the Romans, universal inclusion, making peace, etc. Seen as a form of moral idealism, these ideas are never suspected of being part of a political agenda promoted by Roman governors and their client kings, all of whom are shown in a positive light in the Gospels and the Book of Acts. And yet the teachings of the Gospels are never recognized as expressing the same Flavian agenda that is expressed by the Flavian's own hagiographer, Josephus.

Like the paradox of Jesus's proclamation that his Glorious Second Coming would arrive precisely when the Roman army leveled the Temple under Titus, and Josephus's own claim that his imperial master *was* the Jewish Messiah—in order to solve all of these "problems" all we really need to do is stop resisting history and accept it at face value. If agents of the Roman state authored the Gospels, then what other evidence could we expect but precisely the evidence that we have?

The Romans recognized that it would be impossible to eliminate Jewish devotion to their god or persuade them to relinquish their hope in a messiah who would deliver them. Rather than attempting to destroy their enemies' ideas completely, it is perfectly logical that they would attempt to rechannel their culture into a pro-Roman direction, combining an ideological assault with their military assault. Romans are known to have employed highly sophisticated intelligence gathering, "psy-ops," agent provocateurs and propaganda as an integral part of their military operations.

Romans were self-conscious about the religious changes they brought to their empire, and they were pragmatic about the public purpose religion served. The Roman government was quite accomplished at setting up elaborately organized and funded cults to celebrate emperors as gods, having already done so for three previous Caesars. As we have seen, their ideology was lavishly celebrated on their coinage, often the one form of archeological evidence that survives the passage of time and the meddling of revisionists. We have seen how those coins preserve a catalog of virtues reflected in the New Testament.

The Emperor Claudius wrote a treatise on the religious changes that had occurred during the reign of Augustus. Like all the works of Claudius, this work did not survive the long period of time when only Christian monks copied and thus preserved (or didn't) the great literature of antiquity. And yet, presumably, one of the important topics Claudius addressed in his writings was the arrival of the imperial cult in its first form, the cult of the Divine Julius, which would serve as a model and foundation for all future imperial administrations.

In what is probably the clearest example of the Romans' elaborately organized and funded manipulations of religion for political ends, the Roman Senate officially deified the Caesars Julius, Augustus, Claudius, Vespasian, and Titus by the end of the 1st Century. Yet, while it is common for contemporaries to dismiss the authentic piety and sincere devotion these political gods inspired, this is merely a modern prejudice. Indeed, the imperial cult, in its effort to ground the legitimacy of the Roman monarchy in divine favor, was the direct precedent for the Christian belief in the "Divine Right of Kings," which was used to validate the authority of European monarchs until the 17th Century king, Louis XIV.

The Romans endured because they were relatively flexible as a society willing to add to their citizens and senators political elites from an ever-widening circle of conquered territories. They absorbed rather than destroyed the cultures of the nations they conquered. The first great example was their adoption of the culture and religion of the Greek kingdoms which they had started to conquer. Ironically, in their conquest of the Greeks, Romans were employing a political tactic they had adopted from Greek conquerors like Alexander, welcoming the religious ideas of Hellenized cultures and readily identifying Greek gods with their own deities.

This practice is vividly revealed in the cult of the Divine Julius Caesar, who claimed descent from Aeneas, a Trojan hero of the most ancient Greek epic, *The Iliad*. Aeneas was not only a Trojan prince, but a son of the goddess Aphrodite (adopted and identified as their own "Venus" by the Romans). The Julian family claimed that after the fall of Troy, Aeneas led a group of Trojans to the shores of central Italy where he established the Latin tribe that was a progenitor of ancient Rome. The Julians thus claimed to be descendants of Aeneas's son, "Iulus"—making them living descendants of the Greek goddess of love herself.

Virgil Reading the Aeneid to Augustus and Octavia,
by Angelica Kauffman (1741-1807)

The first dynasty of Roman emperors thus blatantly used foreign religion to establish the legitimacy of their rule over their newly conquered subjects. This is how the Romans conducted war.

What we have been observing is the second dynasty of Roman emperors—the Flavii—employing exactly the same tactic regarding Jewish traditions after conquering Judea (albeit with much more lasting effect). Just like the family of Roman monarchs who had preceded them, the Flavians utilized a foreign religion to demonstrate their divine favor and legitimacy as rulers over conquered people. It would have been strange if they did *not* do this given the precedent set by the first imperial dynasty, which they used as their model. Indeed, the Flavians actually co-opted elements of Greek, Egyptian and Jewish religion in various forms for their own propaganda purposes, as we have seen. The Gospels were just one part of that project, one aimed at a single, if critical, part of their diverse imperial audience.

And it was so effective as a device of religious statecraft that it outlived the entire Roman Empire.

* * * * * * * *

Contributing to our modern ignorance of the New Testament's historical context, Hollywood's retellings of the Gospels have painted the Romans as "the bad guys" who "really" killed Jesus.

Plenty of valid Christian guilt about anti-Semitism, and legitimate Jewish fear of the same, certainly motivated this Hollywood revisionism. In the wake of the Holocaust, Christian guilt finally came to a climax, and in popular retellings of the Christian story they uniformly emphasized the Romans' role in the deaths of Jesus and the first Christian martyrs.

Such an emphasis, however, is a rewrite of the Gospel narratives.

As we have seen, over and over again, the "bad guys" in the New Testament are *always* the Jews. It should now be obvious why: the Gospels were Roman propaganda generated by their war with the Jews during their epical conflict in the 1st Century. Christian anti-Semitism is no coincidence. The Roman's "New" Testament was created to veto the Jewish "Old" Testament.

The one notable exception to Hollywood's trend can be seen in the 2004 film by Mel Gibson, *The Passion of the Christ*. His depiction of the passion narrative as it is told in the Gospels left Jewish and Christian reviewers aghast at its anti-Semitism, with Gibson replying that he was only relating what the Gospels actually say. (8)

When it comes to the portrait of the "Jews" painted by the Gospels, modern Christians are simply in a state of denial. Though recent decades have seen a rewriting of the Gospel accounts in the form of movies and books, the process of "cleaning up" the anti-Semitism in the New Testament actually began long ago.

This drift away from the anti-Semitic politics of the Gospels can, for example, be seen in the shifting perceptions of Pilate, the Roman governor who ordered Christ's crucifixion. The Gospel stories could not be clearer: after announcing his belief in Jesus's innocence, the Jews respond to Pilate by demanding Jesus's execution three times, and only then does Pilate finally relent and accede to their demands. Jesus was convicted of violating Jewish law by Jewish authorities. After unsuccessfully pleading with Jesus to make a defense, any defense, Pilate symbolically washes his hands in a metaphor designed to exonerate the Roman government of his execution. The message is clear: Jesus's message of peaceful acquiescence to Roman rule would never have led to punishment.

Matthew's account stresses this by quoting the Jewish crowd as conveniently proclaiming, "His blood is on us and on our children!" (9) Thus is the bloody war to come justified.

We already asked it, but we must ask again: who but the Roman government would have had the motive to exonerate the Roman government? If Jesus's appeal was to all humanity, why should the Gospels explicitly exclude Romans from any culpability in his sacrifice?

According to Matthew, even Pilate's wife begs him not to do it: "While Pilate was sitting on the judge's seat, his wife sent him this message: 'Don't have anything to do with that innocent man, for I have suffered a great deal today in a dream because of him.'" (10)

Origen actually praises Pilate's wife on this account (11), and, as "St. Procula," Pontius Pilate's spouse is even venerated by the Greek Orthodox Church to this day and honored on her feast day, October 27.

Pilate himself is still venerated as a saint by the ancient Ethiopian Orthodox Church.

Christians in the Latin-speaking West, however, must have rejected such overt admiration of Pontius Pilate early on since they never venerated him as a saint. Over time, Pilate would become more and more the villain in Christ's fate, as he now appears in most presentations of Christ's Passion depicted in the West.

If not the Jewish people, then someone had to take the blame for the murder of Christ. Today, it is invariably the Romans, the very group specifically exonerated by the Gospels, but especially, Pilate himself.

In the wake of the Holocaust, blame had to at last be taken away from the Jewish people for political (and psychological) reasons—just as blame had to be laid at the feet of those same people by the Romans two thousand years earlier, for similar reasons.

The fate of Pilate's reputation is just one example of the gradual reinterpretation of the original text to accommodate shifting political realities over the last two millennia.

We have seen how the Roman political ideology minted on their coins is echoed in the values stressed in the Gospels. New Testament portrayals of Roman officials, governors, and client kings show them to be uniformly sympathetic to Christians, suggesting even an official Roman sanction of Christianity at its earliest stages. Roman authorities repeatedly rescue Paul from angry mobs of Jews and provide him with protection and privileges—and some of them are Jewish aristocrats and personal friends of Titus, the very group to whom the Pauline message of "freedom" from Mosaic Law would have been most welcome.

We have seen evidence that high-ranking Romans like Epaphroditus were simultaneously personal associates of St. Paul, Flavius Josephus, and the Roman emperors Nero, Vespasian, Titus and Domitian.

We have even seen evidence in the Flavian historian Josephus's own writings that he expressed sympathy for the first leaders of the Christian movement, John and James, and that he was, by far, the first person outside Christian literature to do so. That he was a "Flavian" is undoubted. The prolific historian was, essentially, their slave (intellectually, at least) from the moment he was captured by the Romans. And therefore we must reconsider our doubts that he might be the first person to ever mention the existence of Christ outside the Bible.

The political demands of Christ and Paul were exactly those of the Roman government: peaceful obedience to Roman author-ity and the voluntary payment of taxes. The political values of the Gospels perfectly mirror those on Roman coins: peace on earth and good will to all men. Even the first Christians' earliest symbols were taken directly from Flavian coins and art.

None of this evidence has ever been hidden. Most of it has been sitting in plain sight for the better part of two thousand years. It has all been seen, but it has never been believed.

Christianity is simply too pro-Roman to fit with modern misconceptions, so the world has trained its eyes away from seeing the obvious: the New Testament is imperial Roman propaganda designed for a brief political reality that has long since passed and been forgotten.

Conclusion

In the New Testament we read exhortations to obey the Roman government as the appointed agents of God, to pay one's taxes, and even to honor the emperor himself. We also see the earliest Christian leaders laying the foundations for the authority structure of the Church, with an endorsement of Church hierarchy coming even from Jesus long before such developments seem credible. We are presented with benevolent Roman *centurions,* even as Paul's mission uniformly receives official protection from Roman governors, clerks and officials—including sympathy from the Praetorian Guard of Caesar himself.

According to Christ, the faith of one centurion exceeded that of any contemporary Jew. Paul refers to his contacts as those in "Caesar's household" so casually in his correspondence to the Philippians that it must have some basis in fact. Indeed, Paul's contacts reach the highest level of imperial servants and Roman aristocrats, including associates of Vespasian and Titus who had achieved their imperial office by conquering the messianic rebels and becoming Jewish messiahs and Roman man-gods.

This same family of Roman emperors produced a 1st Century "pope." Most of the New Testament was composed during their reign. Their family tomb became the first Christian catacomb. Their family symbol was Christianity's first icon: the anchor.

The founder of the Flavian dynasty, Vespasian, presented himself as "the New Serapis" and performed healing miracles identical to Christ's, syncretizing pagan elements of a mystery religion with his own status as the Jewish Messiah. Vespasian advertised himself as the father of universal peace, a new *Pax Romana*. And he was a monarch born to humble circumstances. Both his ascension to the throne and his death were portended by a *star.*

Jesus, too, was a Jewish messiah, a divine "monarch" born into humble circumstances, and his birth was heralded by a star.

Both Vespasian and his son, Titus, were worshipped as savior gods in the East *while they lived*, and they were worshipped as official state gods in the city of Rome itself long after their deaths. The Gospels, no matter who wrote them, would have been ideal prophetic demonstrations of their divinity and messianic status as Roman Jewish Messiahs.

The cult of Emperor Titus praised his beneficence with propaganda extolling his charity and fatherly love for the masses. Within only a few decades of his death, after his brother Domitian was assassinated, his dolphin-and-anchor motif became the predominant symbol of Christianity.

The Gospels systematically, even melodramatically, absolve the Roman Empire of any culpability for the death of Jesus, laying the blame exclusively on the Jewish people with such a heavy hand that it inspired centuries of anti-Semitic retribution.

The Flavians' own historian, Josephus, favorably portrays New Testament protagonists who are associated with the Flavians. The New Testament expresses inordinate sympathy for Titus's own Jewish friends. Though he became an object of shame to his own people, Christians to this day enthusiastically cite Josephus as frequently as any Church father.

As Jesus explains in the Gospels, he is himself the replacement of the Temple that Titus would destroy: he was the ultimate sacrifice, the complete Atonement for the sins of the People, and the final reconciliation of man with God.

If Christianity was an organic development from Judaism, the product of an evolutionary process, one would expect that the most culturally alienating aspects of the mother religion, such as male circumcision, strict Sabbath observance and Kosher diet, would have disappeared slowly, one-by-one, over a period of time. We have seen how fiercely the first Christians fought for these traditions against Paul. It was those very aspects of Judaism for which the rebels were fighting, the features of their culture that created problems of intermarriage, inter-employment, and even made having lunch with Gentiles a source of heated conflict. In the work of Paul and the authors of the Gospels, however, we see all of these aspects of Judaism swept aside suddenly, stridently, *simultaneously.* And we see it all happening among a group of messianic Jewish rebels, the group least amenable to any modifications of the Torah. More than that: they were done away with at the same time pagan elements and ideas were introduced, transforming the faith into a kind of Mystery Cult that worshipped a man-god.

And all of this radical revision is done all at once in the work of Paul on the eve of the Jewish War and in the Gospels immediately after that war.

Again, if the New Testament is Flavian propaganda, what would the evidence look like other than what we have? It is remarkable just how much evidence still exists, from such a wide spectrum of sources, to support this revolutionary conclusion.

The first Gospels were written during the Flavian era by authors familiar with Jewish religion and history, just like the people who happened to surround the "Messiah" Titus. This same group included Titus's second-in-command, Tiberius Alexander, the nephew of the Jewish Platonist philosopher, Philo; also, the historian Flavius Josephus, who produced a history of the Hebrews from the Creation to their war with the Romans and who received the holy Jewish texts from the Temple after it was sacked; also the long-serving imperial Secretary of Letters, Epaphroditus, who assisted Paul and Josephus; also Pliny the Elder, who endorsed the divinity of helping others, praised as divine this quality in the Flavians, and dedicated his own works to Titus; and even the Jewish royals Agrippa II and Bernice (Titus's one-time fiancée), who appear in the Bible itself.

Some of these figures in the New Testament stood shoulder-to-shoulder with Titus during the Siege of Jerusalem and witnessed the central prophecy of Jesus being fulfilled: the same events recorded by Josephus in terms that match the Gospels' prophecies down to the last visual detail. And both Jesus's prophecies and Josephus's histories were written concurrently, after the events had taken place and during the rule of the Flavians.

The unique combination of means, motive and opportunity, of time, place and people, surrounding the Flavians perfectly coincides with the origins of the New Testament. The oddly organized and widespread administration of early Christianity so unaccountable to scholars implies a top-down governmental hand in its creation. Moreover, that such a widespread effort could have been mounted so publicly in the wake of the Jewish War without Roman sanction is impossible to believe.

The idea that Christians would be so favorable to the Romans, by praising a centurion's faith so extravagantly in the New Testament or adopting an emperor's seal as their own at their gravesites simply in order to avoid persecution contradicts the entire story of Christian martyrdom and their refusal to appease pagans. Occam's razor hovers over all efforts to explain away these facts, which collectively and effortlessly conform with the alternative theory we are presenting.

At the crossroads of Western history, the great Jewish War with the Romans was a conflict of two diametrically opposed views of civilization: one that was exclusive vs. one that was universal. Their epic collision created an urgent need for the exclusive side to protect its heritage against invasion from outside pollution (as evidenced even in the last-ditch depositing of the Dead Sea Scrolls) and the Romans' need to defeat the militant exclusivity that opposed their comparatively pluralistic vision of empire.

The Jewish people's rebellion from Rome sealed their fate. After their brutal treatment by the Romans, theirs was a culture in Diaspora for another two millennia. The Jewish people had already spread far and wide across the Middle East following the Babylonian conquest of Jerusalem in the late 6th Century BCE and, later, in response to the Mediterranean-wide trade opened up by the *Pax Romana*. The final legal exclusion of Hebrews from Jerusalem would be ordered by Hadrian in the 2nd Century, following the Bar Kochba revolt, thus making permanent their status as global exiles until the creation of the state of Israel in the 20th Century.

As we have seen from reports of 1st Century disturbances in the city of Rome, messianic Judaism posed a serious problem not just in Judea but throughout the Empire, including at its very heart. The Romans realized that a military opposition to the Jewish conflict would not be enough. They would need an ideological campaign, as well.

With Christianity, the Romans engineered what they must have thought was the perfect strategy—a demonstration that the Jewish "messiah" did not embody the national or cultural independence of the Jewish people at all, but was, in fact, a pro-Roman, peace-loving, tax-paying, transnational Hellenistic philosopher of the Platonic and Stoic schools who offered a mystery cult-like salvation to all people of all nations.

And they added to this Roman vision of "Christ" that the Jewish people themselves, failing to recognize his true nature as the Messiah, killed him and thus merited their divine punishment at the hands of the Romans.

* * * * * * * *

As radical and new as this hypothesis may seem, it actually reflects insights as old as New Testament scholarship itself. Though there were previous translations of Josephus's writings, when William Whiston, in the 17th Century, first translated the collected works of Josephus into English he set the standard, until recent decades. Whiston was a famous man. He had succeeded his mentor, Sir Isaac Newton, as Lucasian Professor of Mathematics at the University of Cambridge, though he later lost this position because of his theological views. Whiston thought Flavius Josephus to be a secret Christian.

Whiston did not think Josephus was a Trinitarian Christian, however, as were most Christians in Whiston's day. Instead, he believed Josephus must have been a Christian like himself: that is, one who denied that Jesus was one aspect of a single pre-existent divine Trinity. Rather, he believed that Jesus was merely a divine human being created by and subordinate to God the Father. And he, to be sure, did not question the authenticity of Flavius Josephus's *Testimonium.*

Still, Whiston believed that Josephus, the in-house historian of the Roman emperors Vespasian and Titus, was a *Christian.*

In addition, Bruno Bauer, a student of the 19th Century German philosopher G.W.F. Hegel and a teacher of Karl Marx, also recognized that most of the New Testament embodied a Hellenized and Roman worldview instead of a Jewish one. Bruno Bauer was an anti-Semite, to be sure, revealing the dark side of acknowledging the intrinsic anti-Semitism in the New Testament. (1) Well known in his lifetime but almost completely forgotten today, Bauer had debated one of the fathers of critical Bible studies, David Strauss, who helped shape the entire field of Bible scholarship with his book, *Life of Jesus.* (2)

Strauss's book has been available in English editions since 1846. As a result, in so many ways, Strauss set the stage for all Biblical scholarship since. However, at the turn of the 20th Century, Albert Schweitzer wrote that:

> [Bruno] Bauer's 'Criticism of the Gospel History' is worth a good dozen Lives of Jesus, because his work, as we are only now coming to recognize, after half a century, is the ablest and most complete collection of the difficulties of the Life of Jesus which is anywhere to be found. (3)

Bauer's work on Christianity is no longer in print like Strauss's, and it has never been translated into English. The famous philosopher Friedrich Nietzsche once called Bauer "my entire reading public." (4)

Nietzsche himself, of course, a notoriously harsh critic of Christian morality, derided the doctrine of Jesus as a "slave morality" that appeals to weakness, cowardice, and submissiveness in contrast to the life-affirming virtues of the pagans. (5) Whether the consistent Christian advice of submission to authority is a virtue or not on a philosophical level, Nietzsche's insight can now be seen in a new light. And by this same light, even critics of Marxism can re-evaluate the assertion of Bauer's other student, Karl Marx, who famously called religion "the opium of the people." (6)

We must imagine the historical reality that after winning their war against Judea, a conflict that may have taken more than a million lives, the Romans found themselves the owners of tens of thousands of Jewish slaves. Many if not most of these slaves were messianic rebels. Titus alone took many thousands of his own Jewish slaves to Rome to build his triumphal arch, his famous baths, and the Colosseum itself, where so many of their countrymen would later be sacrificed for entertainment.

The Romans needed to opiate these former radicals and recondition them to life as Roman slaves in the wake of their defeat. And the New Testament was precise in this regard. This new form of Judaism repeatedly commands slaves to obey their masters—even cruel and harsh masters—just as it commands free men to obey the Roman state as God's agent on earth.

So effective was this Roman formula that it outlasted their empire, and it would supply kings with a divine right of absolute rule over their subjects for the next 16 centuries as well as conferring on masters a "right" to own their slaves. Europeans are not only still driving on roads Romans built, they are still worshipping a god Romans created in order to legitimize the rule of monarchs they are still honoring.

Romans were ruthless and pragmatic conquerors. They dealt with the Jews as they had dealt with other conquered foreigners—by absorbing elements of their culture and adapting it to their own practical purposes in service of the Empire. It was their instinct and custom to syncretize the religious source of conflict into a cultural justification for both their military incursion and their imperial rule. The Romans did it before with the Greeks—even as Alexander the Great's generals had done it before them with conquered Egyptian and Persian nations.

It would be far more surprising had the Romans *not* attempted to do this in the aftermath of the Jewish War, especially considering how instrumental religion was in that particular conflict. If not for the existence of Christianity, we would need to ask where was the typical Roman response to cultural conflict during the Jewish War?

As its first symbols reveal, Christianity was already syncretizing with the ancient pagan world. The pagan iconography chosen by the Emperor Titus is reflected in Christian symbolism all the way to the Emperor Constantine more than two centuries later, when the prominent symbol of Christianity finally changed. Signaled by Constantine's famous revelation in the sky over a desperate battle of the chi-ro cross (akin to the ichthys wheel we saw earlier) that led the way to his victory, the symbol for Christianity from that point forward would shift... to the Cross.

And so, with the administration of Emperor Constantine and his official instatement of Christianity, the last symbolic link to the Flavian cult was buried.

Constantine the Great

Flavian connections to Christianity became more and more awkward as time passed. By the 4th Century it became necessary to replace the old Flavian symbols entirely.

Dolphins would still adorn Christian sites for some time to come, including panels at Hagia Sophia in Constantinople. Among Constantine's favorite gifts to churches were silver and gold ornaments in the shape of dolphins. But the dolphin-and-anchor motif coined by Titus was finally retired as Christianity was officially rebranded under the sign of the Cross.

None of the Flavian temples remain. Like most pagan temples, they have been ground to rubble and lost to history. And yet, though documents and monuments can be tampered with and destroyed, coins, minted in the millions by the Roman propaganda machine, have survived the last 19 centuries. The last links to that past, scattered and buried under layers of time, still bear witness to the truth.

Most of the evidence has been there all along. By merely taking at face value the New Testament, Josephus, Suetonius, Tacitus, Pliny the Younger, Clement of Alexandria, Origen, Eusebius, Dio Cassius and all the rest, we were able to predict what kind of symbol we would find on the other side of Titus's coin and, conversely, whose face we would find behind the symbol of Christ—long before we found the coin itself.

The witnesses from this time speak a deafening truth in unison with no need for tortured interpretations or speculative somersaults. They tell us what Christianity was when it was invented through the events, politics, people and relationships that they reveal.

There may have lived a man named Jesus, but there remains today no historical evidence that he did. And there need not have existed such a man in order to explain everything that has been passed down to us about him. There is no part of him that is not prophesied by others or prophetic of others, and no aspect of him that is not symbolic, political, syncretized or borrowed from other men or gods.

There is no doubt that the Romans had a motivation to create such a convenient Jewish-pagan "man-god" who would be scorned and mocked as a false "King of the Jews" even while predicting he would gloriously return after his death as a Roman emperor to destroy their Temple. How convenient for Titus, who did precisely that just before those Gospels were actually composed. Attempting to adapt and conform the hostile Hebrew religion to Roman culture, and especially its messianic flashpoint, would have been the Romans' standard practice and, considering the stakes, one of their major priorities.

Thirty years before the publication of this book, while researching the origins of Christianity, the possibility of a Roman provenance for the New Testament leaped out at us when we noticed that Jesus's apocalyptic vision nearly quoted Josephus's historical account of that prophecy's fulfillment 40 years later. When we discovered that the Gospels and Josephus's accounts were written during the same period of time, the possibilities became all the more compelling.

When this glaring coincidence was combined with the political implications of the Gospels' ideology, the evidence began to imply a revolutionary hypothesis about Christianity's origins. Yet it took three decades of painstaking research to finally confirm it—in ways that were ever more predictable and increasingly more astonishing.

As traditional assumptions about Christian origins were challenged by impossible contradictions and coincidences at every turn, we never found any solid evidence to contradict the emerging theory we were testing. Pieces of the mosaic continued to fall into place as an entirely new picture was filled in.

If we were right, we assumed from the very beginning that at some point we would find a Flavian coin that would confirm our suspicions and complete that picture. We did not discover that final evidence until the very end of that long and thorough search, when the Internet finally made the scattered catalog of Roman coinage globally accessible for the first time since they were circulating in the 1st Century itself. And then the last piece fell perfectly into place.

During the course of our research, the works of Robert Eisenman, Francesco Carotta, Joseph Atwill, Rose Mary Sheldon and Thijs Voskuilen appeared, providing us with new details in support of the theory we were pursuing, and the reader will find in their books evidence and arguments on specialized aspects that offer further support to this revolutionary view of Christianity's origins.

This is the only theory that uniquely explains all of the evidence and solves all of the paradoxes that have puzzled scholars for centuries. What we have explored here hardly exhausts the evidence that is sure to confirm and illuminate it further. Much evidence no doubt already occupies a drawer or a shelf in a museum archive, unrecognized for what it is. And much more surely awaits discovery by archeologists.

The historical period that many think of today as an era in which miracles and mystical events frequently occurred was actually no different from today. Culture, politics, and even science took a religious form in that era, when gods like Serapis were readily created by rulers such as Ptolemy and worshipped for centuries. Ironically, it is we in the modern era who mystify such accounts that have become so distant from us that we bestow on them a patina of supernatural authenticity. Likewise, the Flavians counted on the masses in their day to do the same when creating the biography of a Christ who had existed 40 years before their victory and who perfectly and prophetically justified their conquest of Judea.

Rather than adding any validation to other religions, this revelation should serve as a powerful admonishment that all ancient religions were a product of similar human creativity at a time when religious invention was readily employed and widely accepted as a tool of statecraft and conquest.

Certainly, while everything else in our knowledge has evolved— our science, our art, our technology, our forms of government—it is only the supernatural grip of these ancient philosophical artifacts that have kept the most lofty principles guiding our lives from also evolving, freezing them in place from an era of war and tyranny. In the West, science, art, and technological innovation have been liberated from the fetters of the past. Yet, in an age when we have created nuclear weapons, in the realm of philosophy we find ourselves still adhering to primitive agendas hatched during a distant, largely forgotten political war between what were, in fact, two forms of dictatorship.

One thing we can learn from this discovery is that our spiritual insights and ethical wisdom must be allowed to evolve along with the rest of our knowledge, unhindered by ancient ideological expediencies inherited from long bygone times. If not, in the very pursuit of heaven or paradise, we may well bring about our apocalypse here on earth.

As the world has entered the 21st Century and, indeed, the 3rd

Millennium, we are facing many tumultuous transitions and cultural turmoil as a species. Many ideologies experimented with in the 20th Century were ghastly failures and long-trusted institutions have faded. Even as iconoclasm rises on many sides, ancient religion and political radicalism are resurrected. In such times more than ever, many depend on the comfort of ancient norms and established creeds, so much so that any critique like this could easily be viewed as only adding to malaise. For many, the belief in a benevolent God renders the universe with indispensable meaning and morality. Nothing we have discovered and demonstrated here, however, challenges a belief in God or, indeed, the important need for morality. Ethics can, and should, be separate from the study of the actual origins and evidence of religion and what it tells us about its purpose, its nature, and ourselves.

Demystifying Christianity will be seen by some as disarming Western Civilization in the face of a new barbaric assault like that faced by the Romans 2000 years ago. Instead, we believe this revelation will illuminate both sides and help prevent history from repeating itself. On one side of this ancient conflict was a religion of "peace" that bestowed divine authority upon a brutal dictator and upon centuries of kings to come, in the name of order. And on the other side was a religious fanaticism wreaking self-destructive violence to destroy that authority and achieve an even more monolithic domination over the human race.

Philosophy provides powerful answers to our deepest needs by providing a context for all of our knowledge and the vital nourishment of moral values, inspiration, and purpose. As purveyors of this need, religions have endured for millennia by adapting over time to accommodate different eras and cultures. Christianity has proven able to do so, resulting in sects as varied as Shakers and Mormons.

The religion of Christianity is interwoven into the very fabric of Western history. From the evolution of literature encompassing Dante's *Divine Comedy* and Milton's *Paradise Lost*, to the ethical arguments over slavery in antebellum America (on both sides of the argument) and the Civil Rights Movement of the 20th Century, the influence of Christianity on Western Civilization has been profound.

However, denying that Venus was actually born of the sea-foam does not diminish the beauty of Botticelli's art. Disbelieving the gods of ancient Egypt has not demolished the power of the monumental architecture they inspired. To bathe in the glow of the stained glass of Chartres Cathedral, to be transported by the immortal beauty of Schubert's *Ave Maria*, or to be rendered speechless at the sight of Michelangelo's *Pieta* will always be deeply moving experiences for the sensitive human being—just as the majesty of Luxor and Abu Simbel or the dramatic skills of Homer have not been injured by the passing of religions into myth. Indeed, as we have seen, though Christianity eradicated and replaced paganism, it has also carried forward a veritable ark of its cardinal virtues (and vices) into the modern world.

Whether there was a Jesus or not is still a question we cannot answer. The reality of the experience of Christianity for millions of people over thousands of years, on the other hand, is certain.

What is also certain is that other faiths now long gone were just as devoutly followed by billions who lived and died believing them—even as many of the moral teachings behind their religious trappings continue to endure and enrich us.

References and Notes

Introduction

1. The only responsible attitude is skepticism, at least initially, regarding any new hypothesis about Christianity's beginnings. Wild theories based on little evidence have scared away many from seeking a more complete understanding of the New Testament's origins—and quite understandably so.

Therefore, and for the sake of clarity and to anticipate at least some of the many questions such an analysis will inevitably provoke, we aver that our theory *accepts* nearly all of the "hard" conclusions of historical scholarship, unless specifically indicated otherwise in our text, including: the dating of the Gospels, the authorship of the genuine Pauline letters, the insights that Mark was used as a source (along with a so-called "Q" source) in the composition of Matthew and Luke, the nature of and reasons for the images on both Hebrew and Roman coins, the differing perspectives of the various Gospels, the identification of dates, and the like. We also agree with those who see pagan elements, Platonic elements and Hellenized "Mystery" Cult elements in the New Testament. Even when our identifications of certain persons may be controversial, the identification itself is hardly unique to us. We do question some of the traditional understanding of the Dead Sea Scrolls, as many others have of late, as well, but we hasten to add that our theory is not reliant on this fact, and is instead based on both a new integration of the evidence as well as original evidence presented for the first time in this book.

Moreover, the theory articulated in this book takes no position on the existence of an historical Jesus, a fact which has never been (and may never be) possible to verify. If such a person did exist, we believe he was likely to have been quite different from the protagonist of the New Testament. There were a number of Messiahs in the 1st Century who claimed to be the fulfillment of Hebrew prophecy, and thousands of messianic Jews of the 1st Century were crucified for their beliefs. Many messianic fanatics of the era were surely named "Jesus." All of these things are true.

While even most religious skeptics have been reluctant to deny the historical reality of a human moral idealist named Jesus, an altruist and a peace-lover, there is insufficient evidence to claim certainty here. Although most researchers believe there was a real person named "Jesus," they admit this is only a logical inference and that no direct evidence of his existence has ever been confirmed. Some scholars, on the other hand, have gone so far as to argue that there was no historical Jesus at all and that he was entirely constructed from earlier sources. (See, e.g., the work of Wells, G.A., such as *Did Jesus Exist?*, 1975, London: Pemberton.) Indeed, there are earlier precedents for all of the attributes that are ascribed to Jesus, as we demonstrate. Still others think that Jesus did exist but that he was nothing like the person described in the Gospels. Some of these have argued that he was a political revolutionary or an insurrectionist—a "Zealot." However, the question of whether Jesus actually existed is not addressed by our thesis, and perhaps may never be answered.

For the last two or three centuries, during the period when free inquiry in this matter has been possible, scholars have trained a critical eye on the texts of the New Testament, and during this time their arguments weighing the historical reliability of what has been passed down have aroused passionate debate. Most academics today, including many Christians, accept that the Gospels and the Book of Acts are not historically reliable sources. (See, e.g., Ehrman, Bart D., *Jesus Interrupted: Revealing the Hidden Contradictions in the Bible (And Why We Don't Know About Them)*, 2009, New York: Harper One.) We concur and for basically the same reasons (including the obvious contradictions between them), and we agree that the Gospels were written for theological reasons and not as historical documents, and therefore they can only be understood as either articles of faith or as allegorical guides to a deeper meaning. None of the Gospels was written in the time of Jesus, for example, or by anyone who knew him personally. Indeed, no evidence of Jesus from his own time, documentary or otherwise, exists, at all. That Jesus's very name simply means "salvation" complicates the question of his *personal* existence further.

A group of scholars calling itself "the Jesus Seminar" attempted to sort through the earliest Christian texts and answer these various questions by creating an annotated translation of the New Testament—one noting all of their suspicions and doubts about the veracity of each line, phrase and word—in an effort to achieve consensus about what can or cannot be categorized as original, changed or added at a later date. (Funk, Robert W., Hoover, Roy W., and the Jesus Seminar, *The Search for the Authentic Words of Jesus: The Five Gospels*, 1993, New York: Polebridge Press.) Their consensus? The bulk of what the Gospels claim Jesus said was not actually said by the historical Jesus. What the Gospels claim Jesus did was even still less reliable in their view.

In the end, the Jesus Seminar concluded that *most* of the things directly quoted by the Gospels as teachings of Jesus Christ were written later by authors with their own theological motivations. What all of these scholars recognize is that most of what we read in the Gospels is not history at all but often material re-worked from the Old Testament or from narratives later attached to the legend of Jesus. For example, the oldest and shortest Gospel, Mark, contains no "Nativity" stories at all. The two Gospels that are so reliant on Mark, Matthew and Luke each add their own stories about the birth of Jesus—with little overlap between the two and even occasionally contradicting one another. These nativity stories are obvious re-workings of existing material from Hebrew scriptures, such as the slaughter of infants in the story of Moses found in Exodus that is repeated in Matthew's account of Jesus's birth.

Among the copious other evidence that the Gospels are unreliable includes Mark's declaration that Jesus said, before he was ever crucified, "Take up [your] Cross and follow me" (Mark 8:34) If he did indeed say such a thing, no one could have understood it. It is more likely that such words were placed into the mouth of Jesus *later*, after the symbolism of the Crucifixion was established. From across a wide range of disciplines and methods, scholars including many Christians have accepted that the Gospels are fictional and not historical and that their function was *theological*. The reliability of the history contained in the Gospels has long been questioned.

The scholars of the Jesus Seminar do believe, however, that the authentic words of Jesus *can* be discovered through a process of determining the sayings, or parts of sayings, that are most amenable to oral transmission. Thus, by their logic, the more a saying attributed to Jesus is pithy and memorable, the more likely it is to be *authentic*.

They add other factors to their considerations, such as "multiple attestation," i.e., the existence of the saying in multiple sources, and especially its presence in the Gospel of Thomas, which was discovered among the finds at Nag Hammadi, a Gnostic library discovered in Egypt with certain texts dating back to perhaps the 2nd Century. Scholars had long hypothesized that just as Matthew and Luke seem to have used the Gospel of Mark as a source, so the sayings of Jesus shared by Matthew and Luke were probably also once circulated independently. This hypothesized second source was named "Q." The Gospel of Thomas, although itself written in the 2nd Century, looks like it was developed directly from the "Q source."

Unfortunately for the Jesus Seminar's wider approach, many of the sayings that they find to be the most authentic are those which are also the most nakedly pro-Roman and Hellenized parts of his message. For example, Jesus's proclamations concerning taxes ("Give to Caesar what is Caesar's"), his denunciations of Kosher diet ("It's not what goes into a person from the outside that can defile"), his attack on traditional Jewish Sabbath observance ("The Sabbath day was made for Adam"), etc., are among their strongest candidates for authenticity. Indeed, a reversal of standard Jewish expectations is ironically one of their key indicators of authenticity! May we humbly submit, after the evidence we have submitted, that they are some of the strongest evidence that these were inventions of the Roman government.

The Jesus Seminar also falls short in its inability to distinguish material that circulated in an oral tradition originating from other sages like John the Baptist, that were simply attributed later to Jesus in the Gospels or in Q.

Moreover, in an age of widespread illiteracy, much of this material, whether from the Gospels or from earlier Jewish-Christian sources, simply had to have circulated orally, even after being written down. Containing features that were probably passed down through oral preservation, therefore, is simply not enough evidence to source something to an historical Jesus with any confidence.

2. Valliant, James S., "The New Testament Versus the American Revolution," *The Objective Standard*, vol. 10, no. 2, Summer, 2015, pp. 35-47.

3. Mark 4:10-12, emphasis added; cf. Luke 8:9-10, Matthew 13:11-13, and John 10:1-10 (The New International Version of the New Testament is generally used in the notes that follow.)

4. e.g., Mark 5:42-43, Matthew 8:3-4, and Matthew 12:15-16

5. Matthew 16:20; cf. Mark 8:29-30

6. Mark 3:16, Luke 6:14, Matthew 16:17-19, John 1:42; Acts 1:23, Acts 4:36; Acts 13:9

7. John 13:23

8. **NOTE:** There are many outstanding sources on these questions, such as George H. Smith, *Atheism: The Case Against God*, 1974, Nash, new edition, 1979, Prometheus, and Richard Elliott Friedman, *Who Wrote the Bible?*, 1987, new edition and preface, 1997, Harper, and *The Bible With Sources Revealed*, 2003, Harper.

Dolphin and Anchor
I. Crux Dissimulata

1. With the possible exceptions of the epistle credited to James, which we shall consider in some detail, and the Apocalypse of John which appears to contain a combination of elements.

2. The timing of Vespasian's son and successor Titus's own birth—so shortly yet clearly after the Crucifixion of Christ—is strikingly convenient to the purpose of suggesting their separate and successive identities. A widespread belief in some form of such "reincarnation" among Jews, moreover, can be seen in the New Testament, in

which people ask whether John the Baptist, for example, was himself "Elijah returned." Although reincarnation is alien to the traditional Jewish context, John 1:19-23, "Now this was John's testimony when the Jewish Leaders in Jerusalem sent priests and Levites to ask him who he was. He did not fail to confess, but confessed freely, 'I am not the Messiah.' 'They asked him, 'Then who are you? Are you Elijah?' He said, 'I am not.' 'Are you the Prophet?' He answered, 'No.'" John then goes on to identify himself as the voice crying in the wilderness predicted by the prophet Isaiah, an idea certainly more consistent with the theology of the New Testament. However, simply asking if he *believed himself* to be Elijah suggests that there were Jews who did so regard the Baptist and therefore believed in a kind of reincarnation. Furthermore, at Mark 6:14-16, we are told that some thought the same of Jesus. "King Herod heard about this, for Jesus' name had become well known. Some were saying, 'John the Baptist has been raised from the dead, and that is why miraculous powers are at work in him.' Others said, 'He is Elijah.' And still others claimed, He is a prophet, like one of the prophets of long ago. But when Herod heard this, he said, 'John, whom I beheaded, has been raised from the dead!'" Notice that among these notions is the idea that *Jesus himself* might be the Baptist "raised from the dead," someone who was his alleged contemporary(!) This is an idea repeated again at Mark 8:28, and a concept toned down or explained in the Gospel of Luke in its prenatal prophecy about the nature of the Baptist, like this: "And he will go on before the Lord, *in the spirit and power of Elijah*, to turn the hearts of the parents to their children and the disobedient to the wisdom of the righteous—to make ready a people prepared for the Lord." (Emphases added)

3. For an excellent description of the views of the famous Dead Sea Scrolls "sectarians," and a comparison of those views to those of the first Christians, see Eisenman, Robert, *The Dead Sea Scrolls and the First Christians* (1996, Rockport, PA: Element Books).

4. The concept of the Trinity is itself a pagan-flavored one. The three Fates, the three Graces, and the three-faced goddess Hecate are just some of the many precedents of a triple-natured or triple-formed deity in pagan religion.

5. Matthew 4:19.

6. cf. Luke 5:1-11 and John 21:1-14

7. Mark 6:45-52, Matthew 14:22-33, and John 6:16-21

8. Mark 4:35-41, Luke 8:22-25, and Matthew 8:23-27

9. Mark 6:53-56 and Matthew 14:34-36

10. Mark 5:1-20 and Luke 8:26-39

11. Exodus 30:13

12. Matthew 17:24-27, emphasis added.

13. Mark 13:1-30, cf. Matthew 24:1-39

14. Mark 6:31-44, Luke 9:10-17, Matthew 14:13-21, and John 5:6-15

15. Mark 8:1-9

16. Matthew 15:32-39

17. John 6:35, 48 and 51

18. John 4:14-15 and 7:37

19. Mark 14:22-24, Luke 21:19-20, Matthew 26:26-28, and 1 Corinthians 11:23-25

20. Tertullian, "De Baptismo," 1

21. St. Clement of Alexandria, *Christ, the Instructor,* Book III, Chapter XI

22. Herodotus. *The Histories with Introduction and Notes* by John M. Marincola, 2003, Penguin, p. 224.

23. Mark 8:34, cf. Luke 9:23, Matthew 16:24

24. Clement of Alexandria, *Christ, The Instructor*, Book I, Chapter III, "Isaac only bore the wood of the sacrifice, as the Lord the wood of the cross."

25. See, e.g., Moss, Candida, *The Myth of Persecution: How Early Christians Invented a Story of Martyrdom*, 2013, HarperOne.

26. Scarre, Chris, *Chronicle of the Roman Emperors: the Reign-by-Reign Record of the Rulers of Imperial Rome*, 1995, Thames & Hudson, p. 170.

27. *The Letters of the Younger Pliny*, trans. Betty Radice, 1963, Penguin Classics, Book Ten, 96, 97, emphasis added.

28. Tacitus, *The Annals*, in *Annals and Histories*, E. Cowan, ed., trans. Alfred John Church and William Jackson Brodribb, 2009, Everyman's Library (trans. orig. pub. 1876), Book XV, 44, emphasis added.

29. Pasachoff, Naomi E., and Littman, Robert J., *A Concise History of the Jewish People*, 2005, Rowman & Littlefield, p. 67; DellaPergola, Sergio, "World Jewish Population, 2012," *The American Jewish Year Book*, 2012, Springer, pp. 212-283.

30. Suetonius, *Claudius*, 25, this and subsequent references to Suetonius are from *The Twelve Caesars*, trans. Robert Graves, rev. ed. 1979, (trans. first pub. 1957), Penguin Classics. **NOTE:** Suetonius's actual language, *impulsore chresto*, may be rendered simply, "messianic insurgents." This, in either case, would not alter the apparent confusion Tacitus, who obviously was talking about a person called "Christ," exhibits with regard to the violent nature of Christians. Such a translation also still suggests that similar language was then used to describe *both* kinds of messianic adherents. Significantly, the original text of Tacitus read "Chrestiani" rather than "Christiani," seemingly reflecting the same spelling used by Suetonius for his Jewish rebel "Chrestus," helping us to confirm

that these ancient pagan writers shared a similar confusion regarding sectarian divisions among contemporary messianic Jews.

31. Suetonius, *Nero*, 38

32. Flavius Josephus, *Antiquities of the Jews*, Books XIX and XX, hereafter, "Antiquities," *Wars of the Jews*, esp., Chapter 8, Book II, hereafter "Wars," in *The Complete Works of Josephus*, trans. William Whiston, 1960, Kregel. **NOTE:** The very names of the rebel groups are suggestive of religious terrorists. The first, the "Zealots," were credited with being an entirely new ideology or school of philosophy within Judaism by the historian Flavius Josephus, and the name of the other major rebel group, the "Sicarii," actually means "dagger men." Both groups can only be described as "terrorists." The Sicarii, for example, hid daggers under the cloaks and mingled in crowds to disguise their assassinations. (See, Chaliand, Gerard, *The History of Terrorism: From Antiquity to al Qaïda*, 2007, Berkeley: University of California Press, p. 68.) These groups are associated by the ancient historians with both assassinations and kidnappings. Apart from disturbances in both Rome and Alexandria, these terrorists were even accused of arson. When a terrible fire destroyed much of the city of Antioch in Syria shortly before Vespasian arrived in the East, the locals believed it was arson and blamed it on the Jews. Although Josephus tries in his text to absolve Jews of any guilt, both the leadership and the populace of the city were still convinced that Jews had set the blaze. (Josephus, *Wars, ante*, Book VII, chapter 3, sec. 4, and see, Levick, Barbara, *Vespasian*, 1999, New York: Routledge, pp. 147-148.) The Great Fire of Rome would not be the only instance of a major urban fire that was blamed at the time on messianic Jews. Moreover, Tacitus himself provides clear evidence that the fire Nero blamed on Christians was arson, although Tacitus's own implication is that Nero himself was to blame: "And no one dared to stop the mischief, because of incessant menaces from a number of persons *who forbade the extinguishing of the flames*, because again *others openly hurled brands*, and kept shouting that there was *one who gave them authority*, either seeking to plunder more freely, or obeying orders." (Tacitus, *ante, Annals*, Book XV, 38, emphasis added.)

Josephus ultimately blames the burning of the Jewish Temple on the Jewish rebels themselves, but that instance of arson must surely be laid at the feet of the Romans. Writing around the year 400, the early Christian historian Sulpicius Severus, a historian normally given only little credit for the period before his own time, quotes Pliny the Younger as Pliny quotes from the missing volume five of Tacitus's *Histories*. Lost now, only quotations from other authors who quote the missing section from Tacitus's writings survive today, for instance in Pliny/Severus's description of the siege of Jerusalem (which varies considerably from that of Josephus). In this account, Titus is said to have called a meeting in which he discussed the question of whether or not to destroy the Temple—and the reason cited in favor of doing so is stated to be the Temple's inspirational power for both "the Jews and the *christiani*." (S. Severus, *Chronicle*, chapter XXX.) Whether this means "Christians" or not is a matter of scholarly controversy. That it could also mean religiously rebellious Jews is also quite significant. In any case, other instances of arson may well have been part of the Jewish war effort against the Romans.

Of note, while the term that Paul uses to describe himself, "Zealot," on two occasions (Acts 22:3; Galatians 1:14) is usually translated simply as "one who was zealous" for Jewish tradition, that term is actually the name of a group. It may therefore be an assertion on Paul's part that he was a member of the rebel group known as the Zealots. Two recent translations (*The Jewish New Testament* and *The Alternate Literal Translation*) translate this simply, "a zealot." While Jay P. Green's *Modern King James Version* makes this out to be "a zealous one," the passage from Galatians is rendered "being an absolute zealot for the traditions..." in *The Unvarnished New Testament* (1991). This in itself may suggest that the Jewish Christians and the Zealots were one and the same group, if not close rivals. In either case, we must bear in mind that Paul's various self-descriptions, as we shall continue to see, are a moving target and far from reliable as he traveled between an extreme range of ideological groups.

33. Eisenman, Robert, *James the Brother of Jesus*, 1996, Viking, and *The Dead Sea Scrolls and the First Christians*, 1996, Element.

34. Galatians 5:1-6, emphasis added.

35. Ephesians 2:11-20, emphasis added. **NOTE:** At Matthew 21:41 Jesus even informs the chief priests and the elders of the Jews, "Truly I tell you, the tax collectors and the prostitutes are entering the kingdom of God ahead of you." Jesus's context here, the Parable of the Two Sons, is also noteworthy.

> What do you think? There was a man who had two sons. He went to the first and said, "Son, go and work today in the vineyard."
>
> "I will not," he answered, but later he changed his mind and went.
>
> Then the father went to the other son and said the same thing. He answered, "I will, sir," but he did not go.
>
> "Which of the two did what his father wanted?"
>
> "The first," they answered.
>
> Jesus said to them, "Truly I tell you, the tax collectors and the prostitutes are entering the kingdom of God ahead of you. For John came to you to show you the way of righteousness, and you did not believe him, but the tax collectors and the prostitutes did. And even after you saw this, you did not repent and believe him." (Matthew 21:28-32)

So, why are prostitutes and tax collectors mentioned right alongside "sinners" in the Gospels: "When the teachers of the law who were Pharisees saw him eating with the sinners and tax collectors, they asked his disciples: 'Why does he eat with tax collectors and sinners?'" (Mark 2:15; curiously, Matthew, a Gospel directed at a Jewish audience, drops the first "third-person" listing of tax collectors with sinners.) From this should we conclude that all tax-collectors as such are sinners? Tax collectors were already widely regarded as cheats, and while our Gospel references do mention tax collectors in the same breath as "sinners," the distinction between the two is intriguing, especially since the Gospels depict Jesus as being friendly with tax-collectors. Jesus had "many" followers who were publicans (tax collectors) and even recruited a major disciple who was one. (Mark 2:13-17, Luke 5:27-32 and Matthew 9:9-13) So, just as one might have guessed, tax collectors are likely to have been among the most grateful for Christ's message. One Zacchaeus, the wealthy "chief tax collector" in Jericho, was so anxious to hear Jesus speak that he climbed a tree to get the best vantage, according to Luke. Favorably impressed, Jesus insisted on dining at the man's house. (Luke 19:1-10) When the crowd complains that he was dining with "a sinner," Jesus defends him:

> All the people saw this and began to mutter, "He has gone to be the guest of a sinner."
> But Zacchaeus stood up and said to the Lord, "Look, Lord! Here and now I give half of my possessions to the poor, and if I have cheated anybody out of anything, I will pay back four times the amount."
> Jesus said to him, "Today salvation has come to this house, because this man, too, is a son of Abraham. For the Son of Man came to seek and to save the lost." (Luke 19:7-10)

By Christ's reckoning, then, tax collectors can be honest, and he is said to have regarded them as worthy friends and followers, just as Paul did, and, of course, Titus.

36. 1 Corinthians 9:19-23, emphasis added.

37. Galatians 2:2-13, emphasis added. **NOTE:** Galatians is a first-person narrative, a letter, making it far more credible than Acts' historical reconstruction of events after-the-fact. In addition, such a heated debate between the Apostles would have been embarrassing to later Christians and for that very reason Galatians is almost certainly *authentic*, even if it also still contains Paul's own deceptions. Peter and Titus may well have been granted special exemptions from Mosaic Law. In emergency situations, Jewish tradition sometimes permits avoiding strict Torah observance. King David may have cut corners in a time of need at 1 Samuel 21, for example, which Jesus himself cites to justify the Torah-violating behavior of

his own disciples in a non-emergency situation at Mark 2:23-28. Also, during the Hasmonean Revolt, many Jews decided that it was permissible to engage in defensive warfare on the Sabbath rather than be slaughtered (1 Maccabees 2:41).

38. Mark 7:15-16, cf. Matthew 15:10-11

39. Matthew 8:10; Luke 7:1-17

40. Galatians 1:11-12. **NOTE:** Even though the Gospels had not yet been written, if any of the material contained in them suggested that Jesus argued against Mosaic Law (even in an oral form) at that stage, it surely would have been known to both Paul and the previous "Jewish-Christian" leadership in Jerusalem. We must therefore wonder what, if anything, the Jewish-Christians actually believed about a person named "Jesus." Given the dramatic liberties taken in the Gospels by inserting teachings into the mouth of Jesus, and creating whole narrative settings for those teachings, along with their use of Hebrew scriptures as a source of information rather than recent history, we can be confident that very little, if anything, was known with clarity about a historical Jesus during the late 1st Century.

41. Galatians 2:11-13

42. Galatians 2:1-5, 11-12 **NOTE:** If he existed, Jesus is not likely to have been concerned with issues like Kosher diet. His was not the first mission to the Gentiles, as was Paul's, where such issues would have naturally arisen, and the earliest Christians not only seem to have observed Kosher dietary restrictions, as a group, they fiercely opposed Paul for challenging them on that point.

In order to claim that the Apostles ever agreed with him, Paul suspiciously says that he once "met privately" with them and "presented" to them the Gospel that he preached "among the Gentiles," according to Galatians, Chapter 2. However, he does not assert that they agreed with him on the subject of circumcision, but only states that Titus, his uncircumcised Gentile associate, "was not forced to be circumcised." In other words, they may have requested or demanded it, but they simply did not force it to happen. Paul seems to hang his hat entirely on the fact that they did not compel one of his disciples, named "Titus," to undergo circumcision.

Had Paul been able to say that his zealous friends overtly agreed with him, surely, he would have said so explicitly. Reading Galatians carefully, Paul makes no such claim. Indeed, had the Apostles agreed with him, the later efforts of James to "spy on the freedom" of Paul's followers, and their continued general opposition to Paul on these matters, wouldn't make any sense. Paul instead relies on the fact that his companion "Titus" was allowed to keep his foreskin in order to suggest support for his anti-circumcision message that, in fact, he had supposedly already obtained. Paul also seems to rely on the fact that Peter (he can name no one else) likewise was known to "eat with Gentiles" (a rather vague claim) – that is, at least until men from James showed up. Again, rather than any agreement with Paul's anti-Torah message, Paul cites examples of their alleged hypocrisy. And again, this is something rather dubious, if not laughable, coming from a man who boasted to being and acting like "all things to all men"—precisely in order to win their support.

However, in Acts, Chapter 15, we are told by a third-person narrator that James explicitly agrees with Paul: the Gentiles should be given a pass on the matter of circumcision and the full range of Kosher dietary restrictions. If this is true, then the reason why James would later oppose Paul on these very issues is rendered completely inexplicable.

Galatians reports that the Council of Jerusalem, where Acts says that James had agreed with Paul, why, then, did James later "spy on" the freedom of Paul's followers? Why did Paul have to oppose them so strongly? Why is Paul still arguing over these issues in his letter to the Galatians?

Stranger still, if James had explicitly endorsed Paul's anti-Torah message, then why didn't Paul report James's agreement in his letter to the Galatians, even though he reported the hypocritical behavior of Cephas? Why did James's allies, like Cephas, side with James in the later dispute recorded in Galatians? In turn, why doesn't Acts report that same hypocritical behavior by Cephas? Indeed, why has Cephas, after his own vision (reported earlier in the Book of Acts), sided with James in the later dispute recorded in Galatians?

In direct contradiction to the green light Acts acclaims that James gave to Paul's anti-Torah message, we are told that Paul himself still circumcised his own follower Timothy after the Council of Jerusalem "because of the Jews who lived in the area." (Acts 16:3) Apparently, Paul himself contradicted his own message in his behavior. The man who was "all things to all people" was indeed something of a chameleon.

In any case, Acts dramatically amplified the claims Paul makes in Galatians, and in so doing makes entirely inexplicable any later confrontation over these same issues, a confrontation far more credibly reported in Galatians. This section of Acts seems designed to smooth over this very dispute—and it is pure fiction.

43. Romans 3:27-29

44. Galatians 1:11-24

45. Voskuilen, Thijs, and Sheldon, Rose Mary, *Operation Messiah: St. Paul, Roman Intelligence and the Birth of Christianity* (2008, Edgware, Middlesex, UK, and Portland, Oregon, USA: Vallentine Mitchell), and for wider context, see also, Sheldon, Rose Mary, *Intelligence Activities in Ancient Rome* (2005, New York: Routledge) and Austin, N.I.E., and Rankov, N.B., *Exploratio: Military and Political Intelligence in the Roman World from the Second Punic War to the Battle of Adrianople* (1995, New York: Routledge).

46. James 1:17

47. James 1:22

48. James 1:27

49. James 2:10

50. James 2:14-17

51. James 2:19

52. James 4:1

53. James 5:1-5

54. Although its Greek may have been polished by later cura-
tors, a persuasive argument that the Letter of James is among the
earliest New Testament material and predates the Gospels (along
with the authentic letters of Paul), see, Johnson, Luke Timothy, *The
Real Jesus* (1996, HarperOne), p. 121.

55. St. Augustine, *Letters*, 28, 40, 72, 73

56. **NOTE:** There are certainly differences between the theological perspectives in Paul's letters and the Gospels—and between
the Gospels themselves—but they certainly all share with Paul the
same basic position on the Mosaic Law and peace with the Roman
government. Moreover, the differences are easily explicable once
it is understood that each was writing for a different type of audience. In Matthew, for example, while Jesus's defense of virtue as
part of salvation, e.g., Matthew 25:31-46, is slightly different from
the idea of salvation by faith alone found in Paul, both writers agree
that Jewish purity laws and Kosher dietary restrictions are *no longer necessary* and emphasize the virtue of obedience to Roman
authorities and paying taxes, instead. It does, however, seem clear
that the Gospel writers preserved some of the language of the earlier "Jewish-Christian" movement that flatly contradicts many of the
other assertions and actions attributed to Jesus. If the Gospel of
Matthew reports that Jesus commanded obedience to the whole
of the law at Matthew 5:17-20, it also reports that Jesus *attacked*
Kosher dietary laws at Matthew 15:1-20, and that Jesus made the
Pharisees angry with his liberal views on the Sabbath at Matthew
12:1-8. The Gospels may have been written by different authors, as
some have surmised, or, possibly, by one author customizing his
narratives for different audiences from a learned position of authority. In either case, there is little doubt that the Gospel of Matthew
appears to have been aimed at a Jewish audience familiar with
Hebrew scripture while Luke's account seems to have been written
to persuade the more Hellenized or Gentile reader. Compare the

slight differences between the justifications given by Jesus for the commandment to "love your enemy" in each of these Gospels:

> If you love those who love you, what reward will you get? Are not *even the tax collectors* doing that? And if you greet *only your own people*, what are you doing more than others? Do not *even pagans* do that? Be perfect, therefore, as your heavenly Father is perfect. (Matthew 5:46-48, emphasis added)

> If you love those who love you, what credit is that to you? Even sinners love those who love them. And if you do good to those who are good to you, what credit is that to you? *Even sinners* do that. And if you lend to those from whom you expect repayment, what credit is that to you? *Even sinners* lend to sinners, expecting to be repaid in full. But love your enemies, do good to them, and lend to them without expecting to get anything back. (Luke 6:32-35, emphasis added)

Matthew is clearly addressed to a Jewish audience resentful of unfair taxation while Luke omits all mention of pagans and tax-collectors. The Book of Matthew attempts to ground nearly every event about Jesus as a fulfillment of some passage from Hebrew scripture that is seen as prophetic. It draws more direct comparisons between Moses and Christ than the other of the Gospels, and its genealogy descends Jesus from the Patriarch Abraham. Luke's family tree takes Jesus's forebears all the way to the legendary ancestor of all humanity: Adam. Its sequel, the Book of Acts, relates how the message was first taken to the Gentiles by the Apostles, and it is only in Luke that we find the Parable of the Good Samaritan (Luke 10:29-37). In this parable, Jesus tells how a traveler between Jerusalem and Jericho was robbed, beaten and left half-dead on the side of the road. When a priest happened by, he left the man and passed by. The same thing happened when a Levite (another sacred class among the Jews) came upon the scene. Only a Samaritan—a member of a group who adhered to a closely-related religion but whom contemporary Jews thought of as *foreigners*—is shown to stop and render help to the man. The greater virtue of relative *aliens* compared to that of Jewish authority figures is thus once again emphasized in the New Testament.

Once we acknowledge that Matthew was tailored for a more orthodox Jewish audience than Luke, which seems to be aimed at Gentiles and Hellenized Jews, Jesus's claim that a Roman centurion's faith exceeds that of all contemporary Jews (Matthew 8:5-13) only stresses the underlying imperial purpose of all four of the oldest Gospels. Notice, too, that it is in Matthew that the Jewish crowd assumes collective responsibility for the death of Jesus: "When Pilate saw that he was getting nowhere, but that instead an uproar was starting, he took water and washed his hands in front of the crowd. 'I am innocent of this man's blood,' he said. 'It is your responsibility!' All the people answered, 'His blood is on us and on our children!'" (Matthew 27:24-25) Anti-Semitic in its impact, this apparent justification for their subsequent collective punishment was originally aimed at Jews themselves.

The differences between the Gospel of John and the three earlier Gospels (known as the "Synoptics" because of their overlap) are also well-established. In John, Jesus waxes abstract and self-conscious about his own divinity in a way not found in the Synoptic Gospels. For example, Jesus calls himself "the Way, the Truth and the Life." (John 14:6) And for its author Jesus was the pre-existent Logos that was with God and was God, even God at the Creation. This understanding of Christ's divinity is also exhibited in Paul's writings, as well: "...yet for us there is but one God the Father, from whom all things came and for whom we live; and there is but one Lord, Jesus Christ, *through whom all things came and through whom we live.*" (1 Corinthians 8:6, emphasis added) The Synoptic Gospels do understand Jesus to be divine, as seems implicit in a number of ways: the virgin birth, his asserted superiority over John the Baptist (a mere prophet), his resurrection miracles, his own resurrection, and perhaps most strongly by Jesus's forgiving of sins.

> "When Jesus saw their faith, he said to the paralyzed man, 'Son, your sins are forgiven.'
>
> "Now some teachers of the law were sitting there, thinking to themselves, 'Why does this fellow talk like

that? He's blaspheming! Who can forgive sins but God alone?" (Mark 2:5-7, cf. Luke 7:48-49)

However, Jesus himself is never so expansive or overt on the subject of his own status as he is depicted being in the Gospel of John, suggesting this Gospel to be the latest of the four, reflecting a more fully developed theology.

57. St. Croix, G.E.M., "Why Were The Early Christians Persecuted?," *Journal of Historical Studies*, November, 1963, pp. 6–38, reprinted in *Christian Persecution, Martyrdom, And Orthodoxy*, 2006, Oxford University Press.

58. Hebrews 6:19-20, emphasis added.

59. "Anchor," *The Catholic Encyclopedia*, emphasis added.

60. *Ibid*

61. *Ibid*

62. *Ibid*

II. Religion and Propaganda

1. Meshorer, Ya'akov, *Ancient Jewish Coinage, Volume I*, 1982, Amphora, pp. 60-63.

2. Meshorer, Ya'akov, *Ancient Jewish Coinage, Volume II*, 1982, Amphora, pp. 26-27. **NOTE:** Pagan symbols can even be found in some ancient synagogues, and a famous example of Zodiac imagery has been found in a 6th Century CE synagogue in Galilee. Of course, in all such instances, the pagan images themselves were never objects of worship as they never symbolized God. They were aesthetic in nature, never Jewish religious symbols. Zanger, Walter, *Jewish Worship, Pagan Symbols: Zodiac Mosaics in Ancient Synagogues*, 8-24-2012, *Bible History Daily*, http://

www.biblicalarchaeology.org/daily/ancient-cultures/ancient-israel/
jewish-worship-pagan-symbols/

3. Eusebius, *History of the Church*, trans. G.A. Williamson, 1989,
Penguin Classics, Book 4, section 6

4. Philo of Alexandria, *On the Embassy to Gaius,* XXX.203.
NOTE: Some contemporary scholars attribute much of the notorious behavior of the 1st Century Emperor Caligula—such as reports
of his incest with and deification of his sister—to an effort on the
emperor's part to model his monarchy on that of the Pharaohs, the
divine rulers of Egypt. For criticism of this position, see, e.g., Barrett,
Anthony A., *Caligula: the Corruption of Power,* 1989, New York:
Simon & Schuster, Chapter 14.

5. Suetonius, *Vespasian,* 23

6. See Rehak, Paul, and Younger, John Grimes, *Imperium
and Cosmos: Augustus and the Northern Campus Martius,* 2006,
University of Wisconsin Press, p. 93; Brent, A., *The Imperial Cult
and the Development of Church Order: Concepts and Images of
Authority in Paganism and Early Christianity Before the Age of
Cyprian,* 1999, Brill, pp. 17-18, 53-54.

7. *Ibid*

8. **NOTE:** Suetonius retells the fabulous account of Atia, the
mother of Augustus, spending the night in the Temple of Apollo,
where she had a mysterious encounter with a serpent and became
pregnant, bearing the future emperor nine months later. It is
reported that Atia developed a birthmark in the shape of a serpent
after her mysterious encounter at the temple. Moreover, Augustus
constructed a new temple to Apollo that connected to the imperial
palace itself, a structure ranked by the same historian as one of
three most noteworthy of his reign. (Suetonius, *Augustus,* 94, 29)
This echoes the stories told about previous Hellenistic monarchs
such as Seleucus I whose father Antiochus allegedly told his son
that he was, in reality, the son of Apollo. We are told that the god

gave to the mother of Seleucus a ring with the image of an anchor on it, and that Seleucus, as well as his sons and grandsons, had a birthmark shaped like an anchor. (Grainger, John D., *Seleukos Nikator: Constructing a Hellenistic Kingdom*, 1990, Routledge, p. 2.)

9. Suetonius, *Vespasian*, 5

10. Tacitus, *Histories*, in *Annals and Histories*, E. Cowan, *ante*, Book I, 86.

11. Suetonius, *Titus*, 1

12. "Colossus Neronis," *A Topographical Dictionary of Ancient Rome*, ed., Samuel Ball Platner, revised by Thomas Ashby, 1929, London: Oxford University Press. **NOTE:** Even ignoring their construction of the Colosseum, the importance of the Flavian dynasty, both culturally and politically, is hard to overstate. Not only were the works of Josephus and (at least) the first three Gospels written during the Flavian era, Pliny the Elder published his important *Natural History* in Vespasian's reign and dedicated it to his friend Titus. Vespasian subsidized the educator and rhetorician Quintillian who may have taught the author and magistrate Pliny the Younger, the historian Tacitus, and the satirist Juvenal. The historian Suetonius served on the staff of his friend Pliny the Younger when the latter was governor of Bithynia-Pontus. In his youth, the influential Stoic philosopher Epictetus was a slave of Nero's servant Epaphroditus. The Greek historian and biographer Plutarch probably began publishing his works under the Flavians. In the wake of the civil war, the Flavians had to restock the Senate and, in the process, they established the aristocracy that would come to rule Rome in the so-called era of "adoptive" or "good emperors" in the century that followed them. Vespasian advanced the careers of the father of the future Emperor Trajan, who brought the Empire to its greatest size, as well as the ancestors of the future Emperors Antoninus Pius and Marcus Aurelius.

13. John 8:12

14. Stevenson and Madden, *A Dictionary of Roman Coins, Republican and Imperial*, 1889, London: George Bell & Sons, p. 339.

15. *Ibid*

16. *Forum for ancient coins*, http://www.forumancientcoins.com/numiswiki/view.asp?key=dolphin, emphasis added.

17. Venuti, Niccolo Marcello, *A Description of the First Discoveries of the Ancient City of Herculaneum*, trans. Wickes Skurray, 1750, London: G. Woodfall (original Italian edition, 1748, Rome); and *Proceedings of the Antiquarian Society, With Communications Made to the Society*, Volume 12, 1908, Cambridgeshire: George Bell and Sons; and Wollaston, Robert, *A Short Description of the Thermae Romano-Brittannicae, Or, The Roman Baths Found in Italy, Britain, France, Switzerland, Etc., Etc. With Some Notices of the Mosaics and Paintings Which Formed a Part of Their Decorations, Especially of the Thermae of Titus and Constantine*, 1864, London: Robert Hardwicke. **NOTE:** There is evidence Titus himself may have visited the pool at Herculaneum since graffiti apparently made by his physician found nearby, "Apollinaris, the doctor of the Emperor Titus, defecated well here," must have been made in the two months between Titus's ascension to the throne and the eruption of Vesuvius. There is no question that the style of the mosaic places the pool in the Flavian period and, as a large public work, it is all the more likely that it would sponsor their developing iconography. Also of note is that in the center of the cruciform pool a bronze fountain was found:

The fountain is in the shape of a five-headed snake wrapped around a tree and spewing water. It is a clear reference to Serapis and the healer god Aesclepius, whose famous snake-entwined staff is a universal symbol of medicine to this day.

18. Atwill, Joseph, *Caesar's Messiah*, 2005, Berkeley, CA: Ulysses Press, pp. 38-44. **NOTE:** One certainly need not accept all of this writer's various contentions—some of which are highly questionable—in order to see some of these parallels. The Mount of Olives, just to the east of ancient Jerusalem, was a sort of base of operations for the ministry of Jesus when he came to Jerusalem, according to the Gospel of Luke, and so it was the spot where Christ prayed before he was arrested there (Luke 22:39-51). The same text also has Jesus start out on his Palm Sunday triumphal entry into Jerusalem from this location (Luke 19:28-44), and the book of Matthew places Jesus there for his apocalyptic prophecy of Jerusalem's impending destruction (Matthew 24:3, *et seq.*). It is here, also, that Jesus commanded Peter to put away his sword (Luke 22:49-51). This is also where Jesus ascended into heaven following his resurrection, according to Acts (Acts 1:12). Eastern Orthodox tradition holds that Jesus's *Glorious Second Coming* will commence here, as well. Curiously, as Atwill observes, the Mount of Olives was also the camp for the Roman Tenth Legion, *Legio X Fretensis*, under the command of Titus during his siege of Jerusalem, and an important base of operations for his triumphant entry into Jerusalem. Of note, the mountain was already the site of an important Jewish necropolis in Jesus's time.

19. Levick, Barbara, *Vespasian*, 1999, New York: Routledge, p. 33.

20. Levick, *ante*, pp. 68-69

21. Tacitus, *Histories*, *ante*, Book IV, 83 and 84

22. See, generally, Burkert, Walter, *Ancient Mystery Cults*, 1987, Cambridge: Harvard Univ. Press; cf. Plutarch, *Moralia*, Vol. V, *Isis and Osiris*, 1936, Loeb Classical Library, Harvard University Press. **NOTE:** All mystery religions are sometimes referred to as "Orphic

Mystery Cults," although this is inexact. Orpheus, the poet and musician from Greek myth, was said to have visited Hades in an effort to restore the life of his beloved wife. Although his wife was not returned to him, Orpheus had successfully harrowed hell. As a consequence, his devotees believed Orpheus could assist one's soul in the afterlife. His cult believed in punishments following death for the wicked and in a cycle of "transmigration of souls" that could be transcended only by adopting an ascetic lifestyle. Also according to his myth, the famous musician was torn to pieces by the crazed worshippers of Dionysus. The deity of this cult is named as either Dionysus (Bacchus) or Zagreus, and since this god is said to have experienced a similar martyrdom before his apotheosis, their cross identification with the Egyptian Osiris was inevitable. Orpheus was also said to have been a sun worshipper.

A 4th Century BCE Orphic grave prayer reads: "Now you have died and now you have come into being, O thrice happy one, on this same day. Tell Persephone that the Bacchic One himself released you." (Graf, Fritz, and Johnston, Sara, *Ritual Texts for the Afterlife: Orpheus and the Bacchic Gold Tablets*, 2007, London, New York: Routledge, pp. 36-37.)

23. Graves, Robert, *The Greek Myths*, 1955, New York: Penguin, section 50, provides a good list of sources. **NOTE:** Temples to the god Aesclepius were both religious sites/centers of worship as well as the first hospitals and treatment facilities in the Hellenistic world. See, Risse, Guenter B., "Pre-Christian Healing Places, Asclepieion and Valetudinarium: the Confluence of the Sacred and Secular," *Mending Bodies, Saving Souls: a History of Hospitals*. 1990, Oxford University Press, p. 56-59. Such temples, or "asclepeions," became increasingly popular from the 4th Century BCE until the late Roman imperial period.

It was at the asclepeion on his native island of Cos that the famous healer Hippocrates (5th-4th centuries BCE) was probably trained in medicine, and the 2nd Century CE physician Galen was educated at the important asclepeion at Pergamon in the Roman province of Asia (modern-day Turkey), a facility that had been expanded by the Romans.

Pergamon was also the site of an important library, considered to be a rival to the famous library at Alexandria in Egypt, as well as a great temple of the Egyptian deities Isis and Serapis. According to Christian legend, St. Antipas, the first bishop of Pergamon, became such a rival to the priests of Serapis there that he was martyred during the reign of Domitian in around 92 CE by being burnt inside a brazen bull.

Eastern Orthodox Christians still pray to Antipas to relieve their toothaches. The entire "third region" of early imperial Rome, *Regio tertia*, was named *Isis et Serapis* because of the large temple to those deities there. Originally dedicated to Isis alone in the 1st Century BCE, during the Flavian era her worship there came to be associated with Serapis.

After it was destroyed by the fire of 80 CE, Domitian reconstructed and dedicated it to both gods.

The Flavian dynasty appears to have had a pre-existing relationship with the cults of Isis and Serapis, for it was with the aid of the priests of Isis at Rome that young Domitian, disguising himself as a devotee of her cult, was protected from Flavian rivals during the civil war of 69 CE. (Suetonius, *Domitian*, 1) Such a relationship, of course, could also help explain the early and enthusiastic assistance provided to Vespasian at the Temple of Serapis in Alexandria in the first year of his reign.

24. Tacitus, *Histories*, *ante*, Book IV, 81

25. Mark 3:1-6, Luke 6:6-11 and Matthew 12:9-14

26. Suetonius, *Vespasian*, 7. **NOTE:** Another person who was said to have performed healing miracles in the tradition of Aesclepius during the second half of the 1st Century is Apollonius of Tyana, who has been compared to Jesus Christ. Our principal source for the life of Apollonius is Lucius Flavius Philostratus, c. 170-250 CE.

27. Levick, *ante*, p. 69

28. Levick, *ante*, p. 43

29. Mark 8: 22-26; cf. Mark 7:33

30. John 9:6

31. Josephus, *Wars*, Book VI, chapter 5, sec. 4, emphasis added.

32. Suetonius, *Vespasian*, 4

33. Tacitus, *Histories, ante*, Book V, 13, emphasis added.

34. **NOTE:** For a good discussion of Johanan ben Zakkai's messianic assertions about Vespasian, see Eisenman, *James the Brother of Jesus, ante*, pp. 24, 39, 45, 69, 255, 557, 897, 946.

35. 1 Corinthians 13:13

36. Hebrews 11:1

37. Pliny the Elder, *The Natural History*, 2.8

38. Suetonius, *Titus*, 1

39. *Ibid*

40. Suetonius, *Titus,* 3

41. Suetonius, *Titus,* 7; **NOTE:** Before becoming emperor, Titus (like Henry V of England) had a reputation for wild partying. He was also known to have ruthlessly eliminated more than one of his or his father's political foes. In the face of his famous benevolence as emperor, however, it seems that all of that was forgiven.

42. Suetonius, *Titus,* 8, emphasis added.

43. Suetonius, *Titus,* 8, emphasis added.

44. *Ibid,* emphasis added

45. Suetonius, *Titus,* 10

46. Suetonius, *Titus,* 11

47. Philostratus, *The Life of Apollonius of Tyana*, sec. 32, emphasis added. **NOTE:** The "fish" reported to have killed Titus was in fact a mollusk called the Sea Hare, but to most of the ancients almost all sea creatures were called "fish," as was the dolphin.

48. Carotta, Francesco, *Jesus Was Caesar*, 2005, Aspekt, esp. pp. 47-48 and 282-283. **NOTE:** Carotta observes that Julius Caesar's descent from Gaul in the north to a triumphant arrival in Rome where he becomes a martyr to his own compassion and mercy (clementia) parallels the descent of Jesus Christ from Galilee in the north to a triumphant arrival in Jerusalem. Both men are killed by a senate/Sanhedrin for claiming to be "kings." Likewise, Atwill observes, Titus's descent from Galilee to a triumphal entrance into Jerusalem is itself directly foreshadowed—and foretold—by Jesus. For Titus's propagandistic purposes, Jesus provided the ideal bridge—a fusion that demonstrated that he was, in effect, the new Divine Julius. The deeds of both Christ and Caesar were rendered *portents* of Titus. Again, one need not accept all of Carotta's ideas in order to appreciate the range of fascinating insights contained in his work.

Consider how long the pro-government, even pro-Caesar nature of Christian literature persisted. For example, in the first part of the devout Dante's 14th Century epic poem, *The Divine Comedy*, we are led through hell itself and its several descending circles. In each of these circles a different category of sinner is punished. With each new level reached, of course, the sins and the torments punishing them are more hideous. At the very bottom, Satan himself is trapped in a frozen lake with his torso and head above the surface of the ice. He has three faces and in each of his mouths is a sinner—presumably, the three worst and greatest sinners in all of history, chewed eternally by the devil himself.

In Satan's center mouth is the disciple Judas, who betrayed Jesus Christ. More surprising to modern Christian readers, in the others are the ancient Roman traitors Brutus and Cassius Longinus, the men who assassinated Julius Caesar, the pagan god and Roman dictator.

The three mouths chew these damned souls without ever killing them. (Dante Alighieri, *Inferno*, Canto XXXIV)

49. Levick, *ante*, p. 65.

III. Roman Messiahs

1. Mark 13 (emphasis added); cf. Luke 21:5-37 and Matthew 24, et seq. **NOTE:** Another issue with which scholars have long contended involves those occasions when Jesus appears to assert that the "Kingdom of God" (which has been variously translated as "Kingdom of Heaven" or "God's Imperial Rule") has already arrived (see, e.g., John 16:33, Matthew 12:28 and Luke 11:20), despite also predicting it as a future event, something a theory of Roman provenance also helps to explain since, according to the Gospels, Jesus himself lived under Roman rule although Flavian rule had yet to arrive.

2. Mark 15:29-30

3. Josephus, *Antiquities*, Book XX, chapter 5, sec. 1-4

4. Joshua 3:14-17

5. See, generally, Schafer, Peter, *Jesus in the Talmud*, 2009, Princeton University Press. **NOTE:** The pagan origins of the virgin birth claimed for Jesus in the Gospels (Matthew 1:18-25, Luke 1:26-38) are clear. Lacking a mortal father and being miraculous in nature, his divine paternity is demonstrated by an otherwise fatherless birth. Announcing "the Holy Spirit" to have been responsible only further confirms this intention. Divine paternity was common among pagan heroes who enjoyed an apotheosis, but is something that lacks any precedent among Jewish messiahs from the Hebrew Bible for obvious monotheistic reasons.

In addition, the Gospel of Matthew's attempt to ground the idea of a virgin birth in Hebrew prophecy has long been understood by scholars to be artificial. The cited prophecy (Matthew 1:23 quotes Isaiah 7:14) has no direct connection to the coming of the Messiah at all and was a "sign" to be associated with a specific event reported from Isaiah's own time.

Finally, the word used by Isaiah originally meant only "young woman" and only took on the added meaning of "virgin" when Isaiah was later translated into the Greek language in the Septuagint.

Even virgin births can be found in pagan myth, as in the stories of Zeus's matings with Io and Danaë, and, perhaps, in the accounts of the birth of Romulus, the legendary founder of Rome and son of Mars, whose mother was a *Vestal Virgin*.

6. Matthew 8:8-12, emphasis added, cf. Luke 7:1-17

7. Matthew 28:19

8. Matthew 5:41

9. Matthew 5:5

10. Matthew 5:9

11. Matthew 5:43-44 and Luke 6:27-28

12. Qumran Community Rule 9.21-22, and see Eisenman, *James: the Brother of Jesus, ante*, pp. 339, 826, 853-854.

13. Matthew 5:39 and Luke 6:29

14. Matthew 8:1-5 and Luke 18:17

15. Luke 2:14

16. Romans 13:1-7, emphasis added.

17. 1 Peter 2:13-17, emphasis added.

18. Colossians 3:22-24; and see, 1 Timothy 6:1-2, 1 Peter 2:18-20 and Ephesians 6:5-9. **NOTE:** Jesus himself assumes without criticism that masters can and will beat their slaves, as we read at Luke 12:47-49: "The servant who knows the master's will and does not get ready or does not do what the master wants will be beaten with many blows. But the one who does not know and does things

deserving punishment will be beaten with few blows. From everyone who has been given much, much will be demanded; and from the one who has been entrusted with much, much more will be asked."

19. Luke 6:20

20. Mark 10:28-31, cf. Matthew 19:27-30, Matthew 20:16

21. John 13:1-17

22. John 13:12-17

23. Matthew 18:14

24. Luke 22:24-27

25. Matthew 20:25-28

26. Mark 12:17, cf. Matthew 22:21 and Luke 20:25

27. Luke 23:2

28. Matthew 26:60

29. Mark 15:1-15, Matthew 27:11-25, Luke 23:13-25, John 18: 29-40

30. Matthew 27:25

31. The story of Jesus's trial before Pilate, by itself, demonstrates the Roman provenance of the Gospels, indeed, that they are the handiwork of the Roman State.

The story of Jesus's "trial" before Pilate is fiction. The findings of scholars such as those of the Jesus Seminar reflect the wide-spread view among critical scholars: "...the Fellows were virtually unanimous in their judgment that the account of the Judean trial [of Jesus] was mostly a fabrication of the Christian imagination." (Funk, Robert W., Hoover, Roy W., and the Jesus Seminar, *The Search for the Authentic Words of Jesus: The Five Gospels*, 1993, New York: Polebridge Press, p. 121) As these scholars observe, because there were no eyewitness accounts of this trial, and certainly none cited by the Gospels, the details of this episode must be regarded as later invention.

It must be added that certain details, such as the thrice-repeated demand of the crowd to crucify Jesus (reported in all four Gospels), seem entirely hatched. Just as Peter denied Jesus *three* times, so the crowd demands his death *three* times, and the number three is theologically suggestive throughout the New Testament, e.g. the Sign of Jonah, the three favored disciples at scenes such as the Transfiguration, etc.

But if this episode in the Gospels is necessarily fiction, then we must ask what motives shaped it and why its elements were inserted, removed or retained. If that thrice repeated demand to kill Jesus is a fabrication, for example, then what end does it serve— except to exonerate not just Romans, but the *Roman government?* Why does the crowd have to demand his death, *at all?* Only to overcome Pilate's *resistance.* If that thrice-repeated demand by the crowd is fiction, then it was simply to explain how Pilate's belief in Jesus's innocence was overcome.

In fact, as we have seen, the whole underlying cause of Jesus's enmity with Jewish religious authorities as presented in the Gospels, his opposition to the Mosaic Law, appears to have been a post-Pauline invention. This by itself undermines the historicity of the trial before the Sanhedrin, unless it was only an effort on their part to eliminate an advocate of violence and separatism, not a critic of the Mosaic Law, out of fear of the Romans.

Moreover, if, in fact, Jesus had been convicted of blasphemy by the Sanhedrin, as the Gospels assert, then that body could have executed Jesus themselves. That they did not appears to present a problem for which the Gospel of John attempts to provide an answer. According to John 18:31-32, when Pilate told the Jewish authorities to judge Jesus themselves, "the Jews," collectively, replied that they had no legal authority to put "any man" to death. Yet, we know this was not the case: prior to the first Jewish War, the Jews routinely enforced their own law, including its various provisions for capital punishment. Among several other persuasive references, Josephus provides us with verbatim citations from multiple Roman imperial decrees commanding that the Jews be allowed to preserve and enforce their own laws (Josephus, *Antiquities*, Book XVI, chapter 6, sec. 1-8). And the New Testament itself provides us with evidence. For example, we are told that St. Stephen was stoned to death after being convicted by the Sanhedrin of blasphemy (Acts 6 and 7), which was precisely the same context Jesus faced, and Josephus reports the eerily similar stoning of James the Just at the command of the Jewish priesthood (Josephus, *Antiquities*, Book XX, chapter 9, sec. 1).

So why would the author of John's Gospel need to mislead us like that—except in order to explain the unexplainable, namely, why Jesus was not executed by the Jews whom he had allegedly offended?

It is the nature of Jesus's execution, crucifixion, that inescapably required an official Roman command. If Jesus really existed, then the manner of his execution is likely to have been the least flexible aspect of his tradition. If he did not really exist, then this aspect of his tradition seems to have been selected in order for Jesus to fulfill the "Suffering Servant" prophecy of Isaiah, chapter 53, regarding the messianic precursor who will be "pierced" for the "transgressions" of the Jews (Isaiah 53:5). In either case, the Crucifixion appears to have been an inescapable, and earlier, part of the Jesus tradition. Had a historical Jesus actually been executed in this fashion, it is far more likely that he was executed for advocating violence and rebellion against Rome, which would be consistent with what we have argued were the true politics of the Jewish-Christians. Whether this was the case, or whether the Suffering Servant prophecy was the source of this tradition—and even if the idea of the execution had been lifted from some other messianic personage of the period—the responsibility for the execution of Jesus would still have been laid at the feet of the Romans without the Gospel's elaborate account.

Since there was no way to avoid a Roman trial, complex, repeated and unmistakable steps had to be taken to exonerate the Romans. Thus, the betrayal by Judas, the triple denial of Peter, the trial before the Sanhedrin, Pilate's belief in Jesus's innocence, the triple demand by the Jewish crowd for the Crucifixion, are all consistent with the motive to inculpate the Jews and exonerate the Roman state in the face of a method of execution that had in itself otherwise implied Jesus to have been a rebel. Matthew's version, as we argue, simply makes this unified motivation explicit.

Finally, given the fact that the thrice-repeated demand of the Jewish crowd is found in all four of the Gospels, along with Pilate's belief in Christ's innocence, this motive of exonerating the Romans is inextricably linked with the original composition of the Gospel's narrative.

32. Acts 3:13-14, emphasis added.

33. Eisenman, *James: the Brother of Jesus, ante*, pp. 122-123, 492 and 516.

34. Luke 6:14-16, Mark 3:18, Matthew 10:3, Acts 5:36-8, and Josephus, *Antiquities*, Book XX, chapter 5, sec. 1-4

35. Luke 22:29-30. **NOTE:** There may have been several reasons why Jesus had 12 disciples. The Temple Scroll found at Qumran, for example, mentions a leadership council comprised of 12 priests, 12 Levites, and 12 "leaders of the people." (11 QT 57:11-15) But there were also 12 Olympian gods, 12 signs of the Zodiac, and at least one ancient Egyptian priestly college consisted of 12 members, in addition to the "12 Tribes" of Israel.

36. Mark 6:51-52; Mark 9:33-35; Matthew 8:26; Luke 22:54-62; John 20:24-29; Luke 22:3-6 and Luke 22:47-48

37. Mark 6:1-6; Luke 4: 16-30; Matthew 13:54-58; John 4:44; John 7:5. **NOTE:** Mentions of Jesus's family may refer to an actual family, or they may be designed to establish his concrete historical existence. This question is further complicated by the fact that, from the start, Christians called one another their "brothers" and "sisters," and that "Brother of Christ" may have been a title of Jewish-Christian leaders like James the Just. Similarly, the fact that Jesus was said to have been raised in the town of Nazareth may simply have been a means of explaining how Jesus "fulfilled" a Jewish expectation that the Messiah would be "called a Nazarite," i.e. one who vowed

to adhere to an ultra-strict observance of purity regulations. Since Jesus was obviously an opponent of such regulations, the belief of some that he must have been a "Nazarite" had to be altered, garbled, and then transformed into the idea that he was simply a "Nazarene" (from Nazareth). Tertullian preserves the tradition that *"The Christ of the Creator had to be called a Nazarene according to prophecy."* (Tertullian, *Against Marcion*, Book 4, Chapter 8)

The Book of Acts records that Paul was accused of being a leader of the "Nazarenes" and a "troublemaker" (Acts 24:5). The term in Hebrew (*notzrim*) and Arabic (nasara) for *Christian* is based on this word.

This all suggests the "Jewish Christians" may have called themselves as a group "Nazarenes," and that *they* were the "troublemakers."

38. John 6:60-66

39. Mark 11: 15-17; Luke 19:46; Matthew 21:13; and John 2:15-16
40. Matthew 15:21-28; cf. Mark 7:24-30.

41. Josephus, *Wars*, Book II, chapter 6

42. Mark 4:33-34

43. 1 Timothy 3:9

44. Origen, *Contra Celsum*, trans. Henry Chadwick 1980, Cambridge University Press, p. 32.

45. Kallah 51a

46. Matthew 2:1-12 **NOTE:** It is true that Zoroastrianism influenced Judaism itself after the Persian conquest of the Babylonians. Its apocalyptic vision of an End of Days battle between the forces of Light and Darkness had an observable impact on the similar apocalyptic visions of the Dead Sea Scrolls "sectarians," for example. However, the authority of the Magi is never directly invoked in Jewish literature as it is in the Nativity account found in Matthew. On

its face, such a self-conscious syncretism is extraordinary for any religion. Also, the Gospel does not specify the number of Magi, just that they brought three gifts. We infer their number from that fact.

47. Suetonius, *Vespasian*, 23. **NOTE:** Suetonius reports that this was the occasion of Vespasian's deathbed joke about his impending deification. Despite the assumptions of some contemporary scholars, such humor, even if it reflects a genuine cynicism on his part, is not inconsistent with an intention to develop a sincere cult, especially in the east, for good political reasons. Quite the reverse. Also, see, e.g., Tacitus, *The Histories*, II, 78, who reports that Vespasian believed in astrology. The destruction of the Temple itself was also heralded by a star, according to Josephus (Josephus, *Wars*, Book VI, chapter 5, sec. 3).

48. Matthew 6:19-20 and Luke 12:33

49. Matthew 15:10-11

50. See, e.g., Mark 2:23-28, Mark 3:1-6, Luke 6:1-11, and Matthew 12:1-14.

51. Genesis 17

52. Philippians 4:22, emphasis added.

53. Philippians 1:7

54: Isaiah 53, emphasis added. **NOTE:** In yet another borrowing from Jewish scriptures by the New Testament authors, we have the famous story of the reluctant Hebrew missionary from the Old Testament, Jonah, who was famously swallowed and held in the belly of a "huge fish" for "three days and three nights." (Jonah 1:17)

The Lord commanded Jonah to go to the city of Nineveh and preach against the wickedness there. But Jonah instead ran in the opposite direction and boarded a ship. A great storm arose and the ship nearly foundered until Jonah was thrown overboard at his own request.

God's wrath at Jonah was the cause of the storm in response to his disobedience, as Jonah himself realized. After his three days and nights in the fish, Jonah was again commanded by God to go to Nineveh. This time he did so and saved the city from God's wrath, telling the populace that if they did not clean up their act the city would be destroyed in *40 days*. Led by a king who dons sackcloth and ashes, the people repented. (Jonah 1-3)

The elements that the Jesus narrative apparently adopted from this story are noteworthy. We have a storm at sea, a near shipwreck, and a miraculous salvation. A *great fish* is the means of salvation. We have a kind of rebirth after a *three-day period* of concealment symbolic of redemption. Another *40-day period* associated with punishment and redemption is invoked.

The same three-day period appears in the life story of Flavius Josephus who, like Jesus, spent three days in a cave. Josephus may have seen himself as a new Jonah, bringing a message of redemption to a wicked generation.

Jesus himself, at Matthew 12:39-40, compares his upcoming resurrection experience to that of Jonah's "three days" within the fish (cf. Matthew 16:4 and Luke 11:29-32). Recent finds such as the "Gabriel inscription" may suggest that the three-day sign of Jonah was, in some fashion, already becoming associated with Jewish messianic and redemptive expectations at that time.

55. **NOTE:** Josephus reports that the Essenes were also healers who used medicinal herbs and minerals. (Josephus, *Wars*, Book II, Chapter 8, sec. 6) Some scholars believe that the very name "Essene" derives from a word for "healer." It is not clear that their healing involved miracles, and of course it would have been regarded as blasphemy among the Essenes to have identified such practitioners as being in any way divine.

56. Seneca, *On Benefits*, Book II, sec. 1; cf. *On Anger*, III, xii, 2-6.

57. Seneca, *Seneca's Epistles*, Letter 47

58. **NOTE:** Many of Seneca's ideas seem to echo ideas found

in the New Testament. Seneca recommends against seeking vengeance, against being envious, against coveting (even your neighbor's wife) and was a critic of intoxication. Other fascinating parallels include:

1. "A great fortune is great slavery." *Of Consolation, To Polybius*, cap. VI, line 5. The connections to the New Testament's admonition against the "love of money" and Christ's warning against attempting to serve both God and Mammon, are clear. "For we brought nothing into the world, and we can take nothing out of it. But if we have food and clothing, we will be content with that. People who want to get rich fall into temptation and a trap and into many foolish and harmful desires that plunge men into ruin and destruction. For the love of money is a root of all kinds of evil. Some people, eager for money, have wandered from the faith and pierced themselves with many griefs." (1 Timothy 6:7-10)

2. "The sun shines on the wicked" *On Benefits*, 3:25, cf. Matthew 5:45. The direct parallel suggests the existence of an earlier proverb commonly used by both Jesus and Seneca.

3. "The first petition that we are to make to Almighty God is for a good conscience, the next for health of mind, and then of body." *Epistles*, 14. Observe the relationship between this and Christ's rejection not only of violence and adultery, but anger and "lust in one's heart." Observe, as well, the forthright use of the singular "God" by this pagan Roman, a phenomenon that can also be seen in the work of the poet Virgil.

4. "True happiness is to understand our duties toward God and man; to enjoy the present, without anxious dependence on the future; not amuse ourselves with either hope or fears, but to rest satisfied with what we have, which is abundantly sufficient." *The Morals of Seneca: A Selection of his Prose*, based on the transl. by Sir Roger L'Estrange, edit. Walter

Clode (1888, London: Walter Scott, Ltd.) pp. 3-5. Notice how this relates to Jesus's own love commandments, and the duties to both God and other men that he articulates in the Gospels, as well as the Christian conception of happiness as knowledge of God. And compare this to Paul's message at Philippians 4:11-13: "For I have learned to be content, whatever the circumstances may be. I know now how to live when things are difficult and I know how to live when things are prosperous. In general and in particular I have learned the secret of eating well or going hungry, of facing either plenty or poverty."

The forged correspondence between Seneca and St. Paul is also very old, indeed, having been cited by both St. Jerome (*de Viris Illustribus*, 12) and St. Augustine (*Epistle*, 154.4).

The ancient Romans, like today's Christians, believed in the existence of an immortal soul, its judgment following a person's death, and resulting in eternal rewards or punishments.

59. Ephesians 6:6-9

60. Matthew 10:34. **NOTE:** Among the titles of Isaiah's predicted Messiah is also the title, Prince of Peace, as we read: "And he will be called/Wonderful Counselor, Mighty God/Everlasting Father, Prince of Peace/Of the greatness of his government and peace there will be no end."

But this will be a sectarian peace for the Jews: "He will reign on David's throne/and over his kingdom/establishing and upholding it/with justice and righteousness/from that time on and forever."

This suggests such millennial peace will come only after the defeat of Israel's enemies in battle, for the people will "rejoice before you/as people rejoice at the harvest,/as warriors rejoice when dividing the plunder./For as in the day of Midian's defeat,/you have shattered/the yoke that burdens them,/the bar across their shoulders,/the rod of their oppressor." Isaiah 9:3-7.

It should be noted that the Medianites were slaughtered by the Hebrews. All the men, boys and women who had "slept with a man" were killed—only the virgins were spared. Numbers 31.

Jesus seems to bypass the part about *Israel*'s military victory and he advocates peaceful submission to the "rod" of the "oppressors." For Jesus to be urging peace at a stage when that "rod" (of the Romans) was still hammering the Hebrews is also a problematic contradiction of this prophecy.

61. Luke 22;36-38

62. Matthew 26:50-54, cf. Mark 14:47, Luke 22:51 and John 18:10-11

63. Levick, *ante*, p. 170 and 204, and see, e.g., Boyle, A. J., "Introduction: Reading Flavian Rome," in Boyle and Dominik, eds., *Flavian Rome: Culture, Image, Text*, 2003, Brill, esp., pp. 23-25. Langlands, Rebecca, *Sexual Morality in Ancient Rome*, 2006, Cambridge University Press, pp. 359-360. **NOTE:** Evidence exists from Pompeii that erotic scenes were overpainted in the men's changing room at the public baths just three years before the eruption at Vesuvius, see *Sex in the Ancient World (Pompeii)*, 2009, History Channel. In the course of turning messianic Judaism into Christianity, the Romans not only changed Judaism into something else, but, as with the other cultures that they absorbed, they changed themselves, as well.

The influence of Jewish religion and morality on Roman society would be dramatically felt, for example, in the area of sexual standards, especially after Christianity gained official status during the reign of Constantine the Great. It may be safely asserted that the monastic tradition among Christians has its roots in the radical Judaism of 2,000 years ago.

64. Suetonius, *Domitian*, 8. **NOTE:** According to Suetonius, Domitian took a "far more serious view" of the Vestals' chastity vows and the traditional punishments for their violation than his father and brother did. Domitian's special veneration of the deities Jupiter and Minerva (Suetonius, *Domitian*, 4, 5, and 15) may also signal a more traditional approach than his father and brother took by directly associating themselves with both Egyptian gods and the Jewish Messiah.

According to Suetonius, however, Domitian enjoyed it when the *Roman populace* shouted out to him and his wife, "Long live our Lord and Lady!" and during Domitian's reign imperial agents referred to the emperor as "our Lord and God." (Suetonius, *Domitian*, 13)

Moreover, Domitian seems to have continued his family's association with Egyptian gods, since he rebuilt the Temple of Isis and Serapis in the city of Rome. It seems that it was specifically from his family's *Jewish* connections that Domitian disassociated himself.

Domitian was particularly harsh in his collection of the new tax levied against all Jews in the wake of the Jewish War, and he may have even collected it against Pauline Christians or those who admitted any sympathy for Jewish ideas, even if they were not practicing adherents themselves. Our sources indicate that this ruler executed members of his own family who converted to some form of comparative atheism (monotheism) and adopted what were vaguely described as "Jewish ways." The coinage struck by Domitian's successor, Nerva, actually boasts of an easing of his tax:

It reads: "The calumny of the Jewish tax is removed by consent of the Senate." This may have involved relieving Jewish apostates and Christians from the tax, and the harsh collection methods about which we also read, but not much more, as the tax seems to have been collected until the 4th Century.

Curiously, it was the non-Christian member from the family of Constantine the Great, Julian the Apostate, who may have finally ended the tax against the Jews. Among the harsh practices of this ongoing tax before that time we read that old men were physically inspected to see if they were circumcised. This would of course have exempted Gentile Christians of the Pauline variety.

65. 1 Corinthians 7:1-2, Mark 10:2-12, Luke 16:18, Matthew 19:2-12.

66. Deuteronomy 24:1.

67. Levick, *ante*, p. 65; Suetonius, *Titus*, 1.

68. Levick, *ante*, pp. 204-205

69. **NOTE:** There appear to have been some faked ancient coins using the dolphin-and-anchor motif. Though we know of at least one issue by Hadrian of the dolphin-and-anchor on an Alexandrian coin, here is an example of an obvious fake:

While this would appear to be a coin struck by the 2nd Century Emperor Hadrian, careful observers have noted that this emperor never achieved an eighth consulship, as this coin seems to cele-brate. There are no known bronze equivalents, and the die appears to be from a known fake.
(h t t p : / / w w w . c o i n t a l k . c o m / t h r e a d s / dolphin-and-anchor-type-on-a-hadrian-bronze.227771/)

Jews and Christians at the Flavian Court

I. Jews—or Christians?

1. Tertullian, *Prescription Against Heretics*, 32, and Jerome, *On Illustrious Men*, 15.

2. Cassius, Dio, *Roman History*, trans. Herbert Foster, Loeb Classical Library, Book LXVII, 14

3. Suetonius, *Domitian*, 15

4. Eusebius, *History of the Church*, trans. G.A. Williamson, rev. ed. Andrew Louth, ed., 1989, Penguin Classics, Book III, 16, 18.

5. Eusebius, *History of the Church, ante*, Book III, 19

6. Cardinal Annibal Albani, T. Flavii Clementis Viri Consularis et Martyris Tumulus illustrates, 1727, Urbino.

7. Suetonius, *Domitian*, 14. **NOTE:** Christian tradition regarding the martyrdom of St. Clement of Rome is especially specious because the same account of his death also claims that the sea receded three miles to reveal the saint's body buried by angelic forces in a marble mausoleum. Part of this myth appears to be an attempt to explain to later generations why the remains of this officially dishonored martyr should have been housed in such a glorious fashion.

8. Philippians 4:2

9. Suetonius, *Domitian*, 11

10. 1 Clement, Chapter 1

11. 1 Clement, Chapter 14, emphasis added.

12. 1 Clement, Chapter 32

13. 1 Clement, Chapter 47, emphasis added.

14. 1 Clement, Chapter 25

15. 1 Clement, Chapter 55

16. 1 Clement, Chapter 37

17. 1 Clement, Chapter 57

18. 1 Clement, Chapter 46

19. Ignatius of Antioch, *Epistle to the Smyraeans*, trans, Alexander Roberts and James Donaldson, in Roberts, Donaldson and Coxe, edits., *Ante-Nicene Fathers*, vol. 1, 1885, Buffalo, New York: Christian Literature Pub. Co.

20. Acts 20:17-28

21. Matthew 16:18-19

22. **NOTE:** The reader is again directed to Robert Eisenman's pioneering work where some of the following arguments were first presented in a different form, especially, *James the Brother of Jesus, ante*, especially, pp. 788-801.

23. Suetonius, *Titus*, 7

24 Josephus, *Antiquities,* Book IX, chapter 5, sec. 1

25. Suetonius, *Vespasian*, 3

26. Levick, *ante*, pp. 28-29

27. Hillar, Marian, *From Logos to Trinity: the Evolution of Religious Beliefs from Pythagoras to Tertullian*, 2012, New York: Cambridge University Press.

28. John 1:1-5

29. Suetonius, *Vespasian*, 1

30. Eisenman, *James the Brother of Jesus, ante*, pp. 793-801, and "Paul's 'Comrade-in-Arms' Epaphroditus and the First Gospels," 9-04-2013, *Huffington Post*, http://www.huffingtonpost.com/robert-eisenman/pauls-comradeinarms-epaph_b_3862879.html.

31. Josephus, *Antiquities*, Book XX, chapter 7, sec. 1-3

32. Josephus, *Antiquities*, Book XX, chapter 7, sec. 2

33. Josephus, *Antiquities*, Book XX, chapter 7, sec. 3

34. Josephus, *Antiquities*, Book XX, chapter 5, sec. 2

35. Eisenman, James the Brother of Jesus, ante, pp. 797

36. Josephus, *Life of Flavius Josephus*, hereafter, "Life," in *The Complete Works of Josephus*, trans. William Whiston, 1960, Kregel, sec. 23.

37. Galatians 2:3

38. Galatians 2:12

39. Josephus, *Wars,* Book II, chapter 8, sec. 10.

40. *Operation Messiah, ante.*

41. Acts 23:31-24:9

42. Acts 24:23

43. Acts 24:24-27, emphasis added.

44. Acts 25:1-3, emphasis added.

45. Acts 25:9

46. Acts 25:12

47. Acts 25:13- 27, emphasis added.

48. Acts 26:2-30, emphasis added.

49. Acts 26:24

50. Acts 26:25-32, emphasis added.

51. Acts 10, emphasis added.

52. Acts 10:45, emphasis added.

53. Galatians 2:11-13; **NOTE:** Acts places Peter's vision well before its account of the Council of Jerusalem, while the letter to the Galatians makes clear that Paul's confrontation with the Jewish-Christians happened after this event.

54. **NOTE:** Recall that Paul told the Galatians about his meeting with James and the early Christian leaders in Jerusalem, an event that is referred to as the "Council of Jerusalem." Acts' account of this "council" also features Peter's mystical vision, and for that reason is probably not reliable. The only reliable aspect of that chapter of Acts is its account of a falling out between Paul and "Barnabas" (Acts 15:36-40), something that might be embarrassing to later Christians and is therefore unlikely to have been added later.

55. Acts 9:23

56. Acts 9:24

57. Acts 9:29-31

58. Acts 13:44

59. Acts 13:50

60. Acts 14:19

61. Acts 15:30-16:12

62. Acts 16:20-21, emphasis added.

63. Acts 16:26

64. Acts 16:27-34

65. Acts 16:35-36

66. Acts 16:37-40, emphasis added.

67. Hellerman, Joseph H., *Reconstructing Honor in Roman Philippi*, 2005, Cambridge University Press, p. 80, emphasis added.

68. Philippians 4:18, 2:25, 4:3, and 4:22

69. Acts 17 and 18

70. Acts 18:2 and Suetonius, *Claudius*, 25

71. Acts 18:12-16, emphasis added.

72. Acts 18:17

73. Acts 19:35-41

74. Acts 20:3 and 20:19

75. Acts 21:20-25, emphasis added.

76. Acts 21:31-32, emphasis added.

77. Acts 21:39-40

78. Acts 22:22-30

79. Acts 23:10

80. Acts 23:23-24

81. Acts 23:29

82. Acts 27:3

83. Acts 13:1

84. Romans 16:10-11

85. Eisenman, *James the Brother of Jesus*, *ante*, pp. 796-797.

86. Acts 13:4-12

87. Philippians 4:22

88. Philippians 4:18-22, emphasis added.

89. Phlippians 2:25-30, emphasis added.

90. Philippians 1:12-14, emphasis added.

91. Tacitus, *The Annals*, *ante*, Book XV, 55

92. Suetonius, *Nero*, 49

93. Cassius, Dio, *Roman History*, *ante*, Book LXIII, 27 and 29

94. Cassius, Dio, *Roman History*, *ante*, Book LXIII, 14

95. Suetonius, *Domitian*, 14

96. Josephus, *Antiquities*, Preface, sec. 2

97. Josephus, *Life*, sec. 76

98. Josephus, *Antiquities*, Preface, sec. 2; *Life*, sec. 76; *Against Apion*, in *The Complete Works of Josephus*, trans. William Whiston, 1960, Kregel, Book I, sec. 1, and Book II, sec. 42.

99. See, Rajak, Tessa, "Iulius Agrippa II, Marcus", 1996, in Hornblower, Simon, ed., *Oxford Classical Dictionary*, Oxford: Oxford University Press.

100. Josephus, *Antiquities*, Book XX, chapter 8, sec.11, and *Life*, sec. 3.

II. Josephus and the New Testament

1. Josephus, *Life*, sec. 1

2. Josephus, *Life*, sec. 5-8, 75-76, *Wars*, Book VI.

3. Josephus, *Life*, sec. 4-5

4. Josephus, *Life*, sec. 26

5. Josephus, *Against Apion, ante,* Book II, sec. 30

6. Josephus, *Antiquities*, Book XIX, chapter 7, sec. 3

7. Josephus, *Wars*, Book IV, chapter 7, sec. 3

8. Romans 13:1-7; 1 Peter 2:13-17

9. Josephus, *Wars*, Book V, chapter 9, sec. 4

10. Josephus, *Life*, sec. 23

11. Feldman, Louis H., "Hellenization in Josephus' *Jewish Antiquities*: the Portrait of Abraham," in *Josephus, Judaism, and Christianity*, Louis H. Feldman and Gohei Hata, eds., 1987, Detroit: Wayne State University Press, p.145.

12. Josephus, *Wars*, Book VI, chapter 5, sec. 4.

13. Josephus, *Life*, sec. 76

14. Matthew 5:17

15. Josephus, *Life*, sec. 27

16. Josephus, *Wars*, Book III, chapter 8, sec. 3, emphasis added.

17. Luke 2:41-48, emphasis added.

18. Josephus, *Life*, sec. 2, emphasis added.

19. Josephus, *Life*, sec. 2

20. *Ibid.*

21. Eisenman, *James the Brother of Jesus, ante*, pp. 258-362.

22. See Eisenman, *James the Brother of Jesus, ante*, esp. pp. 319-348.

23. Isaiah 40:3

24. John 1:23

25. Acts 23:6; Philippians 3:5

26. cf. 1 Corinthians 7:1-7 and Josephus, *Wars*, Book II, chapter 8, sec. 2 and 13.

27. Josephus, *Life,* sec. 2

28. Feldman, Louis, H., "Introduction," and Feldman, Louis H., "Hellenization in Josephus' *Jewish Antiquities*: the Portrait of Abraham," in *Josephus, Judaism, and Christianity*, Louis H. Feldman and Gohei Hata, *ante*, p. 31 and pp. 133-153.

29. Josephus, *Antiquities*, Book XVIII, chapter 1, sec. 3-5; Acts 23:8.

30. cf. Josephus, *Antiquities*, Book XVIII, chapter 1, sec. 1-6; and *Wars*, Book II, chapter 8, sec. 1-13, esp. 6 and 11; see also, Eisenman, Robert, "Confusions of 'Pharisees' and 'Essenes' in Josephus," *The Jerusalem Post*, January 26, 2014, http://blogs.jpost.com/content/confusions-pharisees-and-essenes-josephus

31. Josephus, *Wars*, Book II, chapter 8, sec. 10, emphasis added.

32. Josephus, *Life*, sec. 44

33. Josephus, *Life,* sec. 3, emphasis added.

34. Acts 27:27-44, emphasis added.

35. Acts 24:1-27

36. Sienkiewicz, Henryk, *Quo Vadis?*, 2006, Aegypan (orig. pub. in Polish, 1896).

37. **NOTE:** Professor Eisenman persuasively rejects the account in Acts as unhistorical. He has suggested that Paul was not even in Roman custody when James the Just was martyred. See *James the Brother of Jesus*, 1997, Viking, esp. pp. 521-597. The death of James may indeed have been the event that sent delegations to Rome from both sides, and this occurred precisely *during the interval between the governorships of Festus and Albinus*, according to Josephus.

38. Acts 5:36-8; *Antiquities*, Book XX, chapter 5, sec. 1-4.

39. Mark 6:17; Josephus, *Antiquities*, Book XVIII, chapter 5, sec. 4.

40. Josephus, *Wars,* Book III, chapter 8, sec.1, emphasis added.

41. As in Matthew's account of the Resurrection, Josephus's cave was carefully *guarded.* Matthew 28:1-10.

42. Josephus, *Antiquities*, Book XVIII, chapter 1, sec. 5, emphasis added.

43. Acts 4:32-35, emphasis added, cf. Acts 2:44-45.

44. Matthew 10:8-10. **NOTE:** As with his admiration for the Essenes' approach to money, one might reasonably ask how any

Romans or Roman sympathizer could have penned the strict regulations of divorce that we read in the New Testament. The Romans, after all, famously had very liberal and easy divorce laws. Josephus himself had divorced, according to his own report. However, it must be remembered that the letters of Paul and the Gospels were not written for a general Roman audience, and indeed, that each of the Gospels and Paul's letters seem to have been written for a specialized audience. In this context, it is worth nothing that the New Testament is not entirely consistent on the subject. According to both Luke and Mark, Jesus flatly forbade divorce (Luke 16:18, Mark 10:2-12), while Matthew says "except for sexual immorality" (Matthew 19:2-12). This is interesting because, of course, under the Mosaic Law any adultery was to be punished with execution by stoning. Matthew's divorce regulation appears to assume that the Mosaic Law is no longer being enforced in this respect. Paul says that divorce is not permitted but curiously adds that if a woman does divorce, she must not remarry (1Corinthians 7:1-28), again, a curious comment if any rule against divorce is actually being obeyed. In these same passages, both Jesus and Paul seem to go beyond such divorce laws and recommend complete celibacy for those who are able to do without sex. Under the Mosaic Law, divorce was permitted (Deuteronomy 24:1), but later Jewish thought was also divided on the subject. The Essenes seem to have practiced celibacy, while the early rabbis sharply differed on the question of whether divorce was permissible. These early Christian documents seem to reflect some of the same divisions of opinion that existed within Judaism at the time. As with a love of poverty, Romans could, and did, admire such rigorous moral practices without themselves adopting them. As we shall see, Josephus very much admired ideals he did not practice.

45. Mark 10:21; Matthew 19:21; Luke 18:22: 1 Timothy 6:10.

46. James 5:1-6; see also, Eisenman, *James the Brother of Jesus, ante,* esp. pp. 496-502.

47. Josephus, *Antiquities,* Book X, chapter 11, esp. sec 7.

48. Daniel 7:13-14, emphasis added. **NOTE:** Christians later suggested that when Daniel spoke of "one like a Man" being given Dominion over the earth, this pointed to a Divine Messiah, a man-god like Jesus. Even though this work was written in an entirely Jewish context, by this logic, it seems to anticipate Christianity. However, this section of Daniel reports a dream by the prophet, one filled with a number of purely symbolic images, such as "beasts" who represent entire kingdoms. Thus, when "the people of the Holy Ones of the Most High" are also granted Dominion over the whole earth, the author is telling us that the Being "like a man" is actually a symbol for that same people. Scholars are almost universally agreed that the "Son of Man" in Daniel represented the "maskilim," the very community responsible for the creation of Daniel. In the hands of later Christians, however, this passage was made to seem like a prophetic anticipation of the Gospels. But in Jewish literature there are no semi-divine humans of any kind—Judaism is a form of monotheism.

49. Mark 14:62; cf. Mark 13:26-27, Luke 21:27, Matthew 24:30-31. **NOTE:** a similar interest in Daniel is not evenly expressed throughout the New Testament.

50. Tacitus, *Histories, ante*, Book V, 13, emphasis added.

51. Josephus, *Wars*, Book VI, chapter 5, sec. 3.

52. Luke 23:34-36. **NOTE:** It is true that St. Stephen at his martyrdom also forgave his killers, but in this case, they were Jewish. However, in the narrative of Luke-Acts (they appear to be the same single work), by then, Stephen is simply imitating Christ in this conduct. Robert Eisenman has persuasively argued that the death of Stephen in the Book of Acts is merely a rewritten form of the death of the important James, a historical event recorded by Josephus, since it happened at the same place, in a similar manner, and James is said to have spoken the same words Stephen did at his martyrdom. (See, Eisenman, Robert, *James the Brother of Jesus, ante*, pp. 521-597.) Stephen's very name means "crown" in Greek and early Christians regarded martyrdom as their own

"crown," making Acts' account of Christianity's first martyr highly dubious. If Eisenman is correct, however, the words Jesus spoke at the Crucifixion were actually first spoken by James and attributed to Jesus in the Gospels. Elsewhere in the Gospels, Jesus forgives sins himself and does not merely ask God to do so, as James/Stephen does.

53. Josephus, *Antiquities*, Book III, chapter 7, sec. 4.

54. Josephus, *Wars*, Book IV, chapter 3, sec 7, and John 19:23-24.

55. Mark 11:15-17; Matthew 21:13. **NOTE:** Of note, at the very moment of Jesus's death on the Cross the earth shook and the curtain of the Temple separating the inner sanctuary from the rest was miraculously torn in two, according to the Gospels. (Mark 15:37-39, Luke 23:44-46, Matthew 27:50-51). Similarly, shortly before the fall of the Temple, its huge and heavy eastern gate opened by itself, according to Josephus, and at the festival of Pentecost, the earth shook and there was a great sound of voices heard to say, "Let us depart!" (Josephus, *Wars*, Book VI, chapter 5, sec. 3). Both the Gospels and Josephus depict God himself ominously signaling his departure from the Temple prior to its destruction.

56. Luke 23:47.

III. The Flavian Testimony for Christ

1. Josephus, *Antiquities*, Book XVIII, chapter 3, sec. 3, emphasis added.

2. Josephus, *Antiquities*, Book XVIII, chapter 5, sec. 2, emphasis added.

3. Galatians 5:14, Mark 12:30-31, Luke 6:31 and 10:26-27, Matthew 7:12 and 22:26-40, John 13:35; cf. Leviticus 19:18, Sirach 31:15, and Hillel, Shabbos 31a.

4. Josephus, *Antiquities*, Book XX, chapter 9, sec.1, emphasis added.

5. Levick, *ante*, pp. 67-68, and see her citations.

6. Feldman, Louis H., "The *Testimonium Flavianum*: the State of the Question," in Robert F. Burkey and Sarah A. Edwards, eds., *Christological Perspectives: Essays in Honor of Harvey K. McArthur*, 1982, New York: Pilgrim Press, pp. 179-199, 288-293.

7. Feldman, Louis, H., "Introduction," *Josephus, Judaism, and Christianity*, Louis H. Feldman and Gohei Hata, *ante*, p. 57; St. Jerome, *Epistula ad Eustochium*, 22.

8. Mizugaki, Wataru, "Origen and Josephus," in *Josephus, Judaism, and Christianity*, Louis H. Feldman and Gohei Hata, *ante*, p. 329, 327.

9. Origen, *Contra Celsum, ante*, Book I, chapter 47, emphasis added.

10. Origen, *Contra Celsum, ante*, Book II, chapter 13, emphasis added.

11. Origen, *Commentary on the Gospel of Matthew*, trans. John Patrick, Alexander Roberts and James Donaldson, eds., 1867, Edinburgh: T&T Clark, X, 17, emphasis added.

12. Carrier, Richard, "Origen, Eusebius, and the Accidental Interpolation in Josephus," *Jewish Antiquities* 20.200, *The Journal of Early Christian Studies*, vol. 20, no. 4, Winter 2012, pp. 489-514.

13. Josephus, *Antiquities*, Book XX, chapter 9, sec.1-3, *et seq.*

14. *Ibid.*

15. Mizugaki, Wataru, "Origen and Josephus," in *Josephus, Judaism, and Christianity*, Louis H. Feldman and Gohei Hata, *ante*, p. 329, 327.

16. Goldberg, G.J., "The Coincidences of the Testimonium of Josephus and the Emmaus Narrative of Luke," *The Journal for the Study of the Pseudepigrapha,* vol. 13, 1995, pp. 59-77.

17. Feldman, Louis, H., "Introduction," *Josephus, Judaism, and Christianity*, Louis H. Feldman and Gohei Hata, *ante*, p. 56.

18. Photius, *Bibliotheca*, Codex 33.

19. Genesis 37:1-11

20. Genesis 37:39-41

21. Josephus, *Life*, sec. 42, *Wars*, Book III, chapter 8, sec. 3.

22. Josephus, *Wars*, Book III, chapter 8, sec. 3.

23. *Ibid*, emphasis added.

24. Genesis 41:12

25. 2 Corinthians 12:1-4

26. Josephus, *Antiquities*, Book VIII, chapter 2, sec. 5.

27. Eisenman, *James the Brother of Jesus*, *ante*, pp. 797-798.

IV. Engineering a Religion

1. John 2:18; cf. Mark 14:58 and Matthew 26.61. **NOTE:** References to Jesus at least symbolically rebuilding the temple make a literal interpretation of Gospel descriptions of Jesus as either being a carpenter (Mark 6:3) or the son of a carpenter (Matthew 13:55) problematic. The word used, "tekton" (τέκτων), could also mean an artisan in stone, the building material for which Jesus named Peter when he predicted that Apostle's "foundational" role in the new Church.

2. Mark 11:15-17; cf. Luke 19:45-47, Matthew 21:12-13, John 2:13-16.

3. Numbers 14:33-34

4. Genesis 7:12

5. Levick, *ante*, p. 199 and p. 205.

6. **NOTE:** "Gnosticism" was a theological approach that influenced a number of ancient religions, including Judaism, the most common elements of it being a radical rejection of the material world in favor of the spiritual and the pursuit of hidden knowledge (hence the name). Such ideas were already starting to have an impact on certain Jewish groups by the 1st Century, if not sooner. Some have argued that the Gospels themselves show traces of Gnostic influence. In any case, it represented another form of syncretism of various religious traditions with ideas developed from Platonism. According to the work of scholar Elaine Pagels, Paul himself may be seen as a proto-Gnostic. See Pagels, Elaine, *The Gnostic Paul: Gnostic Exegesis of the Pauline Letter*s, 1975, Fortress Press, and generally, *The Gnostic Gospels*, 1979, Vintage Books.

7. Levick, *ante*, p. 205.

8. Valliant, James, "First 'Scripts' of 'Passion' Penned by Anti-Semitic Romanophiles," 12-13-2003, *Fredericksburg Star.* (The author did not title the article.)

9. Matthew 27:25

10. Matthew 27:19

11. Sherwin-White, A. N., "Pontius Pilate," *The International Standard Bible Encyclopedia*, revised, ed. Geoffrey W. Bromiley, 2002, Grand Rapids: Wm. B. Eerdmans.